TEACHING COMPOSITION WITH LITERATURE

101 Writing Assignments from College Instructors

Edited by
Dana Gioia
and
Patricia Wagner

A Special Supplement to Accompany
Literature: An Introduction to Fiction, Poetry, and Drama
(Seventh Edition)

 LONGMAN

An imprint of Addison Wesley Longman, Inc.

New York • Reading, Massachusetts • Menlo Park, California • Harlow, England
Don Mills, Ontario • Sydney • Mexico City • Madrid • Amsterdam

Teaching Composition with Literature: 101 Writing Assigments from College Instructors

Copyright © 1999 by Addison-Wesley Longman, Inc.

ISBN: 0-321-02748-5

3 4 5 6 7 8 9 10 – CRS – 0706050403

Contents

FICTION

General Writing Assignments

Writing Assignments on Stories

Writing Assignments on Poems

W. H. Auden, MUSÉE DES BEAUX ARTS

Preface

The design of *Teaching Composition with Literature: 101 Writing Assignments from College Instructors* is unabashedly practical. The volume tries to assist instructors who use stories, poems, and plays in teaching expository writing. The volume is designed to accompany *Literature: An Introduction to Fiction, Poetry, and Drama* (Seventh edition), edited by X. J. Kennedy and Dana Gioia. All the writing exercises and assignments in *Teaching Composition with Literature* use selections from the current edition of *Literature* as their focus or departure point.

In compiling *Teaching Composition with Literature,* the editors asked a cross section of excellent English teachers for help. We approached various instructors from all regions of the country with a request for a composition exercise or assignment they had used in the classroom with conspicuous success. There is no substitute in teaching for practical experience, and the purpose of this book is to share it. Every teacher knows how much one can learn from colleagues who have taught the same or a similar course. We may never be fortunate enough to have the instructors in this volume for colleagues, but this collection will give us the chance to hear and perhaps borrow some of their ideas.

Reading scholarly journals today, one would assume that most college instructors spend their time wrestling with sophisticated theoretical issues. It will come as no surprise to any reader of this book that most teachers face more mundane and pragmatic challenges, especially the never-ending task of teaching entering undergraduates to write competent expository prose. *Teaching Composition with Literature* is not intended to replace the many excellent books in the field of composition. Rather it is designed to supplement one of the most popular approaches, which uses imaginative literature as a means for teaching expository writing. This volume gathers together a representative sampling of proven writing exercises created by instructors to use in their own classrooms.

The initial inspiration for *Teaching Composition with Literature* came from the experience of assembling a new edition of *Literature: An Introduction to Fiction, Poetry, and Drama.* As part of the editorial process for the sixth edition, we sent out a rough draft of our new table of contents to a cross section of instructors for review. Their comments helped develop the final book. As we read through their reactions, we were impressed by how often instructors argued for a particular story, poem, or play by sharing their experiences teaching it in the classroom. Sometimes they would even enclose the assignments they gave to students. Many of these ideas were so good that it seemed a shame not to share them. We incorporated some of the critical ideas in the *Instructor's Manual*, but many of the suggestions were writing assignments and exercises beyond the focus of that volume.

HOW TO USE THIS BOOK

The writing exercises in this book have been arranged to follow the general organization of *Literature: An Introduction to Fiction, Poetry, and Drama*. First, the contributions have been divided by subject into the three major literary categories: fiction, poetry, and drama. All the writing exercises that use short fiction as their departure point, for example, appear together in one section. Second, whenever the instructor focuses the exercise on a particular story, poem, or play, the exercise has been specifically linked to the selection in *Literature*.

The Table of Contents for *Teaching Composition with Literature* has been arranged, wherever possible, to link with specific texts in the textbook, so that instructors can more easily incorporate their exercises into their classroom plan. When a writing exercise is more general in nature (such as Sue Walker's "Dinner on the River," which potentially includes every selection, or William Rice's piece on how authors open and close short stories, the selection has been placed in a General category.

Many contributors discussed several selections in their exercises, especially those listed in the General sections. As its allusive title suggests, Tom Zaniello's "The Use of Force at a Clean Well-Lighted A & P" offers a provocative writing idea equally applicable to stories by Williams, Hemingway, and Updike. Likewise in her exercise, "'Trials and Revelations': Teaching Myth with Joseph Campbell," Diane Thiel mentions five stories that work well with her assignment. A short index, which lists authors, subjects, and titles, appears at the end of the volume. The index also provides an in-depth cross-listing of all works featured in the assignments. Any instructor looking for exercises on particular stories, poems, or plays not mentioned in the table of contents should consult the index.

The exercises in *Teaching Composition with Literature* do not constitute a total course plan for instructors using *Literature* as a text in expository writing courses. Rather, the book is planned to supplement an instructor's class plan by providing new ideas and fresh perspectives. Every instructor finds some topics easier to teach than others. This book may prove most useful by allowing one instructor to hear another teacher's advice on approaching a particular text or topic.

Some instructors, especially new ones, may, however, find it helpful to see a complete course plan that integrates literature and composition. Patricia Wagner's detailed syllabus and weekly teaching plan, which appears in the appendix, provides an example of how one experienced instructor organizes her introductory composition course based on literary texts. This syllabus offers only one model, but at the very least it will help clarify issues of coverage, workload, and organization for other instructors designing their own course.

Finally, we also present two general essays (immediately following the preface) on the advantages of using literary texts in composition courses. Juliann Fleenor discusses her insights and experiences in using stories, plays, and poems in writing courses. Melinda Barth provides an historical and theoretical overview of the issues facing instructors who combine literature and composition in their courses. We do not pretend to be neutral on the ideas they discuss. *Teaching Composition with Literature* was created from a deep and abiding conviction that imaginative literature is not only an appropriate component in expository writing courses but is, in fact, an almost ideal component.

HOW NOT TO USE THIS BOOK

Teaching Composition with Literature is not designed to provide critical commentary or background material to the selections in *Literature*. There is a separate and ample *Instructor's Manual* to accompany the new edition of *Literature*. If you do not have a copy of the *Instructor's Manual*, call your Addison Wesley Longman sales representative for one. It would be a rare teacher who did not enjoy at least perusing the manual, which provides an informal but informed commentary on every selection in *Literature*. In addition to critical ideas, scholarly notes, bibliographical summaries, and additional biographical material on authors, the *Instructor's Manual* also incorporates (with credit scrupulously given) the comments from dozens—indeed over a hundred—instructors who have written us about their experiences teaching the stories, poems, and plays in the book. For this wealth of practical experience alone, many will find the *Instructor's Manual* a valuable aid.

Teaching Composition with Literature is designed to supplement the *Instructor's Manual*, not to replace it, by providing practical proven classroom ideas and assignments for instructors who use *Literature* to teach composition courses or literary courses with an emphasis on expository writing.

WHAT ABOUT CREATIVE WRITING?

As the title indicates, *Teaching Composition with Literature* is not a book intended to be used for creative writing. The editor has, in fact, regretfully turned down several excellent exercises because they focused on poetry and fiction in ways that were beyond the scope of even the most freewheeling composition courses. Several instructors, however, have mentioned that they like to incorporate one or two creative writing exercises in their courses. They do so not only for variety's sake but also because a well-designed imaginative exercise can sometimes dramatize an element of good writing or analytical thinking more memorably than a traditional composition assignment.

I have therefore included about half a dozen creative exercises that may initially strike some instructors as unusual. Robert Phillips, for example, offers a simple first line exercise that can be used in either verse or prose. Although it focuses on helping a student create a new poem or story, this exercise also stresses the importance for all kinds of writing of identifying and building on a good lead. Annie Finch's sonnet-writing exercise is also a creative assignment, but the author makes a strong case that creating an original sonnet compels students to consider syntax, diction, sentence structure, and punctuation in ways they usually ignore. Mark Royden Winchell's revisionary approach to Eliot's "The Love Song of J. Alfred Prufrock" also serves a similar pedagogic goal. Several other assignments, like Fred

Dings's contribution on Tennyson's "Ulysses," can be used either as creative or expository writing exercises.

THANKS

A great many people helped make this book possible. First and foremost are the nearly ninety instructors who contributed writing assignments and classroom exercises. The merits of the book belong to them. Some of these contributors have been long-term collaborators with *Literature*; their advice has helped the book grow and improve with each edition. At Longman, Lisa Moore supported the idea of this volume, capably assisted by Natalie Hart; Donna Campion saw it through production. Katharine Glynn was the ever-resourceful development editor. X. J. Kennedy provided sage senior counsel. R. S. Gwynn, David Mason, Dianne Peich, Melinda Barth, and Bill Rice gave helpful early advice. Jan Carp helped compile the final manuscript. Otto Barz and George Ernsberger of Publishing Synthesis became invaluable partners in preparing the book for publication. They deserve more than the usual debt of thanks. Our greatest gratitude, however, remains to Mary Gioia, who managed every stage of the book's development. Her hard work, good sense, and wry humor made the book better in innumerable ways.

D.G.

Introductory
Essays

Teaching Composition with Literature: One Teacher's Perspective

Juliann E. Fleenor
WILLIAM RAINEY HARPER COLLEGE
PALATINE, ILLINOIS

Over the past few years, I have been disturbed by the widening gulf between literature and composition. I believe that to teach composition without literature is to separate content from skills. It is to reduce the teaching of writing to a service course. How can I teach effective sentences, unless I use well-written sentences such as those used in short stories? How can I teach the use of analogy except by having students read fiction that uses analogy or metaphor? Students learn from reading poetry, fiction, and drama how to read a text closely. They also learn critical thinking. By separating the content of my discipline from the skills of writing, I lose the fervor, the imagination, and the love that I feel toward literature. I lose the heart of who I am as a teacher.

How did I arrive at this heretical position, nailing the theses to the church door? I was dutifully teaching students to write multiple drafts. When my students refused to do them or did them twenty minutes before class, I worked the drafts into the evaluation. But whatever I did, it continued to be a struggle between me and the student—I who valued revision and the student who did not. Recently I began to remember how I myself wrote as a freshman. I went to a public university, working part-time, while also taking care of my husband and child. No one suggested to me that I write drafts. I worked essays out in my head as I drove to school or outlined them to myself while I was working at home. Eventually, I sat down and wrote the essay in class under pressure. It wasn't until years later, after I became a professional writer, that I began to value drafting and love revision almost as much as the initial draft. If I had been forced into multiple drafts, I probably would have rebelled as my own students do. I began to ask myself, why did I not allow my students to have the same experience I had had?

3

I believe the separation of the study of literature from composition accompanied the fragmentation of the literary canon and that fragmentation accompanied the loss of authority of the English teacher. Don't misunderstand me. I was one of many feminist scholars who were trying to integrate women's writing into the canon and on whom it was not lost that I had read very few women in my undergraduate and graduate courses. Through opening the canon to many voices and cultures, however, we who teach English found that we couldn't say what was important to read any longer; nor could we claim to be authorities in our discipline. I was expected to learn new works and teach them. When I joined a learning community with four other teachers, I was expected to teach Latin American Literature. I needed months of preparation to do so. And even so I never really reached the level of understanding that I have with Nineteenth-Century American Literature, my specialty in my discipline.

A related change was that group work was in and the authority of the teacher was out. But how do you teach complex ideas without doing it in stages or without the teacher as the authority? Otherwise we will never rise above the group in class. These observations do not mean that I don't value group work—I do. But if students bring poor reading skills to the group and no experience with reading critically, how can they benefit from working in a group?

Not only do I teach literature in my composition classes—both English 101 and English 102—but I no longer emphasize process writing, the multiple drafts that I have assigned in the past. I begin my English 101 classes where many teachers begin, with a discussion of the three stages of writing: prewriting, first draft, and revision. We practice brainstorming, scratch outlines, freewriting, and clustering. I return to freewriting over and over throughout the semester as a way of garnering the students' initial responses and fostering the discussion of an assignment.

I also use Angelo and Cross's "One Minute Paper" to see if my students understand an assignment. These responses help me gauge what I need to cover again or have them practice. Tests are another such gauge. But why wait for a test when I can find out with little effort what the students do and do not understand?

At this point, I also begin to review grammar; complex, compound, and simple sentences; along with punctuation. I test them on grammar and punctuation as well. I might include an in-class presentation on date rape—about which they then write an argument paper.

I do not include descriptive or narrative papers, although I work descriptive and narrative writing into the course assignments and into their writing. If I include a date rape presentation, I include a short story such as Joyce Carol Oates's short story, "Where Are You Going, Where Have You Been?" I then link the argument paper to the short literary paper. I could also use William Carlos Williams's "The Use of Force." Many times I ask that it be a short library report, which uses only reference works such as *Short Story Criticism* or *Contemporary Authors*. I usually shape the assignment so that it is unique.

One semester, for example, I taught Stephen Crane's "The Bride Comes to Yellow Sky." I arranged for a library tour and had students complete a library quiz. Questions on the quiz asked that they turn to the *Oxford English Dictionary* along with a medical encyclopedia and works like *Contemporary Literary Criticism*. I asked the students to look up the entry on tuberculosis in the medical encyclopedia and the word *courage* in the OED. These with other questions were worked into the five-page library paper. The students then had to consider the effect dying from tuberculosis would have on a writer and how that might shape the short story. As you might recall, "The Bride Comes to Yellow Sky" features a bride who is neither young nor pretty and a gunfight that never happens. The paper is crafted from the students' interpretations of the story and what they learn in the library, which in turn is influenced by readings in *Contemporary Literary Criticism* or *Short Story Criticism*.

Thus, I assign the paper in pieces and then help the students bring the pieces together. But I do not assign drafts as such. The writers do begin, however, to see different facets of the story. They gradually proceed to a deeper understanding of the 1891 story written by a man who was himself wasting away from tuberculosis. From the first day, I discuss a writer's use of analogy—argument by analogy, and analogy to explain a concept. Because I end the semester with the library paper, we explore carefully the use Stephen Crane makes of analogy, and the students see how vivid language becomes with the use of analogies. In fact, the entire semester is built around analogy and culminates in the assignments relating to "The Bride Comes to Yellow Sky." They will write in-class essays on foreshadowing along with the library quiz and the library paper.

Another assignment I have made in the past requires the students to go to a public place—a restaurant, a zoo, a mall perhaps—and to eavesdrop. Most writers eavesdrop. They pick up phrases with which they build character and action. I ask the students to write out dialogue they overheard and then speculate on the meaning of the dialogue. I stress that most people won't reveal strong emotions in public places but that such emotions exist nevertheless under the dialogue. Then I assign Ernest Hemingway's "A Clean Well-Lighted Place," and as a class we discuss the sparse dialogue in that story. We speculate on its meaning. Then we go back to the earlier assignment and look again at the dialogue they quoted. What emotions lie beneath the surface? I then ask the students to write a paper that combines both assignments and that presents the student's interpretation of the story.

Another assignment I have used in English 101 is the "Ladder of Abstraction." The students are taught to move down the ladder of abstraction, from love to the definition of love to kinds of love to one kind of love to an analogy to a personal experience of love to a person they love. This ladder could be applied to an analysis of "A Rose for Miss Emily." Or it could be applied to Kate Chopin's "The Storm." Another abstraction and other stories could be used.

In my department, we have made our English 102 classes literature-based. Until recently, however, the English 101 classes have been non-fiction and non-poetry. That is now changing. I find my colleagues interested in teaching literature. And I hear them questioning the overuse of drafting and group work. In our English 102 classes, most now teach Shakespeare. I sense a shift back towards the authority of the teacher. What other discipline has trained its members to do one thing and then insisted they learn something else? It is like taking an ophthalmologist and asking her to become a podiatrist instead. For me, the first year students I teach are well served by a return to the authority of the teacher and teaching composition with literature.

Encouraging Voice and Thought: Using Literature in the Composition Course

Melinda Barth
EL CAMINO COLLEGE
TORRANCE, CALIFORNIA

Nowhere is it written, but the commandment against teaching imaginative literature in the freshman composition class is as understood as if it has come down from the mountain top chiseled in stone. Adjunct instructors change their plans if they know they are going to be observed while teaching a short story or even a narrative essay in a freshman comp class. Composition textbook writers incur critics' disdain—and threats of nonadoption—for texts incorporating even an occasional poem or short story among the predominant essays.

The arguments against teachers of composition assigning literature for the content of their students' essays have their origins in the political realities and class biases embedded in the history of the English Department. As education became less the intellectual property of the elite and increasingly a way to train a work force, the essay's value was in the information it gave rather than in the form it had or the diversion it provided. The comments of Matthew Arnold, who called journalism "literature in a hurry" (qtd. in McQuade 489), and Virginia Woolf, who regretted the "heart-breaking task" of good writers needing to write for people "catching trains in the morning or for tired people coming home in the evening" (qtd. in McQuade 489) reflect the social and economic changes that moved the essay from the creative to the functional. McQuade believes that the lower, "utilitarian" status of the essay, and the focus of textbooks in composition, have established the hierarchy that assumes literature to be "elegant," "aesthetic," and "elite," whereas composition is "commonplace" and "déclassé" (491).

Another historical fact that helps explain the gap between rhetoric and literature is the shift in perceiving the focus of rhetoric and language study from the creative to the interpretive act. Until the eighteenth century, Winifred Horner observes, the study of rhetoric had been the study of composing, "discovering and communicating truth" (3). As the emphasis shifted from composing to reading and interpretation, the results were an incredible body of scholarship in critical theory and a further disassociation of literary scholars from rhetoric and freshman composition.

It is interesting to note that as early as the mid-nineteenth century, professors at major universities in Scotland and at Harvard in America were complaining about the freshman college student's inability to write, and one professor complained that he had "enough student papers to roast an ox" (Aytoun qtd. in Horner 5). The solution to the problem was to delegate writing instruction to the "lower schools, or to graduate students, or to adjunct part-time faculty" (4). At large universities, senior tenured faculty continued to teach and do research in literature, and the graduate students studied literature but taught composition. The economic advantages were clear to all college administrators, and the senior faculty approved of the distribution of labor; the graduate students who were underpaid to teach writing continued to fill their literature seminars.

Graduate students, until recently, continued to study literature but teach composition, even after it was clear that if they were finally hired with their new Ph.D.s, it would be in composition. But it was conveyed to them that the "serious business of the department is not research or teaching in composition but research and teaching in literary studies" (Horner 6). By the 1970s, enrollments at universities dropped or leveled off, and as positions were cut, and funding for composition teachers and programs increased, English scholars competed for the few openings. Literature offerings have continued to decrease, and the number of writing courses increase, as the population shifts and study preferences of the new students—medicine, law, and engineering—mandate a new view of the English Department.

Within this Department are scholars who feel "threatened, angry, and deeply discouraged" that their educations in literature are considered expendable (Horner 7). The venerable and old professors who have their Ph.D.s in Milton or Melville, or the somewhat younger but also tenured professors who have their degrees in Beckett, Barthes, or Barthelme are all reluctant to give up their career aspirations to teach literature to upper-division students just because every entering college freshman is in need of some level of writing instruction. These professors undoubtedly guard their courses and contribute to the bias that maintains that composition instructors should not invade their turf. Compelling arguments—even pedagogical ones—insist on a separation between the disciplines. But as many critics and my own teaching experiences verify, literature provides subject matter that students can write about confidently, in real voices. Writing about literature also encourages sound critical thinking. Let's examine some of the positions in the debate about teaching literature in Freshman Composition.

Those devoted to Writing Across the Curriculum programs advocate other than literature as subject matter for freshmen writers. Elaine P. Maimon is one composition theorist who believes that "the required composition course should be an introduction to composing academic discourse in the arts and sciences" (117). She says that we need to help "students enter the larger community of academic and public conversation" (117), and this "larger" community is outside of literary studies. She believes that the English Department must not only serve the greater community but protect itself from the "dreariness" of contrived research papers, with "quotations strung together like sausages," by implementing a cross-disciplinary view for student writing assignments.

The cross-disciplinary view is also held by Erika Lindemann, a Professor of English and Associate Dean of the Graduate School at the University of North Carolina at Chapel Hill who argues that if freshman composition is "the only required course remaining in most college curricula," it must "provide opportunities [for college freshmen] to master the genres, styles, audiences, and purposes of college writing" (Lindemann "No Place" 312). This course must offer "guided practice in reading and writing the discourses of the academy and the professions" (312) because Lindemann believes this is what "our colleagues across the campus want [the course] to do [and] that is what it should do if we are going to drag every first-year student through the requirement" (312).

Lindemann emphatically excludes courses "preoccupied with grammar, or the essay, or great ideas" (312), no one of which can take the place of the freshman writing course that is linked with a content course in history or the sciences because these courses have "an immediate connection to the assignments students confront in college" (312). Not merely skill courses or professional training for fields that students may enter after graduation, these courses raise questions about "audience, purpose, and form that rhetorical training has always prepared students to address" (313). In Lindemann's view, then, is the assumption that Freshman Composition is the course that prepares students for all their college studies, an obligation that holds English teachers responsible for mastering the various forms, voices, and audiences required by their colleagues across the campus. As Hamlet might say, "Oh heavy burden."

In addition to favoring what she calls the second generation Writing Across the Curriculum courses—the linked course—Lindemann absolutely denounces literature as a subject for freshman English. She sees the standard procedure for teaching literature as one where texts are "consumed" rather than "produced," and where the "teacher talks 75 to 80 percent of the time" (313). She imagines literature classes where students must "assume the disembodied voice of some abstruse journal as they analyze the ingrown toenail motif in *Beowulf*" (314). Lindemann believes that students' voices are silenced by assignments that ask them to respond to literature in such a stultifying way, a way she must feel predominates in the universities. She also believes that students see no examples of good writing styles in literary journals. Thus Lindemann argues against the use of literature in the freshman writing course.

However, even the critics who ultimately argue for a composition course that is not literature based concede that literature is an attractive subject matter for most instructors because English teachers have been brought to the love and teaching of literature during their own studies and want to teach writing courses with content that they know best. Edward P. J. Corbett, for example, acknowledges that "professors of English are usually more familiar and comfortable with literary text than with the expository essays that serve as the stimulus and model for writing assignments in most freshman anthologies" (178). Frederick Crews, who advocates the use of literature in freshman writing, also recognizes that "instructors who are issued sections of freshman English tend to be literary types," and he agrees that "if they are allowed to choose the works of literature they consider most engaging for both the students and themselves, they will surely be more alive in the classroom" (Crews 165). Richard Lanham recognizes that instructors return from the teaching of literature "excited and rejuvenated" (112), and that for most people "teaching composition does not bring the same feeling of renewal" (112). In fact, Lanham admits that teaching composition "takes grotesque amounts of time," and to do it for long turns the instructor's "mind to oatmeal" (112).

Gary Tate challenges the assumption that the freshman composition course is "a place to teach students to write academic discourse" ("Place" 319). Tate rejects the idea that the writing class is a service course for other disciplines. He asks, "Does the vast apparatus of our discipline—all the journals, books, conferences, graduate programs—exist in the cause of nothing more than better sociology and biology papers?" (319). Tate also insists that this utilitarian view of the freshman writing course reduces a college education—and the English teacher's role in it—to "job training."

Tate takes a personal stance, but probably reflects the thinking of many humanists—including writing instructors—when he asserts that he refuses to look at students as "primarily history majors, accounting majors, nursing majors" ("Place" 320). He writes that he does not wish to spend his teaching years helping students write "better papers in biology or better examinations in the health sciences" because he would find these goals "restricted, artificial, irrelevant and . . . boring" (320). Rather, Tate prefers to think of his students as people "whose most important conversations will take place outside the academy, as they struggle to figure out how to live their lives—that is, how to vote and love and survive, how to respond to change and diversity and death and oppression and freedom" (320). He observes that in spite of their affluence and freedoms, many of his students come to college "bruised" by alcohol, drugs, or parents (Tate, "Place" 320). Although he does not turn his writing courses into therapy classes for the "battered," he does believe that the needs and interests of students must be addressed. Tate asserts that the resources found in literature for helping our students should not be censored by the composition theorists he calls the "Rhetoric Police."

Even Edward P. J. Corbett, who describes how vigilant he must be to stop writing instructors who "sneak" literary texts into their writing courses (181), acknowledges that we need to get freshman composition students "hooked on books" (Fader qtd. in Corbett 178), especially if some of the "vocationally minded students are foolish enough to want to avoid any exposure to courses in the humanities" (Corbett 178). More emphatically, Frederick Crews sees that even the "wariest" students will discover in literature a world "full of images, stories, and enacted values that interest their lives in any number of ways" (165–166). Crews believes that "a freshman whose brain turns to sludge when he is asked to write about world disarmament is likely to have a definite impression of a literary character" (166).

Gary Tate reports another value for students of studying literature in the classroom: "His experience with literature gives him stature" ("Dying" 307). His reading of literature gives him "something to communicate, something he can pour out in an understandable manner. . . . His depth of thought and his pondering are turned from his reading to his expression" (307). The stature that students gain in writing about literature comes from the fact that they can be experts on, for example, character analysis—as they never, as undergraduates, will be experts on disarmament, or abortion, or capital punishment. Crews also points out that students may feel freer to write about literature because they don't suspect they have to "kowtow to an [instructor's] approved line about gun control or abortion or offshore oil leases" (165). Some teachers do have a social or political agenda, and yet they may be open to divergent views in students' papers about literature. Michael Gamer reasons that students who have difficulty writing about concepts, "for example, individual rights, responsibility, or violence" even though they may have firsthand experiences, find in imaginative texts "particularized material with which [they] can interact" (284). Literature also provides an opportunity for students to "negotiate among conflicting viewpoints," and to entertain "multiple points of view"; by its nature literature is "multidisciplinary" (Gamer 282). When a student can both interact with material that connects to her experience and see the material from multiple points of view, she is able to both think and write with meaning and voice.

Voice is a real concern for teachers of writing, as Nancy Comley and Robert Scholes perceive, in part because "students have undergone prior training designed to purge them of all impulses toward individuality" (102). Comley and Scholes illustrate how students can model different voices by examining them in literature, but perhaps more importantly establish their own confident voices by sensitively responding to well-chosen literature that they have read. The authors argue that "the condensed richness and complexity of poetry, its appeal to both the emotions and the intellect, make it stimulating to work with" (108), and if the poem is used as an "intertext" for writing in other forms, or as a "pre-text" around which to develop highly structured but not constrained writing, students' competence and commitment to the work will grow (Comley and Scholes 108).

Students' ability to think critically also will improve. In his essay "Rhyme and Reason: Why the Study of Poetry is the Best Preparation for the Study of Law," George Gopen, who holds a law degree and Ph.D. in English from Harvard University, writes from his work and observations in both fields, and his experience as a Director of Writing Programs at Loyola University of Chicago. Gopen argues first that the study of poetry, more than any other academic discipline, requires students to see how many ways a text can have meaning. Second, because "no other discipline communicates as well that words are not often fungible" (334), or "interchangeable," the study of poetry helps us teach and admire perfectly selected words. Prompting students to understand the multiple definitions of key words chosen by poets not only encourages them to admire a poet's skill but also to see the multiple levels of meaning within the poem because of the poet's word choice.

The concept of words not being fungible leads to Gopen's third and fourth points, that studying poetry teaches us to concentrate on the effects of individual words and phrases (340) and the "concept of contextuality" (342)—that the meaning of a word or phrase changes within the varying syntactic and semantic contexts of the poem. Gopen believes that the study of poetry "helps students learn how to analyze language, to recognize ambiguity, and . . . to perceive with new eyes, not merely to see new things" (347). It would appear that if we want our students to understand word choice, multiple viewpoints, and be able to support their positions by returning to the text, the study of literature— and I would agree with Gopen—especially poetry, will encourage such important critical thinking.

Wayne Booth insists that we must develop academic programs that "educate bachelors of arts who can read, think, and write in educated ways—B.A.s whose critical capacities will not shame us" (60). I believe that the scholars whose positions I have summarized here all have something worthwhile to say in the literature-in-the-composition-course debate, but I think that Booth's goal—producing students whose critical capacities will not shame us—will be met if we use some literature in the freshman composition course.

Love of literature is what brought most of us to study it and want to teach it, and it does make sense to teach a subject matter that we know and relish. This is not a default mode so much as it is an affirmation of our teaching well and most enthusiastically what we know best. We will be far more convincing teaching a subject that we know rather than frantically studying global warming, nuclear energy, the Vietnam War—or any of the other Writing Across the Curriculum subjects we have tried to prepare one step ahead of the students in order to design writing topics for them. My own WAC experiences have varied from interesting (when the subject was mythology or fairy tales) to experiencing hard work and futility when I spent eighteen weeks trying to learn philosophy well enough to design writing topics for the philosophy teacher with whom I was paired and whose papers I would ultimately read and grade. I have come to believe that Tate is correct when he argues that the English Department does not exist to service all other departments on the campus.

However, I don't think that we can ignore our students' general academic needs and teach them our version of our favorite graduate school literary theories. The students in a freshman composition course need to be given help in reading better, not select lenses for reading what isn't there. Deconstruction, Marxist, or Whateverist critical interpretations when applied to literature may give students opportunities for admiring the amazing intellectual gifts of their instructors, but I think we will be doing the students more good if we help them realize and develop their own amazing voices and gifts. If the writing course is going to help students learn to write, they must write—not listen to their instructors talk 75–80 percent of the time, as Lindemann observes.

Lindemann is unfair when she implies that writing about literature must have students reading about the "ingrown toenail motif in *Beowulf*" and paralleling the "disembodied voice of some abstruse journal" (314). Well-selected literature will not only help students learn to live their lives, as Tate believes, but provide "particularized material with which [they] can interact" with experiences from their own lives, as Michael Gamer believes (282). Further, literature provides opportunity for students "to negotiate among conflicting viewpoints," for literature presents, as Gamer observes, "multiple points of view" (282). Literature is multicultural and cross-cultural, reflecting the many worlds and the between worlds our students inhabit.

Lindemann is also inaccurate when she concludes that all students will take a literature course before they graduate and therefore need not study literature in their first year of college. I don't imagine that California institutions are unique in offering students an option of a course in critical thinking to follow their freshman writing course and complete their English requirements for general education transfer. For many, many students, the critical thinking course supplants the writing about literature course that once traditionally followed the freshman composition course. Most often taught as an argument course using expository materials, or as a formal logic class, the critical thinking course is characteristically also devoid of imaginative literature. That means that if no literature is taught in freshman composition, students can leave the community college—and perhaps the transfer university—without having read a single short story or poem, novel, or play.

Literature can be used to teach critical thinking, and some of us are using literature in just this way in both our freshman composition courses and our critical thinking classes. As George Gopen argues, there is no better way to teach students the value of word choice than to help them learn, and write about, the multiple meanings of key words in a particular poem. For example, I have students look up and write about the multiple denotative definitions of three seemingly ordinary words in Robert Frost's poem "Nothing Gold Can Stay." They show in their papers how knowing each dictionary definition of "gold," "green," and "flower" helps them understand the theme of Frost's poem. For another paper, students consider all the denotative and connotative meanings of a "border" in order to understand and connect their experiences to the speaker in the poem "To Live on the Borderlands Means. . . ." Students can write from their own life experiences, in real and confident voices. I have had students from other cultures convince me that Mrs. Ardavi, in Anne Tyler's "Your Place is Empty," is worthy of empathy, that her traumatic history influences her thoughts and behavior. Students who connect with the substance of literature write vividly, convincingly, purposefully, and perhaps cathartically.

All my literature-based assignments cultivate critical thinking, increase the students' knowledge and appreciation of literature, permit them to write in authentic voices, and let me teach what I know best. Even as I read my students' literature-based papers, my mind may turn to oatmeal, but there will be lots of sugar sprinkled on it—just the way I like it.

WORKS CITED

Booth, Wayne C. "'LITCOMP': Some Rhetoric Addressed to Cryptorhetoricians about a Rhetorical Solution to a Rhetorical Problem." Horner 57–80.

Comley, Nancy R., and Robert Scholes. "Literature, Composition, and the Structure of English." Horner 96–109.

Corbett, Edward P.J. "Literature and Composition. Allies or Rivals in the Classroom?" Horner 168–184.

Crews, Frederick. "Composing Our Differences: The Case for Literary Readings." Horner 159–67.

Gamer, Michael. "Fictionalizing the Discipline—Literature and the Boundries of Knowledge." *College English* 57 (1995): 281-86.

Gopen, George D. "Rhyme and Reason: Why the Study of Poetry Is the Best Preparation for the Study of Law." *College English* 46 (1984): 333–47.

Horner, Winifred Bryan, ed. *Composition & Literature: Bridging the Gap*. Chicago: U of Chicago P, 1983.

Lanham, Richard A. *Literacy and the Survival of Humanism*. New Haven: Yale UP, 1983.

Lindeman, Erika. "Freshman Composition: No Place for Literature." *College English* 55 (1993): 311–16.

Maimon, Elaine P. "Maps and Genres: Exploring Connections in the Arts and Sciences." Horner 110–25.

McQuade, Donald. "Composition and Literary Studies." *Redrawing the Boundaries*. Ed. Stephen Greenblatt and Giles Gunn. New York: MLA, 1992: 482–519.

Tate, Gary. "A Place for Literature in Freshman Composition." *College English* 55 (1993): 317–21.

———."Notes on the Dying of a Conversation." *College English* 57 (1995): 303–9.

Literature

Getting Started:
How to Begin an
Analytical Paper

Sharon Adams
IDYLLWILD ARTS ACADEMY
IDYLLWILD, CALIFORNIA

When I assign the first paper in my literature class each fall, I know that my students have a range of experience with this type of assignment. Some consider themselves old hands at analytical writing. Others have never had to write this type of essay before. Still others have failed miserably with similar assignments in the past because they never figured out "what the teacher wanted." I know they will be grateful for some initial guidance. I also know that the more I teach them, the better they will perform, and the easier it will be for me to face the pile of papers I will have to grade a few days hence. The best way I know to teach students to write a paper is to show them how I do it. For the first writing assignment, therefore, I take my class by the hand and lead them each step of the way.

The prewriting activity for this assignment is to read a short story of interest to both the young men and young women in my class. Two stories that never fail to captivate my students are "Greasy Lake" by T. Coraghessan Boyle and "Where Are You Going, Where Have You Been?" by Joyce Carol Oates. Each story is sufficiently complex and provocative to inspire a thoughtful essay, and the more ambitious students can find a number of ways to compare them.

Day 1

The first step of the writing process is to generate topics. I list the ideas volunteered by the class on the board. I then demonstrate the second step, which is to select a topic and write a thesis statement. I actually write several thesis statements to demonstrate the variety of approaches to any one topic. That night's homework assignment is to choose a topic and write a minimum of three thesis statements to bring in to class the next day. I hand each of them a copy of my attempts to do this step. My thesis statements are handwritten, obvious working drafts that clearly demonstrate my efforts at finding the best expression of my ideas.

Day 2

The following day I start the class with students in small groups sharing their thesis statements to be sure everyone has a workable thesis. I then discuss the ways to incorporate that thesis statement into an introductory paragraph, a first paragraph that serves as a road map to the reader indicating where the essay is going and how it is going to get there. Again I hand each of them some sample introductory paragraphs I have written and send them home to start writing their paper.

Day 3

The third day I discuss documentation from the story or stories they are writing about to support their analysis. I give them some samples of ways to integrate direct quotations into their text. I also remind them of the correct way to punctuate quotations.

Day 4

On the fourth day, the students share their rough drafts in response groups. They now have concrete examples of an appropriate standard of writing against which to measure their own and each other's work.

COMMENTARY

When I think of my own experience as an English major in college, I know that it took me several years of figuring out through trial and error how to write a good literary analysis. I don't remember ever seeing a model paper written by another college student or by a professor. It was definitely a well-kept secret. Consequently, my goal as a teacher is to make sure that the process of writing about literature is neither difficult nor mysterious.

SAMPLE PAPER TOPICS

- Flirting with Danger
- Surviving Adolescence
- Comparison/Contrast of the Two Protagonists
- Facing Fears

TWO SAMPLE THESIS STATEMENTS

- To Connie, the young protagonist of Joyce Carol Oates's short story "Where Are You Going, Where Have You Been?" being pretty was everything.

- In "Where Are You Going, Where Have You Been?" Joyce Carol Oates explores the danger and potential tragedy inherent in a young woman's promiscuity.

TWO SAMPLE INTRODUCTORY PARAGRAPHS

- The young woman protagonist in Joyce Carol Oates's "Where Are You Going, Where Have You Been?" finds herself in a dangerous situation, lured by a young man to whom she is attracted. However, the consequences for each are very different as a result of the way they handle their fear.

- A desire to be pretty and popular and to engage in innocent flirtations is normal behavior for adolescent girls. But what happens when that desire crosses the line and becomes obsession, when flirtation becomes sexual encounter? In "Where Are You Going, Where Have You Been?" Joyce Carol Oates explores the danger and potential tragedy inherent in a young woman's promiscuity.

Becoming Involved as a Reader and Writer

Jennifer Black
McLENNAN COMMUNITY COLLEGE
WACO, TEXAS

WRITING ASSIGNMENT

Write an essay (which will be mailed by me) directed to the author you've been reading or to the editors of our text. You must do *one* of the following:

1. Show the reader how to see the piece through your eyes.

2. Explain what you like or dislike about the piece.

3. Persuade the reader to keep this piece or to delete it from the next edition of the text.

THE RATIONALE BEHIND THE ASSIGNMENT

Often, for students, reading and writing are nothing more than words on a page, graphic squiggles to be gobbled in a hurry; syllables, phrases, sentences, paragraphs, paragraphs, and endlessly more paragraphs. They read, they parrot back, but they don't really listen—and they don't engage in the conversation when it's their turn.

My hope, with this assignment, is to sketch in the humanity behind what students read and to provide them an opportunity to have a voice when they write. In short, my hope is to help the students experience reading and writing not as rote activities but as acts of communication (which is what they really are, right?).

EXAMPLES OF PAST ASSIGNMENTS

The success rate of the assignment is, of course, varied. Some students seem to love writing something "real"; others are flustered by the reality of it. Whether individual students are flustered or not, I do insist on mailing all essays. (I mail them together in a large manila envelope with a cover letter attached explaining the assignment.) One semester I gave students the option of not including their names, and that was a mistake: I got the worst work I've ever gotten in response to this task.

Here are samples of past assignments and responses from authors/editors:

1. The students read Mike Rose's *Lives on the Boundary* and wrote what they liked or disliked about it. Although many of the students agreed with Rose's points, most of them chose to argue with something he had said. I got a letter back from Rose, indicating that he had loved reading the essays, largely due to the argumentative nature of their letters. It seems that critics had reviewed his work as a narrative, but—to his delight—the students had easily seen his argument.

2. The students read two essays from a freshman composition II reader but could choose to respond to only one. If they chose the piece from the living author, they wrote to that person; if they chose the author who was deceased, they wrote to the editor, indicating whether the piece should appear in the next edition of the text. Most of the students chose the latter angle, seeming to enjoy having a say in what might appear in a future edition. It turns out that the text was being revised, and I got a call from the editor thanking us for the responses.

3. The students read Dana Gioia's poetry and chose to respond to one poem (or theme or point of style or other aspect). Gioia wrote an open letter in response to the essays, and I sent a copy to each student (the semester was over). I got several calls and e-mails from students amazed at Gioia's response. Two semesters later, students are still talking about what Gioia "said" in his poems.

SOME ADVICE

I carefully prepare the students for this task, both so that they understand what they need to do (and don't embarrass themselves) and so that they concretely see the connection between themselves and the written word.

First, I want them to understand that reading is listening, and writing is talking. So I talk about how a book (or poem or story) can be seen as someone talking to them in written form. I bring in books on tape so that they can hear the words—especially when I can get them in the author's own voice—and CDs with songs adapted from poems (such as Joni Mitchell's version of Yeats) so that they can hear other interpretations. I show them my own books with notes in the margins—places I listened and agreed; places I argued and fumed.

Secondly, I want them to understand that they're engaging in the art of communication, not a "did not/did too" type of argument. So I go over possible elements of effective arguments; the students role-play their essays—one student pretends to be the reader, and another talks through his or her essay—then we all respond or critique; and the students write several drafts and go through at least one peer critique session.

Thirdly, I don't want the students to be embarrassed. So I have at least one peer editing session before the letters are mailed. Also, if an essay is truly horrible, I talk with the student about revising it again before it gets mailed. Ultimately, though, the decision is the student's.

A RELATED TASK

When I was an undergraduate, a professor of mine had us pretend to be one of the authors we had read, writing a letter to another author we had read. I really liked that assignment and found that it made me think more deeply about both works. In that case, both authors had been long dead, so there was no real communication, but the task worked nonetheless. By the way, if you use this assignment, say a silent thank you to Dennis Kratz of the University of Texas at Dallas.

What is Literature?
A Double Assignment

Janis Adams Crowe
FURMAN UNIVERSITY
GREENVILLE, SOUTH CAROLINA

In my "Introduction to Literature" course, I ask students to do a short, in-class writing assignment on both the first and the day-before-last day. This assignment uses four quotations I include on an introductory information sheet:

> "Writing and reading are not all that distinct for a writer. Both exercises require being alert and ready for unaccountable beauty, for the intricateness or simple elegance of the writer's imagination, for the world that imagination evokes. Both require being mindful of the places where imagination sabotages itself, locks its own gates, pollutes its vision. Writing and reading mean being aware of the writer's notions of risk and safety, the serene achievement of, or sweaty fight for, meaning and response-ability."
>
> *Toni Morrison*

> "Literature, in the widest sense, is just about anything written. . . . In the sense that matters to us. . . literature is a kind of art, usually written, which offers pleasure and illumination."
>
> *X. J. Kennedy*

> "I will simply take the position that the spoken word, like the written word, amounts to a nonsensical arrangement of sounds or letters without a consensus that assigns 'meaning.' And building from the meanings of what we hear, we order reality. Words themselves are innocuous; it is the consensus that gives them true power."
>
> *Gloria Naylor*

> "Literature, we're told, is one of the arts, along with painting and music; and, after you've looked up all the hard words and Classical allusions and learned what words like imagery and diction are supposed to mean, what you use in understanding it, or so you're told, is your imagination."
>
> *Northrop Frye*

THE FIRST ASSIGNMENT

X. J. Kennedy says that literature "in the widest sense, is just about anything written. . . . In the sense that matters to us . . . literature is a kind of art, usually written, which offers pleasure and illumination." Read the other definitions of literature on your intro sheet and think about your own notions of what literature is—from the college catalogue, high school or other English classes here, friends' experiences, and popular culture.

Write, in a sentence or two, your definition of what literature is—based on your reading and academic experience.

RESULTS

Most of these first-day definitions tended to be vague and rather awkward; they relied heavily on a few words—"symbol," "great," and "creative." They mentioned few genres, usually just "novels" or "books" and "poems." Many were thought of in the contexts of academic class experience; literature has hidden meanings that classes reveal; and literature is somehow composed of works that schools own the listing of. No one mentioned literature as work that he or she might write. I read all these in class and kept them until the end of the term, when I asked them to write another definition.

THE SECOND ASSIGNMENT

Now that we've read a great variety of writing in this class, what do you think literature is? Is it what you said it was in March? Do you have more focused ideas about what you enjoy? About what is difficult? About different genres? *Now*, how would you distinguish literature from your infirmary excuse notes, overdue book statements, letters from home, and Subway menus? Define literature this time in the context of what you have read and found of value.

RESULTS

This time the definitions— I handed both back the last day— were more confident and more specific. Students talked about literature as if they knew some! They said it communicates feelings. It moves us. Literature "gives us a voice," one said. It "separates the human race from all other life forms." They put themselves in the definition and connected organization with particular effects. After commenting on their definitions, I tried to focus on the point that literature—as I define it—is *crafted* writing. It is writing arranged according to the vision of an individual artist. Marcel Proust says that style comes from vision, and this idea gives us a chance to talk about their point that literature lets us speak, shows us the world from each other's eyes. I raised the issue of a canonical approach to reading literature, *and* to what I think is the purpose of this intro course: the development of their analytical skills and knowledge to the point where they feel that no literature is inaccessible—even some prize-winning, experimental piece of contemporary writing. They should at least know where to get on the path into what looks at first like inhospitable territory.

Some Writing Assignments for Literature Class

Kathleen De Grave
PITTSBURG STATE UNIVERSITY
PITTSBURG, KANSAS

In my literature classes I assign many different kinds of writing. Many of the assignments students write in class, to help them learn the material and focus on certain elements of the genre we are concentrating on. But I also give outside assignments, formal and informal. The formal assignments consist of two- to three-page typewritten papers. The informal assignment is a Response Notebook. I describe each in detail.

GENERAL RULES FOR WRITING ESSAYS

I have my students write essays of two to three pages on specific stories, poems, and plays after we have discussed the elements of the respective genre and studied several pieces closely in class. Because one way to learn to write about literature is to see what other students have done, I have students bring a rough draft of the essay to class and work in peer groups. It always helps if I can show a model of the kind of essay I am looking for on the overhead first. The students bring at least one photocopy of their rough drafts with them so that everyone in the group of three or four can read along as they deal with one paper at a time. I stress the difference between interpretation and plot summary and remind them that quotations should be short so that interpretations of the quotations can be full.

WRITING ASSIGNMENTS FOR SPECIFIC STORIES

"A & P"
Explain what Sammy in "A & P" is rejecting when he says "I quit." Think about what the store and Lengel stand for from

Sammy's point of view and what his new relationship to the "hard" world will be.

What is Sammy's attitude toward women? He quits his job, he says, because he wants to look like a hero in Queenie's eyes. Is he egalitarian, defending the young women's right to dress as they please, or is he sexist?

"The Jilting of Granny Weatherall"

Granny Weatherall has a spiritual crisis the first time she is jilted. Why is she able to stand up so well to what she perceives as her second jilting? What has she learned? What *is* the second jilting?

What are the crisis and climax in "The Jilting of Granny Weatherall"? Argue that a particular moment is the moment after which there is no going back, and that another moment is the high point. Be sure to focus on Granny's death as the story, not on her memories; the memories shape her death, but I don't want the crisis of her past—give the crisis of the present.

"Everyday Use"

The quilt in "Everyday Use" plays a symbolic role in several ways. Explain how the quilt functions as a symbol, both in itself and in how it partakes in the action of the story.

The mother in "Everyday Use" has an epiphany near the end. Describe the epiphany and show how it is both the crisis and the climax of the story. What brings the epiphany on? What is the result of it?

"Barn Burning"

Why does Abner Snopes burn barns? Is he a hero? An antihero? Be sure to explain the class system involved in being a tenant farmer.

At what point does Sarty decide to betray his father? Argue that this point is the crisis of the story. *Why* does Sarty betray him?

WRITING ASSIGNMENTS FOR SPECIFIC POEMS

General Assignment

Write a letter to a friend in which you explain why you like a particular poem. Pretend that you have sent a copy of the poem to your friend and that your friend has read it. You will need to interpret the poem for your friend and explain some of the more difficult images and metaphors. But your main purpose is to tell your friend why you would really like him or her to read *that* poem.

"Facing It," "The Death of the Ball Turret Gunner," and "Dulce et Decorum Est"

Pretend that Yusef Komunyakaa, Randall Jarrell, and Wilfred Owen were able to meet and talk. What would they say to each other about the meaning of war? Remember that each poet experienced a different war (Vietnam, World War II, World War I). Use word choices, images, and metaphors/similes from each poem to make your point.

"In Memoriam John Coltrane"

This is a poem about a great jazz saxophone player. Argue that the poem re-creates a sense of jazz by its use of sounds and rhythms. In particular, talk about all the sound connections you see (alliteration, assonance, consonance, exact rhyme, slant rhyme) and try to describe the sound and rhythm effects.

"My Papa's Waltz"

Some people argue that "My Papa's Waltz" is about an abusive relationship between a father and son. Some people say the poem is just about a rollicking, friendly dance—about love. What do *you* think the poem is about? Is this an abusive family relationship? Is it a loving one? Could it be love/hate? Analyze imagery, sound relationships (including rhyme), and rhythm in order to make your case.

WRITING ASSIGNMENTS FOR SPECIFIC PLAYS

Trifles

Show how props are used symbolically in *Trifles*. Explain the use of the prop and what the prop symbolizes in each case. Look at all of the props and try to group them somehow. (For example, you could find symbols of Minnie's emotional battering, symbols of Minnie's hard work, symbols of the women's growing comprehension.)

Pretend that you are the prosecuting attorney and argue that Minnie Wright murdered her husband. Show that she had the opportunity, means, and motivation.

OR

Pretend that you are the defense attorney, faced with the evidence Mrs. Hale and Mrs. Peters discovered. Argue that there are extenuating circumstances in the case and that therefore the judge should be lenient in his sentencing. Put yourself into the time period of the play as you discuss Minnie Wright's alternatives. Remember that in the era the play is written, the judge and jury will be all men.

A Doll's House

Decide what the moment of recognition and reversal is in *A Doll's House*. What does Nora recognize, and how is her situation at the end of the play reversed from the beginning? Show how the action leads up to this moment (or these separate moments if they are not the same) and explain why the dénouement is then inevitable. Use specific quotes.

Many people were outraged that Nora would leave her husband and children at the end of *A Doll's House*. In fact, some versions of the play have her going into the children's room at the last minute and deciding to stay. Which ending do you think is the better one and why? Be sure to refer to the main themes of the play and to keep in mind Nora's and Torvald's characters.

Oedipus the King

In *Oedipus the King*, trace the successive changes in the attitude of the chorus towards Oedipus and towards the gods, because Oedipus comes into conflict with the gods as the play proceeds. Look at each choral section and decide what the attitude is in each. In some sections, the chorus might focus on just Oedipus or just the gods; in some the chorus talks about both. Decide whether the respective attitudes change, and if so, how. Use quotations from the choral sections to argue your case.

The Glass Menagerie

Argue that Laura is or is not a dynamic character. Show when and how she changes, if she does. Do not speculate on what she will do after the play. Simply describe her character at various stages of the play, *always* using evidence from the text.

Discuss the ambiguity of Tom's leaving. Show how it is both necessary and cruel—how to escape his "coffin" he has to "drive out at least one nail." What will be the effect of his leaving on Laura and Amanda (not speculation, but using evidence from the text)? Why is it necessary nonetheless that he leave?

Explain Jim's intentions. Why does he talk to Laura about

her "inferiority complex" and dance with her and kiss her? Is he being kind? Is he trying to help her? Is he being self-centered? Is he an insensitive lout? Perhaps he has a complex mixture of intent.

Whom is this play about? Which character—Tom, Laura, or Amanda—is the protagonist? Decide what the "center" of the play is for that person, and interpret the plot in light of that person's development. Also, given this protagonist, who or what is the antagonist?

Laura Wingfield is "crippled." Discuss several speeches or dialogues that show *how* Laura is crippled (in what ways, physically, emotionally, socially, she is crippled) and *what* she is crippled by.

Consider the various coats in the play to be symbolic. Discuss the symbolism of each scene in which a coat plays an important role.

JOURNALS

A regular assignment that I make as I teach the three genres is a journal, although the form differs for each.

FOR FICTION, the journal assignment looks like this:

Write from one to three pages on four stories of your choice (from those we are reading this semester). For each story, give three kinds of response: a personal response, a social issues response, and a literary comparison. I want you to engage the story personally and intelligently. Do not summarize the story—we will do that in class. Rather, *react to* the story; make it your own. This is a place to take risks. I will not grade the response notebook on grammar or form, only on your willingness to use your thoughts and emotions as you read.

Personal Response

Relate the story or parts of the story to an experience you have had, to people you have met. If you have a strong emotional reaction to the action or to a character, explain *why* you have that reaction. It might be just a phrase or a part of the setting that affects you. Let the story mean something personal to you. (**Caution:** If the story is *too* personal, don't write on that one.)

Social Response
Relate the story to a larger social or philosophical issue, like problems of race, gender, class, age, religion, or problems in government, education, law—whatever.

Literary Comparison
After you have read all four stories, see if you can find some comparisons or contrasts among them. Are themes similar? Do settings seem to repeat? Might some character from one story help you understand the characters from another? What light might one story shed on another? Let the stories interact, have a dialogue in your mind, rather than sit separately in little compartments.

FOR POETRY, the journal assignment is a bit different:

The poetry response notebook will have two parts. For the first part, write an emotional response to any four poems we read. Choose poems that you really like or some that make you very angry or depressed. Think about the lines in the poem, the sounds and the images, that affect you and explain why they do. I'm not asking that you talk about yourself but about the poem and what it does to you, although sometimes it is easier to explain what the poem does by describing the images or experiences it calls up. Reading poetry is most enjoyable when you put some of yourself into it, even if you don't understand the entire poem on your own.

For the second part, write a poem. You might try imitating one of the poems you write about for part one. Or you might write a poem about an experience that one of the poems recalls for you. In the poem, try to use the poetic elements we discuss. Use *concrete images,* not just abstract language. Use unusual comparisons—*metaphors* and *similes.* Use *sounds* to connect ideas and heighten them. Try very hard to make your poem *not* rhyme.

FOR DRAMA, the journal is very simple:

Keep a journal of entries on the plays that we both see and read. Write a page or two on each play, discussing the differences you notice between the written play and the play as it is performed. Always talk about how the differences affect you and affect the theme and characters. Decide which version you like better. Keep in mind what you gain from stage directions on the one hand and from seeing an actor or actress interpret a part and a director interpret a play on the other. Discuss the effect of costumes, stage effects like lighting and music, entrances and exits, blocking, and interpretation of specific lines or scenes.

Outside the Anthology

Frank X. Gaspar
LONG BEACH CITY COLLEGE
LONG BEACH, CALIFORNIA

Elizabeth Bishop once remarked that she did not like to use an anthology when teaching because too often the students came away thinking that the anthology wrote the work. It is a classic Bishop witticism, but it comes with an underlying truth: Too often our students are overwhelmed with the sheer breadth of selections in an anthology, and often they can only refer to a poem as "the one about all the laundry hanging out the window," or a story as "the one where the woman kills the guy and leaves him on the bed." But, of course, the anthology, especially a good anthology, is indispensable to us.

Here is an assignment in plain vanilla, designed to make each student a resident class expert on one author contained in the anthology. The aim here is to break the boundaries of the anthology and allow students to explore the vast world of literature that the anthology necessarily samples. We can learn that Emily Dickinson had a family, and that "I like to see it lap the miles" in another version reads, "I like to *hear* it lap the miles," and according to one writer, may have had something to do with her brother Austin. I generally give this assignment near the end of the course. It can be varied in any number of ways, but here is a template:

1. The students review the selections they have read and pick one that they especially liked for whatever reasons they are prepared to give.

2. The student declares that a particular author is his or her subject.

3. The student, using the library and other sources of data, assembles a small preliminary bibliography. (The resulting paper or presentation can vary in length to suit the needs of the course—I usually use this as a "documented essay" exercise, practicing MLA style, but I have seen this used with panels and individual oral presentations).

4. The student, using the following guidelines (or your version of them), builds a preliminary outline.

INFORMATION REQUIRED FOR AUTHOR PROJECT

- Biographical information

- Context in which this person wrote (historical period, concurrent writers or discoveries, geographical area)

- Precursors to this person's work (groundwork laid by those who came before, and the like)

- Major works, their significance and impact

- People or schools of thought this person subsequently influenced

- Evidence of this person's importance or stature in current times

- What you have gained from this study (how your thinking or perception has been affected, or some similar impact this study had on you)

- Why this writer's work appealed to you in the first place (what value you found in it, how it spoke to you, and other features that struck you)

The students then write or prepare the assignment. I often teach note-taking techniques, research skills, and other related matters as part of helping them through this. The variations are endless, and, despite the essentially homely quality of this assignment, the response is overwhelmingly positive. Oral presentations, small group presentations, and read-arounds are generally lively. The students simply like being experts and sharing their new knowledge—and the boundaries of the anthology have been extended.

Weekly In-Class Writing Assignments

Francie Kisko
SKAGIT VALLEY COMMUNITY COLLEGE,
SAN JUAN CENTER
FRIDAY HARBOR, WASHINGTON

WRITING ASSIGNMENT

1. Divide the class into four groups. As a homework assignment, have each group read one story from a single chapter in *Literature: An Introduction to Fiction, Poetry, and Drama.* For example, if you are using the chapter on Point of View, assign "A Rose for Emily" to group one, "The Tell-Tale Heart" to group two, and so on. (**Note:** If the chapter contains only three stories, use one of the stories from "Stories for Further Reading" so that the number is even.)

2. As an in-class writing assignment, give each group a question regarding the reading assignment, such as:

   - Would "A Rose for Emily" have been more effective if told from Miss Emily's point of view?
   - How do you think "The Tell-Tale Heart" would have changed if it had been told from the third person objective instead of the first person point of view?

3. Give the students in each group ten to fifteen minutes to discuss their readings and to generate ideas on how to answer the question effectively.

4. Then have each student individually write a short one- to two-page essay answering the question, emphasizing the need for a thesis statement and supporting evidence from the story itself (or from examples drawn from other stories read during the class).

5. After the writing assignment is completed, have a number of students read their question and response aloud and let the other students comment whether they feel: (a) that the ques-

tion was answered with an appropriate thesis statement; and (b) that the thesis was adequately supported with evidence from the story. This should open up the subject for discussion by the students who shared the story; the others can participate by discussing style and logical application of support.

COMMENTARY

This short in-class writing assignment helps the students focus on a particular characteristic of literary writing that is being discussed in the chapter, and gives the students practice at supporting their main ideas as well as documenting their sources. The oral discussion after the writing assignment emphasizes to the students that their writing is read by others and must therefore make sense.

Reading and "Really Reading"

Kim McCollum-Clark
MILLERSVILLE UNIVERSITY
MILLERSVILLE, PENNSYLVANIA

Upon encountering a group of students in an "Introduction to Literature" class who freely identified themselves as "nonreaders," I inserted into my traditional syllabus several activities to honor their very real question: "What is this literature stuff for, anyway?" The following activities were created to bridge the students' self-understandings and the aims of the course. As I relate them here, these inquiries seem like a great deal to accomplish before the "real" work of the class begins, but in the case of nontraditional or reluctant students, I believe they were critical in creating a realistic setting in which to talk about literature, how it works, and what it "means."

THE READING SURVEY

We began with a brief passage from Adrienne Rich: "You must write, and read, as if your life depended on it" (*What is found there: Notebooks on poetry and politics.* New York: Norton, 1994) and continued with an inquiry into the habits of "regular readers" to find out if reading did indeed play a role in life outside of formal school assignments. Each student interviewed five people who identified themselves as readers, asking the respondents why they read, who were their favorite authors or types of books, how reading fit into their choices as to how to spend their time, who was responsible for supporting their reading habits, and how they decided what to read. Results were returned and collated in class to provide a profile of typical readers. Our class poll concluded the following: readers reported that they read mostly for enjoyment and to experience new things; women were more likely than men to attest to the personal importance of reading; and families with strong reading habits were cited as the most important influence on individual reading. Students were surprised with the ubiquity of reading across gender, age, class, and employment tracks. They quickly pointed out, however, that the reading the respondents identified was not the kind of reading promoted in our class and literature anthology. "We do read," they acknowledged, confronted by the data and recognizing themselves in it, "but we don't *really* read."

FAMILY TALES AND CULTURE TALES

An inquiry into the term *really reading* revealed that students believed that "literature" had little or nothing to do with the reading they did. They suggested that only specially trained people "really read" when they are confronted with special types of stories, novels, plays, and poems for reasons they could not describe. It was in trying to bring these reasons to our inquiry that we began by describing "family tales" and "culture tales"—stories told by groups, large or small, to create representations of themselves, defining those inside and outside the group. In one activity, each student wrote and shared a story important to his or her family, pondering the way the story defined the family and the student's role in it. In another, students described objects that held special meaning in the life of their families and its members. This activity led to our reading and discussion of Alice Walker's short story "Everyday Use." We briefly expanded our notion of family tales to "culture tales" with an examination of "patriotic" stories about the United States and an analysis of advertisements that function (among other things) to "tell stories" about the core values of being an American. (Interestingly, the students decided that one such core American value was the injunction, "Love yourself first.") As a part of all of these activities, I continually cultivated the question, "How are these core values or meanings represented?" We used Wilfred Owen's poem "Dulce et Decorum Est" to explore how a culture's tale can be promoted or undercut in a work of imaginative literature.

At the end of these inquiries and activities, the class decided that humans use "story," and hence literature, to construct or seek meaning in life's events, to transform what is confusing and ineffable into something we can grasp and even share with others, to try to explain things, and to build solidarity within groups and identify those outside groups. The notion of the unspeakable, the ineffable in everyday life, resonated with the group. They wrote for a long time in their journals of personal experiences in which they either had no words to communicate emotions they recognized or no words to help themselves understand the emotion itself. These ideas led us to explore the rest of our readings as expressions of individuals with stories to tell and special gifts and techniques for telling them.

Putting Together a Literature Paper

Todd Scott Moffett
COMMUNITY COLLEGE OF SOUTHERN NEVADA
LAS VEGAS, NEVADA

ASSIGNMENT

When you write a paper for courses involving literature, you usually perform a literary analysis. In your analysis, you interpret short stories, poems, or plays that you have read for the class. This interpretation will either explain the function of the elements (plot, setting, rhyme, author's background, and the like) in the readings or set out your response (Did you like the play or dislike it? What do you think of the main character? and so on). To complete your analysis, you may want to use the following models for your thesis sentence and your body paragraphs.

THESIS

Your thesis represents your interpretation of the work. To complete your thesis, you need to have a clear understanding of your assignment. If your instructor has given you a question, then your thesis should be your answer to that question.

Sample Question: What motivates Iago, the villain in Shakespeare's *Othello*?

Sample Thesis: Iago is motivated by his jealousy of Othello and by his ambition to rise through the ranks of the Venetian army.

If your instructor has asked you to decide on your own topic, then you may find the following frames useful:

1. (The author) uses ___x___ to show___y___.
2. Through the use of ___x___ (the author) shows (how) ___y___.
3. The development of ___x___ reveals___y___.

Here is an example of how this form might be filled in.

1. (Shakespeare) uses_the X-plot_to show_Iago's growing influence over Othello._
2. Through the use_of the grotesque,_(Faulkner) shows how _Miss Emily's secrets represent ugly truths about the American South_.
3. The development of_the flea as a symbol for love_ reveals_the desperation behind the speaker's attempt to seduce the lady he is addressing._

BODY PARAGRAPHS

After you have stated your thesis, you must support that thesis in your body paragraphs. To support your thesis, you must cite and explain passages, from the work itself, that give rise to your interpretation. Remember that you are explaining and interpreting the work and NOT summarizing it (that is, simply retelling what happens). You should assume that your reader is familiar with the work. By following the model given here, you can create any number of body paragraphs to support your thesis.

The Five-Step Paragraph
1. Topic Sentence
2. Narrow Down Sentence
3. Quotation
4. Explanation
5. Conclusion

Topic Sentence

In the topic sentence, you should present some portion of your thesis to be proven in the paragraph. If you are working with a thesis created from the three models presented earlier, you can present the information you inserted into spaces x and y. Early paragraphs in your essay should focus on the information in space x, and later paragraphs should focus on the information in space y. Each new paragraph should either develop a new portion or expand a point made in a previous paragraph.

Narrow Down Sentence

The narrow down sentence should point the reader's attention to a specific passage that supports your topic sentence You should name the source of the passage (who is speaking here?), name the location of the passage (is it toward the beginning of the work? toward the end? in what paragraph?), or describe the content of the passage (who's doing what? what is the speaker saying?).

Quotation

In this sentence you should write out the passage you pointed out in the narrow down sentence. If you write the passage word for word, you must put it in "quotation marks." If you paraphrase the passage (rewrite it in your own words), then you won't need quotation marks. However, whether you quote word for word or paraphrase, you need to document your source by giving the last name of the author and the page number on which the quoted passage appears in the original work (Kennedy 1860). Give only the page number if you mention the author's name in the narrow down sentence or if you are writing about a single work (233). If you are quoting from a play, you may cite the act, scene, and line(s) instead of the page number. This citation will appear in parentheses after the quotation (2.2.14–17).

Explanation

In this sentence you need to explain the meaning of the passage you just quoted, and/or explain how that passage supports your topic sentence. Refer to specific words in the passage that carry special meaning or extra importance and how those words give rise to your interpretation.

Conclusion

To conclude the body paragraph, you need to finish your explanation of the passage and sum up the points just presented. You may also need to provide a transition to the next paragraph.

Following is an example of a worksheet based on these instructions:

Analysis Checklist

Thesis _____
_____
_____

Topic _____
_____
_____
_____

Narrow Down (location/speaker/content)   _____
_____
_____

Quote " _____
_____
_____
_____ " (reference).

Explanation of quote's key word(s)   _____
_____
_____
_____

Conclusion (relate meaning of quote to topic)   _____
_____
_____
_____

Analysis Checklist

Thesis In "The Chrysanthemums," John Steinbeck uses Elisa's dress and the fence surrounding the garden to show the many boundaries Elisa has imposed upon her life.

Topic The attention given to the characters' movement around the wire fence shows that this boundary has been created to protect her from intruders.

Narrow Down (location/speaker/content) Steinbeck draws his readers' attention to the Drifter's movements as he works his way from one side of the fence to the other.

Quote "He drew a big finger down the chicken wire and made it sing" (Steinbeck 242); then "He leaned confidentially over the fence" (242); and finally, "The man leaned farther over the fence" (243).

Explanation of quote's key word(s) The fence, designed to keep out barnyard animals and others who might trample and uproot the flowers, here also keeps the Drifter away from Elisa, and a major turning point in the story comes when she allows him into the garden.

Conclusion (relate meaning of quote to topic) She has lowered her protection from this intruder and becomes vulnerable to his lies and schemes.

Looking for Fresh, Crisp Language

Mark Todd
WESTERN STATE COLLEGE
GUNNISON, COLORADO

This exercise introduces students to *catachresis*—that is, writing that uses apparently inappropriate word substitutions, inappropriate because the relationship between the words substituted is not obvious or even definable. I usually illustrate on the blackboard or overhead a sample of each of the steps to give students a leg up. I frequently stop them and ask them to try out their latest locutions on neighboring students.

When I finish the exercise, I make a writing assignment that requires them to use instances of this syntactic construction. I also end by encouraging them "to spank their writing lovingly" with catachresis. If they've been paying attention, I can tell from their reaction to this catachretic quip whether or not they understand the trope.

Step 1
Write down the five senses across the top of a piece of paper, creating a column for each. Under each sense, write a variety of adjectives, nouns, and verbs appropriate to that sense, but paying no attention to similarities between categories. Write at least five words under each category.

Step 2
Combine descriptions that blend two senses—in other words, that take words randomly from two categories and join them into a phrase:
- a *loud plaid screech*, or a *sour hum*

Step 3
Juxtapose unexpected combinations of the same sense:
- a *silky shudder*, or a *clang of silence*

49

Step 4

Experiment with combinations that include modifier-modified, noun-prepositional phrase, and subject-verb:

- *a clanging silence*
- *a clang of silence*
- *silence clanged through the room*

Step 5

Finally, try varying the degrees and nuances of a single phrase of Step 4. Think of a scale of 1 to 4, in which "1" represents a subtle instance and "5" a blatant instance. Situate your phrase on the scale and invent other phrases that precede or follow that one, as appropriate. For example, if I decide that "a clanging silence" from Step 4 were a "4" on the 1-to-5 scale, then I might propose these phrases as well:

- *a sweet silence*
- *a billow of silence*
- *clanging silence*
- *a silence roared*

Student Writing Exercise

Sensory Language

Bernadette Wagner
WESTERN STATE COLLEGE
GUNNISON, COLORADO

Step 1   Words for Each of the Five Senses

Sight	Hearing	Touch	Taste	Smell
Bright	Quiet	Smooth	Sweet	Fresh
Colors	Loud	Rough/Sticky	Sour	Flowers
Light	Voice	Solid	Bitter	Rich
Darkness	Whisper	Liquid	Sugary	Heady
Lightning	Thunder	Sensitive	Salty	Aroma
Glance	Silence	Fur	Spicy	Clean

Step 2   Random Combinations That Blend Two Senses
    rich flower voice
    bitter liquid whisper
    sweet smooth darkness
    liquid lightning glance
    salty thunder
    thunder voice
    lightning glance
    liquid fur

Step 3   Unexpected Combinations for the Same Sense
    rich aroma
    rough liquid
    ·color glance
    sticky breath

Step 4   Experimental Combinations
a sweet smooth darkness
a salty thunder
the sweet smoothness of dark
the thunder of salty
the smooth darkness of sweet
darkness sweet and smooth
flower-rich voice
her voice was rich with flowers

Step 5   Nuanced Phrases
a subtle darkness
a smooth cloak of darkness
a rich salty darkness
a bitter darkness
a thunder of darkness

Dinner on the River

Sue Walker
UNIVERSITY OF SOUTH ALABAMA
MOBILE, ALABAMA

> "If music be the food of love, play on."
> —*Shakespeare*
>
> *Please join us for a grande repast*
>
> *Baron and Baroness D'Agneau*
>
> *Place: Houseboat on the river Styx*
> *Time: 8:00 p.m.*
> *Dress: Optional*

The occasion is a dinner party given individually by each student, who may invite no fewer than eight guests. The guests may be any characters from any story or poem that has been covered during a specific period. I like to use this assignment for either a mid-term or a final exam, because it tests the student's knowledge of authors and literary works, and the students have fun determining the guest list, menu, music, and flowers and creating who says what to whom under a variety of circumstances. They can be as inventive as they like, in addition to using quoted passages from stories and poems. When I have given this assignment for a final, the students have been so enthusiastic that they asked to gather at a nearby restaurant to eat and to read their papers. The papers have been excellent, and the literary party produced a post-exam party as well!

A word about placements and anachronisms. Students are free of time constraints and strictures. Any character may share the table with any other, though one may have strut and fret his hour across the stage in New Smyrna, Florida, in 1897 or in any clean, well-lighted place in 1933. Who keeps up with chronometers when Lethe water flows freely with spirits of all kinds?

I have found in giving this assignment that William Faulkner's

Miss Emily is a favorite party guest in spite of the fact that she has become somewhat bitter about men and property taxes. The last time I was with her at one of these feasts, she was not in good health. Her hair was *cut short, making her look like a girl, with a vague resemblance to those angels in colored church windows—sort of tragic and serene.* She was, however, not a typical angel by any means. I sat across from her and observed her closely as she talked with an old lady who kept protesting that she did not want to go to Florida. "A Misfit's on the loose," she said, and I agreed that a woman can't be too careful these days. "You know," the grandmother went on, "a good man is hard to find." Emily said she thought she had found one once, but he wasn't the marrying kind.

Granny Weatherall was also at dinner, and, typically, she chimed in the conversation though she was sitting at least three seats down from Emily and me. Love always seems to produce such a reaction in her. Everyone says that in spite of being eighty-years-old, she's never gotten over that young man who jilted her. I thought the woman seemed quite demented, leaning over her plate and shouting down the table: *"I want you to find George. Find him and be sure to tell him I forgot him."* Crazy Jane was so startled that she broke off the conversation she was having with the bishop and said "Granny Weatherall, didn't anybody ever tell you that *nothing can be sole or whole that has not been rent.* You don't want to find George, and we aren't going looking for him." She went on about love being pitched in excrement. I thought it was best to change the subject, so I asked Billy to tell me about his accident in an open boat. "Who drowned?" I asked, and he said that the sea was a bucking bronco, and that he and his comrades were so busy bailing out the boat that *none of them knew the color of the sky.*

Life seems to be one tragedy after another. I can't remember her last name, but Jane told a horrifying account of the Weir Mitchell rest cures. Her husband is a doctor too, and he took her out to a run-down country estate and virtually confined her to an attic. Well, Jane pulled her chair up beside Emily and made the waiter set her a place. She said there was a woman creeping about behind some ugly yellow wallpaper and she had to peel off the monstrous paper and get her out.

I hope I wasn't rude, but the conversation got to be too much! I made my excuses as soon as we finished the chocolate mousse. It was a beautiful night on the river Styx. Charon was gallant as he reached out his hand to help me off the boat. "Great party," he said.

Fiction

What Will It Take to Get Your Attention?

Adrienne Bond
MERCER UNIVERSITY
MACON, GEORGIA

This exercise can be used after reading "The Use of Force," "Everyday Use," "I Stand Here Ironing," "A & P," "Araby," "Barn Burning," or almost any story of self discovery.

What will it take to convince you? What will it take to get your attention? What will it take to make you realize? Most of us find this sort of question irritating when it's directed toward us, but it is the central question the author is asking his character in a certain kind of story.

ASSIGNMENT 1

Think back through your life. Was there an event that changed the way you looked at the world, or altered your self-image, undermined some idea or value you previously held, or caused you to act out of some higher value that had just been words to you before? What was it? Make several pages of notes about this event and what you learned from it—or unlearned.

ASSIGNMENT 2

Now think hard. Can you remember (or make up) several previous times when you might have made this discovery, faced the facts, learned this hard lesson, but didn't? Other opportunities that didn't quite get your attention? Write about each of these inconclusive events in order, then end with the dramatic event you first made notes on. Voilà! You have the first draft of a short story!

Scripting a Story

Paul Buchanan
BIOLA UNIVERSITY
LA MIRADA, CALIFORNIA

I have noticed that many of my students come to college lacking confidence in their ability to write or read analytically. This trend is probably due to the fact that so much of the typical student's life has been spent in front of a television set.

But rather than belittle my students for wasting their youth, as I was inclined to do in the past, I have found that their savvy about the conventions of film and television can be exploited to discuss the elements of good writing. Although they lack confidence in writing and reading, they are supremely confident in their ability to watch a movie.

I find myself creating analogies between what goes on in a typical film with what goes on in the writing process, and by discussing these analogies, I find my students more inclined to enter the dialogue. They feel that they aren't learning new techniques, but rather new ways of talking about techniques they already thoroughly know. The *establishing shot* of a new scene in a movie becomes the *topic sentence* of a new paragraph. The *visual transitions* between scenes become *thematic transitions* between topics.

I like to have my students read five or six short stories from the Kennedy reader at the beginning of the semester, posing as studio executives. After reading, we vote to buy one of these "properties" to make into a film. Once a story has been chosen, we begin scripting our film as a class. One of the students becomes the "script supervisor," whose job it is to keep the official version of the script as we go along.

The process of scripting one of these stories serves as an excellent jumping-off place for talking about writing in the weeks ahead.

For example, the students are invariably concerned with making sure that the first scene is action-filled while still introducing the main character and the conflict. Their concerns about what goes into the first scene of their movie is easily used later on to explain what should go into the first paragraph of an essay.

Students are also careful to make sure that their film is easily followed. We spend a lot of time talking about transitions between scenes, and elements that can be used to link scenes together—topics that the students naturally bring up themselves. The students are also careful to try to put scenes into a logical, causal order, and they often want to establish the order at the outset—which can become a powerful argument in favor of outlining later in the semester (a habit to which most of my students have an aversion).

Specific stories also present their own unique problems that can be used in discussions later on. For example, one class chose "The Tell-Tale Heart" and had trouble coming up with a way to present the final scene. Should the heartbeat be audible to the audience? How can the sound be suggested without implying that it was an actual sound? The obvious problem is that the story is a first person narrative, whereas film is almost always third person. This became an excellent way to discuss the advantages and disadvantages of the different points of view.

If I spend the first week of class talking about film, I find that my students are much less intimidated by the writing process, and I find almost every aspect of writing to have a parallel in filmmaking, so the analogy can be used throughout the semester to explain what happens in an essay and why it happens.

Using the Elements of Short Fiction

Mary Piering Hiltbrand
UNIVERSITY OF SOUTHERN COLORADO
PUEBLO, COLORADO

English 130 at the University of Southern Colorado is a one-semester Introduction to Fiction course. It tends to have a large enrollment because it fulfills one of the humanities requirements for all undergraduates. Because it fulfills one of the core requirements, it attracts a high number of students who are not English majors. (In my spring section, only two out of thirty-three students were English majors.)

This assignment is the second of two short-story writing assignments. (For the first assignment, students are required to write a critical analysis of one of a list of designated stories. For this, the second assignment, they may either write a second critical analysis, or they may choose this option.)

WRITING ASSIGNMENT

Write a short story, For this assignment you may submit one that you have already written. In addition, please attach a one-page description of how you have used at least two of the short story elements in constructing your story: plot, setting, characterization, tone, and symbolism are all examples of the elements you might address in this one-page description. For this assignment, you will be graded not on whether you have composed a sophisticated, professional story, worthy of inclusion in this text, but on the consciousness of the short story elements that you demonstrate in describing your story. Have fun!

I find this assignment valuable for a number of reasons. First, students who have struggled to write a 500 word critical analysis essay have sometimes turned in 15 page short stories! Next, it demonstrates that students often are capable of the kinds of critical consciousness that more traditional and academically oriented assignments don't reveal. Moreover, the assignment allows me to treat students as serious writers with unique and individual voices. (I comment both on their observations of their story and write some of my reflections on their use of the basic elements. Not surprisingly, my comments on their stories are often at variance with theirs. For example, a young man recently wrote extensively that the dance in his story was a symbol. I commented that I really thought that the first-person point of view was the most striking aspect of his story. It revealed a narrator who seemed decidedly obsessed and unbalanced, one about whom I felt decidedly uneasy. There was a profoundly sinister sense created by him, possibly a bit reminiscent of that of the narrator in John Fowles's *The Collector*. [I have the feeling that this student may read this book this summer.] The disparity in viewpoints often allows students to see unexpected aspects of their story, however. It also reveals to them that they, like the professional writers studied, do manipulate the short-story elements, and they do have an effect on their stories.) Finally, I have urged students to submit their stories to *The Hungry Eye*, USC's fledgling literary magazine. This latter provides support for my colleagues who are working to get this publication established on campus, and it provides some further positive encouragement for students.

Following is an example of one student's description of her short story. This piece was submitted by Adele Knisley, a student enrolled in my Spring 130 Introduction to Fiction course. It reflects, I think, a fairly sophisticated understanding of the short-story elements and a considerable measure of engagement with her story.

Student Essay

Two Elements in My Short Story

Adele Knisley
UNIVERSITY OF SOUTHERN COLORADO
PUEBLO, COLORADO

In this short story, I have tried to utilize two different elements of the short story—point of view and symbol. First, in choosing the point of view I decided on a nonparticipating narrator with limited omniscience. Initially, I thought that Jack would be too young to comprehend the meaning of some of the events to have him tell the story himself. After working on the story, I also discovered it was easier to comment on the events rather than trying to express the emotions that Jack felt (although I think this might be an approach I would like to try as well).

The symbol I incorporated into the story was the deserted, old mill. This represents the emptiness and frustration of the town, which contributes to the events at the ballpark. Breathing life back into the mill is meant to show how the people need to put the past behind them and get a fresh start. Jack's symbolic gesture in the end is his way of expressing this need.

It would be impossible to write a story without utilizing the other elements as well: character, setting, plot, and so on. For this story, however, I did not concentrate much effort on these areas. In rewriting this story, I would like to focus more attention on character, Jack's in particular. He is the more rounded character of the story. Focusing more attention on developing him might add more life to the story. Also, working more on the setting of the story, the town, and the ball field might make the symbol more clear.

How Authors Open and Close Short Stories

William Rice
HARVARD UNIVERSITY
CAMBRIDGE, MASSACHUSETTS

The question that interests us in this assignment is one that fiction writers agonize over: how to begin and how to end a short story. With a typical minimum of eight and a maximum of thirty pages, the genre of the short story puts great pressure on each word, sentence, and paragraph. Every image, detail, and idea, all imaginable parts of a short story need to count. Wasted words can be ruinous.

Nowhere is this more true than in both the opening and the closing paragraphs. Writers say these parts of the story can be excruciatingly difficult to get right.

Consider the example of "A Rose for Emily" by William Faulkner. Read the opening paragraph. Already there is a sense of the unknown concerning "the inside of her house." The narrator engages our curiosity. What is in the house? Why has "no one save an old-manservant" entered it for so long? These are questions of the "what happens next" type. But there are other questions—about tone, for example. Will the voice of the narrator remain wryly matter-of-fact to the end? The social sentiments expressed and the metaphors and imagery—found, for instance, in the men's "respectful affection for a fallen monument"—all help clue us into the culture and society we are about to observe.

Now read the story through to the closing paragraph. Here we learn the macabre answer to the "what happens next" question. How does Faulkner, word by word, maintain suspense in the close of the story? Why is it that one particular detail—the "long strand of iron-gray hair"—serves so well to bring us to the horrific end? Has the narrator's voice changed? If it has, how? If it hasn't, why? What does the ending tell us about the society portrayed in the story—its "monuments," its good opinion of its own past?

If you read the story again carefully, keeping the opening and closing paragraphs clearly in mind, you'll see more and more. The short story will begin to resonate within itself, and you can write about what you've discovered.

You may want to write an expansion of these initial observations about the opening and closing of "A Rose for Emily." Or you may choose another short story in *Literature* to analyze. Some stories are especially suited to this approach, but this short list is obviously not complete:

Jorge Luis Borges, "The Gospel According to Mark"
John Cheever, "The Five-Forty-Eight"
William Faulkner, "Barn Burning"
Ernest Hemingway, "A Clean Well-Lighted Place"
Charlotte Perkins Gilman, "The Yellow Wallpaper"

In an essay or exercise, consider these kinds of questions:

- How does the first paragraph set up the main features and problems of the story? What expectations does the writer create?

- How does the last paragraph conclude the story—in plot, theme, significant detail, tone, idea? Do the first and last paragraphs echo each other?

- How might the author have opened and closed the short story differently? Why do you think he or she chose to fashion the beginning and the ending in this particular way? What choices were involved?

These aren't the only questions you can ask. You can expand or limit your inquiry. No mater how narrow or broad your focus, this essay does require you to speculate about the artist's craft, and to do this sensitively and persuasively, you'll need to read closely and write from the evidence of your reading. Once you see how much care authors have put into the opening and closing of their short stories, you'll be alert as well to similar challenges of starting and finishing—as these occur in poems, novels, essays, and plays—and in your own writing.

Fiction and Creation:
The Art of Naming

William Rice
HARVARD UNIVERSITY
CAMBRIDGE, MASSACHUSETTS

Some painters remark on how hard it is to give names to their paint-ings. Working as they do in a world of color, line, and shape, rather than in the realm of words, their predicament is understandable. But even the best writers, who are masters in the world of words, face immense challenges in naming. As creators of fiction, they have to give names to their stories and characters—and, at times, to dogs, cats, and horses, towns and businesses, counties and countries, creeks and rivers, even gods and religions.

Authors sometimes try various titles before settling on the one we come to know their short stories by. (This is true of novels, poems, essays, and plays, too.) Some titles seem straightforward and even inevitable, as in Charlotte Perkins Gilman's "The Yellow Wall-paper." What other title, one wonders, could that powerful story possibly bear? But many titles are not so necessary or obvious. Wil-liam Faulkner might have called "A Rose for Emily" something like "This Old House." But that title wouldn't resonate.

Think about the titles of stories you've read. Choose one that puzzles you. The most interesting titles to think and write about tend to be the odd ones—those that seem initially ambiguous, mys-terious, suggestive. Consider these questions:

1. Does the title describe—or not describe—the action of the story, its theme or point, its language?

2. What might be the purpose of the title—description, predic-tion, bafflement?

The names of the characters usually deserve attention—even when there are no names but just a procession of "I," "he," or "she." This is the case in Raymond Carver's "Cathedral," narrated by an

68

unnamed "I." But even here the author's choice *not* to name the narrator—or the narrator's wife—is worth pondering. Consider:

1. What is the effect or purpose of anonymity? Why is this information kept from us? Does the lack of a name create mystery?

2. Do we feel closer to or more distant from the two main characters because they lack names? At what points does the author resist the opportunity to give the characters names?

More often than not, however, characters are given names. Try scrutinizing them for meaning in the stories you have read. Ask:

1. Is the meaning overt, as in Nathaniel Hawthorne's "Young *Goodman* Brown"?

2. Is the meaning suggested, as in Katherine Ann Porter's "The Jilting of Granny *Weatherall*"?

3. Is the meaning so indirect that you want to be cautious about drawing conclusions?

Make a list of names—not just of characters, but, where appropriate, of towns, roads, and so on—and ponder their relation to the themes, events, and ideas dealt with in the short story. Look up the etymologies of given female and male names, and those that are shared by the sexes, and ask if their meanings make sense in the framework of the plot. (Most hardback college dictionaries have an appendix of names.) Similarly examine last names (surnames). Do they add a dimension to the short story?

Titles and character and place names aren't always crucial to understanding a short story, but careful attention based on close reading can prove revealing. Stories that repay study of their respective author's choices of names include those mentioned here and also a great many others. ("A Good Man Is Hard to Find," by Flannery O'Connor, is a particularly outstanding example.)

Some of what you find in your inquiry will seem speculative, not altogether "provable," but this shouldn't deter you. Offer your readers honest—if tentative—readings, based on the evidence of the fiction and your own best hunches. We cannot read the minds of authors as we can read road maps and flowcharts. Authors, as creators, work on the boundaries of the confirmable, and to appreciate the greatness of their accomplishments, we must try to understand the choices they faced, including the choice not to name—or even not to title, which was the poet Emily Dickinson's choice. You can take your heightened awareness of this naming aspect of the writer's craft into your reading of other genres (poetry is a good place to start) and into your own writing—as when you create titles for the papers you write.

"Trials and Revelations": Teaching Myth with Joseph Campbell

Diane M. Thiel
UNIVERSITY OF MIAMI
CORAL GABLES, FLORIDA

Early in the semester, I introduce students to Joseph Campbell's work, particularly "The Hero's Adventure" in *The Power of Myth* (one could use the book or the video series). Campbell is an excellent source to raise discussion about archetypal ideas, myth, and story-telling from different cultures. Campbell's philosophies about the hero sequence of action (the going, fulfillment, return) and the trials and revelations each character must undergo can be applied to much of what follows in this course. By mid-term, I have students choose from the stories we have read and answer the following assignment.

ASSIGNMENT

Choose three of the stories we have read and develop a thesis that connects them, using Joseph Campbell's notion of trials and revelations that each character undergoes in the hero sequence of action.

Such an assignment is particularly useful because it introduces the use of secondary source material. Students will create a thesis, quote from Campbell and the three stories, many without realizing that they have, in fact, written a mini research paper. When students choose topics for the research paper, many choose to delve further into Campbell. They often choose one or more of the five coming of age stories I briefly discuss here.

T. Coraghessan Boyle's "Greasy Lake"

Almost every student can relate to this story. Often they can also relate a similar account, although perhaps not as extreme. One might ask the students to write about their own "Greasy Lake." The story also raises quite a bit of gender discussion. One journal assignment I have used successfully with this story is to have the students

71

write from the "fox's" perspective, giving the voiceless woman a voice. And certainly, Campbell's insights about the motifs of death and resurrection can be applied to "Greasy Lake." The narrator literally goes into the festering murk of Greasy Lake and emerges a new individual.

John Updike's "A&P"

"A&P" is another story that certainly reveals the notion of trials and revelations. One might note, for instance, Sammy's thinking of himself as a "knight in shining armor" and his subsequent realization of "how hard the world was going to be hereafter." He rejects "policy" and the system. The system is, according to Campbell, the dragon he must slay. In a setting as mundane as a supermarket, the boy experiences a major epiphany.

Doris Lessing's "A Woman on a Roof"

Lessing's story works very well as a comparison to "A&P." We again have the main character crossing a threshold that may appear insignificant, but, in reality, it proves to be a major life event. The story is also a good one to expand the notion of setting—the heat that contributes to the sequence of events in the piece. The class issues raised by the story can also form a good basis for comparison to "A&P." Both stories feature a working class male and a female of leisure. And good discussions about gender can arise from the comparison of the "fox" in "Greasy Lake," Queenie in "A&P," and the nameless woman of "A Woman on a Roof."

Alice Munro's "How I Met My Husband"

Students love this story and enjoy the debates that rise in class. Some students seem to feel that the young girl settled for the mailman, while others argue that the story is, in fact, a good representation of the way life really works: The paths we take lead to other unforeseen paths. "How I Met My Husband" is also an excellent story to discuss the power of a title. The title effectively places us in the position of the young girl, Edie. We are led from the beginning to give Chris Watters the benefit of the doubt.

Munro's story is also useful for a discussion of symbols. Although the symbols in this story are somewhat more subtle than, for instance, "The Found Boat" (another story by Munro), they are clear enough for good discussion. Students might be asked to identify them, discuss what they represent, and perhaps compare them to symbols from other pieces they have read. The plane, for instance, is the shining armor Chris wears, also a symbol of the freedom Edie romanticizes. The dress Edie wears the day she meets Chris is the symbol of her desire to cross some sort of threshold of maturity. In a discussion about irony, one might ask the students how the ironic end of the story "makes" the story.

Two other Munro stories that I have used as comparisons to the above and that have produced some fine research papers are "Boys and Girls" and "Wild Swans."

Joyce Carol Oates's
"Where Are You Going, Where Have You Been?"

Students like the macabre nature of this story and draw immediate comparisons to any of the preceding stories. One might ask students, for instance, to notice symbols in the story—how the hamburger joint is like Greasy Lake. One might note the way Connie dresses—the "two sides to her"—and compare that to Edie in "How I Met My Husband." One might also focus on the rich fantasy life that all the previous characters have, or explore the evidence of pop culture influencing their lives—particularly in "Greasy Lake" and "Where Are You Going, Where Have You Been?"

I use Campbell's ideas numerous times throughout the year. One of the main assets to using Campbell is that all his theories help students to think in terms of lineage. They begin to realize the connections that can be drawn between works of literature—from the earliest stories to the contemporary. Such awareness is certainly necessary as you begin to treat drama and poetry in the class. I find that we return to Campbell's ideas numerous times through the semester.

The Use of Force at a Clean Well-Lighted A & P

Tom Zaniello
NORTHERN KENTUCKY UNIVERSITY
HIGHLAND HEIGHTS, KENTUCKY

Whenever I feel I've taught the same story too many times the same way, I like to offer the writing assignment in which a student takes a secondary character from a short story and retells the "story" from that character's point of view. Retelling of course means confronting the original telling: What was the original point of view? Why is one character of primary importance and the student's character not? How does retelling remake the story? What follows is a composite version of a number of these teaching moments.

In theory any story would lend itself to this exercise, but some are more equal than others: Switching Sammy's first-person narration to one of the "three girls in nothing but bathing suits" in John Updike's "A & P," for example, rearranges the furniture of the store quite a bit. Changing Angelina, William Carlos Williams's patient in "The Use of Force," into the teller rather than the told makes even the original version quite different on subsequent readings. A few brave students take on Ernest Hemingway, but find that the virtually invisible narrative style of a story such as "A Clean Well-Lighted Place" is tough to challenge. When there is consensus that Katherine Anne Porter's "The Jilting of Granny Weatherall" had better be left totally alone, I feel that at least some of the students are reading from the inside out and well.

This assignment lies in a curious zone somewhere between passive deconstruction and active reader-response. I like to treat the new stories primarily as performance pieces with classroom readings whenever possible. (I don't require the new story to be as long as the original.)

Sometimes I group the students by story title, and let them first have an internal story-slam that culminates in one group entry for the out-loud portion of the day's program.

But whether in groups or out-loud or both, we inevitably face The Big Question: Is this fair to the Author? Or a corollary: Doesn't this retelling reflect the new teller's attitude rather than the original author's? Here I sometimes push the analytical portion of the program a bit, suggesting two characters as locked in struggle or tension, with the author clearly favoring one but not surrendering the hope of the other making a play for the reader's attention.

At different moments of the debate I launch samples of the way "reader-response" has already generated the interest—and amusement—of professional writers. (Part of my hidden hand is to demonstrate that some of our professional betters have been doing this all along.) Here's a short list, with a brief comment or two, of some of the pieces I have used (and a few I haven't got around to using yet):

- Shirley Jackson, "A Biography of a Story": These letters to Jackson c/o *The New Yorker* where "The Lottery" first appeared must be read to be believed. Having the story in *Literature* helps, but at this point virtually all the students have already read it.

- Mary McCarthy, *Memoirs of a Catholic Girlhood:* I suspect that most of these are fiction in the first place, but any given interchapter is her reader-response (and rearranging) of the previous chapter.

- Mary McCarthy, "'General Macbeth': She Who Must Be Obeyed": She has always been a reader-response critic, often of her own work (see No. 2), but here she calls Macbeth a "golfer . . . on the Scottish fairways" and "one you could transpose into contemporary battle dress or a sport shirt and slacks."

- James Thurber, "The Macbeth Murder Mystery": If you want more Macbeth . . . excerpts from this classic reader-response comedy can be read aloud.

- Laura Bohannon, "Shakespeare in the Bush": A cultural anthropologist's (relativist's?) dream, as the West African elders set Bohannon straight about Hamlet's real problem.

- Aldous Huxley, "Wordsworth in the Tropics": Not many of our students know Huxley anymore, but they certainly know some English Romantic (genteel) poetry and what Huxley is trying to do here.

A day or two of this and you will have trouble teaching point of view in the old way, whatever that way was.

Naturalism and Character

Elizabeth Oness
VITERBO COLLEGE
LA CROSSE, WISCONSIN

WRITING ASSIGNMENT

The following is a sample assignment containing some open-ended prompts for a four-page essay.

John Updike's "A&P" and T. Coraghessan Boyle's "Greasy Lake" are two very different coming-of-age stories. Read the definition of literary naturalism in our *Literature* book, then go to the library and read at least one additional essay on naturalism. In light of your reading, consider the following questions. *Beyond the differences in generation,* how are these young men different? How are they similar? (Don't simplify these stories to a good-boy versus bad-boy model.) How do these writers use language to reflect their different worlds? Consider the spatial metaphors in these stories: the neatly labeled aisles of the A&P and the murk of Greasy Lake. How do these metaphors reflect the characters' situations or the authors' points of view?

ELEMENTS TO INCLUDE

1. Include the basics: a simple introduction, **a clear thesis,** smooth, clean prose, and a conclusion.

2. Remember to refer to the story itself to support your ideas.

3. Use quotes, summary, and paraphrasing from critical articles to support your points.

4. Make sure that your quotations (both from the story and

from critical sources) are accurate and that you understand your sources.

5. Include an accurate Works Cited page, and correct MLA documentation.

6. An excellent essay does not have to be large in scope. Original thinking, connections between ideas/images that may appear separate, unique and subtle perceptions, are all elements that raise a modest essay to an outstanding contribution to our discussion of literature.

Comparing Two Cases of Cather's "Paul's Case"

Donald Weinstock
CALIFORNIA STATE UNIVERSITY, LONG BEACH
LONG BEACH, CALIFORNIA

I assign Cather's "Paul's Case" for discussion on a given date. On that day, before the class discusses the story, I play a videotape of PBS's *American Short Story* version (1980). Then I invite the class to focus on the differences between the two versions: What is missing in the film version? What's been added? What kind of "spin" does the film present? (For the second question, the narration by Henry Fonda before and after the story is helpful. The film version presents Paul as a sensitive, artistic boy crushed by a Philistine world unfriendly to such people. The narration also states that this is a persistent theme in Cather's fiction.)

The film offers a lovely interpretation. The only problem is that it is not all of the story Cather wrote. Hers is a far more tough-minded tale. First of all, there is the subtext of homosexuality. There are also the prevalent comparisons to fairy tales and the like. More important for the purposes of this assignment, there are the explicit references to Paul's lack of any artistic talent or ambition. Cather clearly shows him as a passive character—not far removed from our contemporary "couch potatoes." He takes no initiative. He plays no instrument. He reads almost nothing. He creates no art—not even bad art. He can't distinguish between good art and inferior art. He has no notion that there's a relationship between art and hard work. Finally, there are key references to Paul's characteristic lying. There are ironic references to what Paul believes is his clarity of thought, especially as he prepares for his suicide.

WRITING ASSIGNMENT

Discuss how the film and written version of the story portray Paul as an immature boy in search of instant gratification, a kid who wants to succeed but is unwilling to do anything to bring that success about. How does the more condensed film version change or lose important elements of Cather's story?

The Beginnings of Self-Respect: Responding to John Cheever's "The Five-Forty-Eight"

Robert McPhillips
IONA COLLEGE
NEW ROCHELLE, NEW YORK

When I teach John Cheever's short stories in my freshman writing classes, I often do so in conjunction with a number of essays by Joan Didion, including her essay "On Self-Respect." In this personal essay, Didion discusses how she herself began to develop self-respect when she failed to be elected to Phi Beta Kappa, an occasion she equates with the loss of innocence. "The day that I did not make Phi Beta Kappa," she writes:

> I lost the conviction that lights would always turn green for me, the pleasant certainty that those rather passive virtues which had won me approval as a child automatically guaranteed me not only Phi Beta Kappa keys but happiness, honor, and the love of a good man; lost a certain touching faith in the totem power of good manners, clean hair, and proven competence on the Stanford-Binet scale. To such doubtful amulets had my self-respect been pinned, and I faced myself with the nonplused apprehension of someone who has come across a vampire and has no crucifix at hand. (142–43)

Didion's experience leads her to take responsibility for her own actions, to begin to develop self-respect. In John Cheever's story "The Five-Forty-Eight," the two main characters, Blake and Miss Dent, in very different ways, are forced by their encounter to reflect upon their actions and confront the possibility of self-respect.

Blake is, in many ways, an archetypal Cheever hero, albeit perhaps his least sympathetic one. He is a married, middle-aged, white Anglo-Saxon male with a respectable job in Manhattan to which he commutes each day from the Cheeverian suburb of Shady Hill, a mythologically real Westchester town along the Hudson River with its own Metro North train station located parallel to the river. Blake, like so many of Cheever's heroes, is also strongly libidinous. In addition, like Neddy Merrill in "The Swimmer" and Cash Bentley in "O

Youth and Beauty!," two other fine Cheever stories, Blake tends to ignore how his actions affect both himself and the people with whom he is involved. Despite his age and apparent respectability, he resembles the nineteen-year-old Didion in "On Self-Respect;" both of them feel "curiously exempt from the cause-effect relationships which hampered others" (Didion 142). His seemingly casual affair with Miss Dent, an office temp—"a dark woman, in her early twenties, perhaps—who was slender and shy" as well as "competent, punctual, and a good typist"—and its *Fatal Attraction*-like aftermath, jolts him out of complacency, leaving himself to contemplate the fragile stability upon which his suburban paradise is built in the shabby landscape abutting the Shady Hill train station.

By contrast, Miss Dent is a character who seems to have wandered into Cheever country from the more violent, contemporary, psychic fictional terrain of Joyce Carol Oates. For during his perfunctory sexual encounter with Miss Dent, Blake learns that she has been hospitalized for emotional problems, and he deals with this knowledge in as impersonal a way as his position within the business world allows him: "When she was out to lunch, he called personnel and asked them to fire her." But she is not as easy to shake as all that. She begins to stalk him at his office, but he refuses to speak to her. So Miss Dent takes more desperate measures: she follows Blake to Grand Central Terminal and on to his commuter train, "the local—the five-forty-eight."

Miss Dent's presence on the train is eerie, uncanny: she transforms Blake's ordinary routine into an extraordinary nightmare. Her presence—she has a gun in her purse, he is to learn—forces him to reflect on his strained relationships with his neighbors on the train, and by extension, with the pathetic state of his marriage. For her part, Miss Dent, who forces Blake down on his hands in the wasteland beside the suburban train station, causing him to fall "forward in the filth" and to weep, regains a sense of psychic wholeness. " 'Now,' she declares, 'I can wipe my hands of all this, because you see there is some kindness, some saneness in me that I can find and use. I can wash my hands.'" She has regained her self-respect both by humiliating Blake and by proving herself capable of both "kindness" and "saneness" by sparing Blake's life and calmly walking back across to the other side of the train tracks to return to the city and to her life, free of Blake.

Miss Dent has attained a kind of psychic stability, then by

the end of the story, regained a sense of self-respect. Blake, contrarily, though "saved," is also at the beginning of the journey toward self-respect.

In my usual assignment to composition students, I ask them to examine the role of self-respect in their own lives. Have they ever found themselves forced by life to reflect upon the values that determine their actions? Has any painful personal experience proven to be ultimately useful in helping them to develop a more mature understanding of life and affected their behavior accordingly? Who do they identify with more strongly in the story and why? Is Miss Dent's behavior both understandable and justified, given the circumstance of the story? Or is the threat of violence always an unacceptable option in a civilized world? Is Blake to be admired, pitied, or despised—or some combination of all three? A more advanced student may want to explore how the situation, dramatized in the story, reflects the values of mid-century America, and whether the problems it confronts are still prevalent today. (And given the high profile that has been given to the incidence of sexual harassment in the workplace, one would have to say that, to a large extent, they are.) Some students might, then, use this story as a springboard for an essay on sexual power politics in the workplace, or focus more personally on experiences of this nature that they may have encountered either in their part-time or summer jobs or in the classroom.

Depending on the assignment, then, the writing teacher can use "The Five-Forty-Eight" as the basis for either a personal narrative or a more objectively analytical essay in place of more traditional essays of literary analysis.

WORK CITED

Didion, Joan. "On Self-Respect." *Slouching Towards Bethlehem.* New York: Noonday, 1990. 142–48.

Exploring Paradox

Elizabeth Oness
VITERBO COLLEGE
LA CROSSE, WISCONSIN

When students begin to write about literature, they sometimes run into trouble because they simplify their reading to make their ideas fit a thesis. My students are smart enough to resist the idea that the teacher has the last word on the reading of a story, but when it comes to writing, they often retreat to the notion of a single "correct" interpretation. Some myths must be debunked gently, and I try to debunk the idea that a strong argument relies on a simplistic interpretation by addressing what students already know. At the edge of adulthood, they know that life is complex. Paradox is trickier. They are uncomfortable with contradiction in their reading of a story; they hope for a single, concrete truth. I try to let them explore the ways in which literature reflects the complexities they instinctively understand.

I begin the semester by talking about short stories. Stories are intimate, confiding, and students seem to have a certain self-assurance in talking about short fiction. In the first few class sessions, aside from assigning a story in *Literature*, I also have them read about a particular type of criticism from the "Critical Approaches to Literature" section in the back of the book. For some students, reading different types of criticism is a wholly new exercise. I try to help students see how a certain school of criticism might by aligned with their own instincts in approaching a story. As we progress, I encourage students to view stories from a critical perspective they might not have considered at first.

After several classes, I put students into small groups and, using a story such as Cheever's "The Five-Forty-Eight," I have each group examine the story in light of a different type of criticism. One group will examine gender issues, perhaps approaching the story from a feminist perspective. The students begin by discussing the power politics of the workplace, but they disagree about the responsibility of Miss Dent. Some students see her as a victim, others do not. Another group examines the story from a psychological perspective. A few people feel that Blake's self-centeredness and mean-spiritedness border on the pathological. Other students have varying opinions about the way Miss Dent defines her sanity. I tell another group a little about Cheever's life, and see what they come up with in a biographical reading. Then each group addresses the class. As the students listen to their classmates emphasize, and disagree about, certain aspects of the story, they begin to understand the paradoxes that even a seemingly simple short story contains. In discussing "The Five-Forty-Eight," my students disagreed about whether Blake, at the story's end, was truly changed by his encounter. Some felt that Blake's being forced to his knees represented merely outward complicity, whereas others felt that it was the beginning of a new humility and understanding.

I try to emphasize that paradox can be rich, rather than merely troublesome. When some aspect of the story doesn't fit neatly into a thesis, an intelligent argument addresses this anomaly directly rather than pretend that aspect doesn't exist. Most importantly, through exploring paradox within a story, students learn to consider the assumptions they bring to their reading and therefore their writing.

Kate Chopin's "The Storm"

Dianne Peich
DELAWARE COUNTY COMMUNITY COLLEGE
MEDIA, PENNSYLVANIA

The first impulse of most composition instructors teaching Kate Chopin's "The Storm" is probably to ask students, "What do you think of *this* action?" Calixta and Alcée's sexual encounter will certainly elicit reactions from students about the morality of the action, especially because no real conflict (the focal point of all narratives) exists within the story. All the characters are so obviously happy! Where are the recriminations? Where is the betrayal? Where *is* the guilt? In light of the social, economic, and political realities for women during the era in which Kate Chopin wrote, the story becomes even more intriguing. The subject, sexual infidelity, is timeless. Even the sexual revolution has not helped to clarify opinions about infidelity.

"The Storm" is an accessible story for freshman students and offers many excellent topics for writing, but I like to have students write about the story's setting, either in brief analyses of specific aspects of the setting or in a detailed analysis for a thesis-based paper, perhaps one that answers the question "Could the action in 'The Storm' have occurred in any other setting?" or "What influence does the setting have on the action of the story?"

I often consider this story early in the semester when I want to stress the importance of basic essay writing techniques, so I prefer to have my students first write brief papers in class that analyze specific aspects of the setting. I often ask my students to write one or more paragraphs that support topic sentences that I provide. Asking students to support these statements works nicely to emphasize the importance of coherence, unity, and development in a brief format that is easy for me to review. Following are some topic sentences about the setting of "The Storm" that are easy for students who may never have written about literature before to investigate and support with both paraphrased details and quotes from the story.

Class as an Element of Setting

"Alcée and Calixta are from two different social classes." If the students have enough background information about the social dictates at the turn of the century in America, I might add another clause to the topic sentence, or ask the students to add their own, which demands a reaction to or interpretation of the topic—for example, "Alcée and Calixta are from two different social classes and as such, would have been unlikely to marry even if they had been in love."

The Natural Setting

"The weather causes important elements in the action." One might add, "without the storm, the tone of the story would change dramatically." Another topic sentence concerning the natural setting of the story might read, "Elements other than the weather serve to isolate the characters." One might add, "This isolation helps assure that sexual infidelity does not have to equal betrayal."

Pathetic Fallacy

"The storm mirrors the spontaneous emotions of Alcée and Calixta," followed perhaps by "and serves to strengthen the intensely passionate nature of their encounter."

These topic sentences require that students analyze an entire story for a specific element (in this case, setting), isolate details relevant to that element, and effectively paraphrase and quote details supporting the topic sentence. I have found that these types of practice paragraphs encourage many of the skills necessary to write full-length college essays about literature without overwhelming the student. The instructor can give valuable feedback about such writing before the student attempts to write something longer.

Many instructors might want students to incorporate some or all of the paragraphs into a thesis-based, college-length essay about "The Storm." Students can express their own interpretation of the importance of the setting in a thesis and choose supporting details accordingly.

Writing Assignments for "The Storm"

Betty Jo Peters
MOREHEAD STATE UNIVERSITY
MOREHEAD, KENTUCKY

Sometimes our personal beliefs make teaching specific works difficult. I have always faced this problem with Kate Chopin's "The
Storm." Because I had been almost embarrassed to teach this story of
an overt act of adultery, I decided to focus my writing assignments
about it on several other aspects. Some approaches I have used include the following:

- The author's failed marriage to an "Aracadian" in comparison
  to the protagonist's loneliness—students have to research
  Chopin's life and to read carefully the dialogue of the story
  and write their findings.

- The feminist approach—students write about the earlier feminist movement and the author's bent in that direction.

- A social statement on morality—students write a "debate,"
  playing the devil's advocate on the right and wrong of the
  character's actions; they write a persuasive paper.

- The five steps to the plot as outlined in the five "chapters" of
  the story—students study and analyze the parts according to
  E. M. Forster's *Aspects of the Novel* and write a process essay.

- The story as seen as a "drama" with the five "acts"—students
  write stage directions, blank verse and/or rhymed couplets,
  and dramatic lyrics for the "story."

- Akin to this, the "unities" of Aristotle—students write about
  the singularity of time, setting, and unity of action.

- A VHS film "Don't Drop the Potato"—students watch this
  sixty-minute tape about the history of the "Cajun" people,
  from the time they left Europe until their settlement in
  southern Louisiana, and about their culture here and now,

and write their reactions in contrast to mainstream America. We even bring in Justin Wilson's cookbooks, look at the pictures in the books, and may try a simple recipe or two.

- One of the most rewarding comparisons to use with "The Storm" is the Old Testament's Song of Solomon—students read passages from this book and write how they believe the syntax and diction of Solomon influenced the writer of "The Storm."

- It can also be interesting to focus on the natural occurrence of a storm in the world of weather. My scientific-minded students enjoy writing about how a storm comes about, especially a summer storm, while also writing about symbolism and allegory.

Exploring Point of View: Kate Chopin's "The Story of an Hour"

Donna Haisty Winchell
CLEMSON UNIVERSITY
CLEMSON, SOUTH CAROLINA

Kate Chopin's very brief "The Story of an Hour" provides an excellent means of teaching point of view. Chopin's choice of limited omniscient point of view is crucial to understanding the irony of the story's conclusion. Because we readers are allowed inside the head of Louise Mallard, who has just been informed of her husband's death in a railroad accident, we are with her not only as she cries immediate tears of grief in the arms of her sister but also as she sits alone in her room upstairs and feels a sense of joy and impending freedom steal over her. An interesting exercise in point of view asks students to consider how the story would have been different had Chopin made a different choice.

WRITING ASSIGNMENT

Kate Chopin chose to tell "The Story of an Hour" from the limited omniscient point of view with Louise Mallard as the character from whose perspective the story is told. Consider how that choice affects our perception of her reaction to the news of her husband's death. Retell the story from the perspective of her sister, Josephine. Remember to limit yourself to what the sister knows. For example, she is outside the bedroom door while Louise experiences her terrifying revelation and thus is not privy to Louise's thoughts. Consider these questions: What does the sister see? What does she think? What does she do? Tell the story from Josephine's perspective, but keep it in the third person.

Miss Emily
vs. Miss Brill

David Peck
CALIFORNIA STATE UNIVERSITY, LONG BEACH
LONG BEACH, CALIFORNIA

I often assign in-class papers that compare and contrast two short stories. One particularly successful assignment uses William Faulkner's "A Rose for Emily" and Katherine Mansfield's "Miss Brill," two stories that students almost always respond to strongly.

WRITING ASSIGNMENT

In a well-organized paper (including plenty of detail from both stories), write an analysis in which you compare these two fictional characters. Which protagonist is the more successful in her story? How? The focus (thesis) of the paper is your own, but the analysis should include the most important elements from each story. Show how the form of the story—point of view, imagery, and the like—reinforces the themes or ideas you are discussing.

Student Essay

Comparing Miss Emily
and Miss Brill

Karen Humphrey
CALIFORNIA STATE UNIVERSITY, LONG BEACH
LONG BEACH, CALIFORNIA

In both William Faulkner's "A Rose for Emily" and Katherine Mansfield's "Miss Brill," the reader is given a glimpse into the lives of two old women living in different worlds but sharing many similar characteristics. Both Miss Emily and Miss Brill attempt to adapt to a changing environment as they grow older. Through the authors' use of language, imagery, and plot, it becomes clear to the reader that Miss Brill is more successful at adapting to the world around her and finding happiness.

In "A Rose for Emily," Faulkner's use of language paints an unflattering picture of Miss Emily. His tone evokes pity and disgust rather than sympathy. The reader identifies with the narrator of the story and shares the townspeople's opinion that Miss Emily is somehow "perverse." In "Miss Brill," however, the reader can identify with the title character and feel sympathy for her because of the lonely life she leads. Mansfield's attitude toward the young couple at the end makes the reader hate them for ruining the happiness that Miss Brill has found, however small it may be.

The imagery in "A Rose for Emily" keeps the reader from further identifying with Miss Emily by creating several morbid images of her. For example, there are several images of decay throughout the story. The house she lived in is falling apart and described as "filled with dust and shades. . . an eyesore among eyesores." Emily herself is described as being "bloated like a body long submerged in motionless water." Faulkner also uses words like "skeleton," "dank," "decay," and "cold" to reinforce these morbid, deathly images. In "Miss Brill," however, Mansfield uses more cheerful imagery. The music and the lively action in the park make Miss Brill feel alive inside. She notices that the other old people that are in the park are "still as statues," "odd," and "silent." She says they "looked like they'd just come from dark little rooms or even—even cupboards." Her own room is later described as a "cupboard," but during the action of the story, she does not include herself as one of those other old people. She still feels alive.

Through the plots of both stories the reader can also see that Miss Brill is more successful in adapting to her environment. Miss Emily loses her sanity and ends up committing a crime in order to control her environment. Throughout the story, she refuses to adapt to any of the changes going on in the town such as the taxes or the mailboxes. Miss Brill is able to find her own special place in society where she can be happy and remain sane.

In "A Rose for Emily" and "Miss Brill" the authors' use of language and the plots of the stories illustrate that Miss Brill is more successful in her story. Instead of hiding herself away, she emerges from the "cupboard" to participate in life. She adapts to the world that is changing as she grows older, without losing her sanity or committing crimes, as Miss Emily does. The language of "Miss Brill" allows the reader to sympathize with the main character. The imagery in the story is lighter and less morbid than "A Rose for Emily."

"A Rose for Emily" and "Barn Burning"

Deborah Ford
UNIVERSITY OF SOUTHERN MISSISSIPPI
HATTIESBURG, MISSISSIPPI

What has been most effective in my classrooms is the pairing of texts. I have used two of Faulkner's stories, "A Rose for Emily" and "Barn Burning," in this way:

After reading both stories, I have students imagine that Sarty ("Barn Burning") meets Miss Emily ("A Rose for Emily"). I ask students to write a conversation that Sarty and Miss Emily might have.

After a discussion of Faulkner's tone and style in each story, I ask students to invent a dance called "The Faulkner." I ask them to describe the dance (modern, ballet, hip-hop, and so on), to describe the costumes, the music, the scenery, the dancers. They should also describe the mood of the dance and should articulate how and why the dance has been so named.

Making Strange:
The Effective Use of the
Unexpected in Descriptive Prose

Peggy Hesketh
CHAPMAN UNIVERSITY
ORANGE, CALIFORNIA

Every Monday morning I start my Basic Writing Skills class off with the same question: "Did anyone read anything interesting this weekend?" At the start of the semester, the answers typically fall somewhere between blank stares and flat-out denials. I might as well ask if anyone enjoyed his or her latest root canal. Reading for pleasure is an anomaly to most of my students. That is why they must learn to appreciate the difference between "correct" writing in grammar textbooks and great writing in works of literature before they can start to enjoy reading, let alone hope to approach anything resembling good writing themselves. To do this, they must see and hear and examine in detail how language works in the hands of a truly fine author.

This assignment is designed for prebaccalaureate or beginning composition students. It is based loosely on the theories of the Russian Formalist Viktor Shklovsky, who advocated a technique in art and literature that he called "defamiliarization," or "making the familiar seem strange."

IN-CLASS EXERCISES

For homework, I have asked my students to read "A Very Old Man with Enormous Wings" by Gabriel García Márquez. In class, I ask them what they thought of the story. This generally prompts comments like "It was weird" or "I didn't get it." (This is not surprising.) I assure my students that sometimes even experienced readers have to read a story several times before they "get" it. I also tell them that it is perfectly all right to think that this story is strange or somewhat confusing—some ambiguity is intended. I ask them, however, if they can at least picture what the town and the angel in the story look like. Most of them say they can.

Now I ask the students if they think the opening passage of the story is very descriptive. Again, most say yes. I ask them to underline all the adjectives in the first paragraph. (There aren't very many.) Then I ask them to find places where García Márquez has used more than one adjective to modify a single noun. (There are even fewer.) I ask them if they can think of any reasons why García Márquez might have made a point of using additional adjectives to describe the "single ash-grey thing" and the "very old man." Next, I have them find an example of a noun standing on its own without a modifying adjective. (This isn't hard to do. There are lots of these.) I ask them what effect this has. Finally, I ask them to tell me in their own words what they know about the setting of the story from the descriptions in the first paragraph and what they know about the very old man who is found there.

The purpose of this first exercise is to get the students to examine the author's economic, yet very effective use of adjectives. Most inexperienced writers assume that the more adjectives they use, the more descriptive their prose will be. As a result, they often produce long strings of synonymous adjectives that bog down rather than elucidate their descriptions. Students are generally surprised to discover how sparingly adjectives are used in what they all agree is a very descriptive passage.

Now, I ask my students to circle all the verbs in the same opening paragraph. I then ask them to tell me which verbs describe the actions of the characters and which ones describe the state of mind or being of the characters. Then, I ask them to point out any verbs that describe something about the place or setting of the story. And then I question them about what the beach is usually like on March nights, and what it is like when the story opens. Finally, I ask them to describe, in their own words, the mood of the opening scene.

The purpose of this exercise is to help the students see how much of the descriptive load verbs can carry in well-written prose.

Finally, I ask my students to come up with a list of ten words that they associate with angels. Then we list these words on the board. (Students usually choose nouns like *halo, harp, wings, feathers, clouds,* and *robes,* and adjectives such as *white, golden, beautiful, good,* and *wise.*) Now I have them turn to the second paragraph of the story, and I ask them to underline all the descriptions of the old man that they can find. I ask them if they know what the old man is supposed to be. (An angel, they say. Why? Because he has wings, and the neighbor woman says he's an angel in the next paragraph.) I ask them if any of the descriptions of the old man in the story match their idea of what an angel should look like. Then I ask them to compare their list of words on the board with the words García Márquez used to describe the old man. (Often, the only common word is "wings," but I make sure to point out that it is paired with the unlikely adjective, "buzzard.") Next, I ask them to tell me, without looking at the story, what other unusual descriptions of the angel they can remember. (Most recall his bald head and his missing teeth. They also tend to remember that he is dressed like a ragpicker and that he speaks like a sailor. They are surprised, in fact, by how much they do remember.) I ask them if the angel is a memorable character. Most agree that he is. We conclude by discussing what makes this angel so memorable.

The last part of this exercise is designed to show students how effective an unexpected adjective, simile, metaphor, or verb can be in descriptive prose. The angel stands out in their memory because he is dressed "like a ragpicker" instead of being clothed in white robes. García Márquez has made the familiar seem strange.

WRITING ASSIGNMENT

Following the preceding discussion, students are asked to write a short personal narrative describing a significant event in their life. They are asked to concentrate on the moment this event transpired and to describe where they were, and what they saw and heard and did. They are advised to set the scene with care by using adjectives judiciously and by using active verbs to convey mood as well as movement. Finally, they are asked to find unexpected ways to describe familiar objects and actions.

Student Essay

My Sonogram

Trina Ruiz
CHAPMAN UNIVERSITY
ORANGE, CALIFORNIA

I waited, silent and alone, for the doctor to come back into the small examining room. I could feel the cold drafts of air from the vents sweep over my revealed stomach. I was almost five months pregnant and waiting to have my first sonogram done. I was finally going to see the little life growing inside of me.

For the past few months friends and family kept reminding me that a tiny baby was slowly developing inside of me. The only problem I had was trying to convince myself that it was real. Being able to believe that I could create another life wasn't easy. I had a friend who was also five months pregnant. The fact that she was always feeling the little life inside of her made it more real. As for me, I didn't feel any movement inside of my stomach. If I did, I never believed that it was the baby.

The doctor finally walked in with a man. She explained that the machine she was using for the sonogram was new and he was there to help her. "This won't hurt at all," she whispered to me with a friendly smile. Then she squirted the ice-cold jelly on my stomach to help the monitor slide smoothly across my skin. As she turned the machine on, the sound of my baby's heartbeat filled the room. This wasn't the first time I had heard the heartbeat, but each time was unforgettable. Every beat reminded me of the sound of a rope whipping through the air.

My utter fascination was interrupted when the doctor asked, "Are you ready to see your baby?" Before I had a chance to respond to her question—there it was. The vision on the screen wasn't very clear at first, but after a few seconds I could see it perfectly. It looked like the silhouette of a small body lounged back in a chair. Then in an instant it came to life. The hands and feet began to move, and I could see the mouth slowly open and close. My realization started the flow of tears from my eyes. It was real. The baby inside of me was real. Then to add to my astonishment, I heard the doctor say, "Let's see if it's a boy or a girl." Finally, I was convinced. He was real.

Just knowing that I had another life in me was never enough to be real. Believing I had another life in me was all I needed. From then on, every twist, turn, and kick inside of me had an importance. Every day became another day closer to the real baby boy inside of me coming into the world.

Understanding Myth:
What Makes a Hero Heroic?

Patricia Wagner
CALIFORNIA STATE UNIVERSITY, LONG BEACH
LONG BEACH, CALIFORNIA

When confronted with an analytical paper, few students are able to discuss a text in a relatively simple yet focused and detailed manner. They either retell the plot step-by-step, slide off into an unrelated tangent, or bury themselves in the library to research the text to death. To break them of any of those extremes, I ask students to look at the story, poem, and/or play from one perspective. That is, I tell them to look at one aspect of one character, one aspect of the setting, or one aspect of a theme. Their goal with this method is to discuss the text thoroughly and without taking for granted that the reader will understand what they mean.

WRITING ASSIGNMENT

Write an essay in which you discuss the nature of a "hero" and how it applies to "Godfather Death" by Jakob and Wilhelm Grimm. This is a classic tale, and though the characters are merely sketches, they clearly have a dramatic role. Who is the hero? Does he act heroically? Why or why not? Within your discussion of the hero, you might also address some of the following questions: Of what importance is the overall shape of the tale to the hero's plight? Is there a moral or lesson to be learned from the hero's actions? Is there a symbolic significance to the light and dark imagery? Though the tale is both old and strange, does the situation of the hero have a lesson for us today?

COMMENTARY

Students usually fight me when I rein them in and demand such a tight focus. They have rarely, if ever, had to pinpoint a topic so clearly or write with such precision. Once the essay is done, however, they get over their reluctance. How can they resist? They have written better and longer essays with less effort. They have also improved their critical skills and become better readers—though they may not realize that until my class is long over.

Student Essay

The Nature of Heroism in "Godfather Death"

Diane Smith
CALIFORNIA STATE UNIVERSITY, LONG BEACH
LONG BEACH, CALIFORNIA

In our culture, folktales are often classified as "children's stories." But folktales have always been an important part of man's universal heritage. The fact that a whole society "creates" its folktales means that the symbols, characters, and actions in the stories usually have a particular cultural significance. Folktales often are about critical stages of life.

The Brothers Grimm were able to look at many of these conflicts through the retelling of ancient German folk stories. "Godfather Death" is one of these traditional folktales. The story looks at the difficult decisions parents face in raising a family. At the same time it addresses issues about religious beliefs and what the implications of a virtuous life mean in context with Western religion. The Grimms' tale, like all myths and folktales, is a reflection of the culture in which the audience lived. The cultural views in this tale mirror the value system of Christianized Northern Europe.

This story fits many of the archetypal patterns that most myths and folktales possess. It combines an imaginative attempt to solve the mysteries of life with social consciousness to express the author's point of view on religion and morality. To express these views, the tale follows the mythological traditions of all cultures by featuring a heroic figure who performs extraordinary feats in the course of laying the foundations of human society. In "Godfather Death," there are two heroes: a poor father who must sacrifice his youngest son to save his other twelve children, and the young son who must learn the truth about life and death.

The journey starts with the poor man forced to make an impossible decision. Knowing that he must give up his son, the man looks to his religion to find the answers. In many traditions, creation is brought about by sacrificial death. Here, the creation of a better society starts with the sacrifice of his youngest son to humanity's great equalizer, Death. In making his choice, the man faces a common dilemma, his faith versus reality. In this case, God should be the man's first choice to take care of his son, but bitterness blinds him to what the morally correct choice would be. He turns his back on God because of his own misfortunes. But his moral conflict does not corrupt his judgment. He is still able to turn his back on the wrong choice, the Devil. Without God or the Devil, the man must choose what is essentially the only choice humanity has, which is Death.

Heroes are the models of behavior for their society. They earn lasting fame, the only kind of immortality possible for human beings, by performing great deeds that help their community, and they inspire others to emulate them. In "Godfather Death," a poor man's son is given his role as savior of man by Death, the ultimate destroyer. Death teaches the boy about an herb that can cure any ailment. Here, the boy learns of the healing powers of the earth, a common theme in mythology. He earns his enduring renown through his extraordinary feats as a doctor with the ability to keep Death at bay. With his fame and fortune, however, there is a price to pay. He must make a pact with Death, allowing some people to stay on the earth while others must die. It is up to Death to determine who will live and who must die. It is up to the boy to heed the wisdom of Death and to make the right choices. His choices are the base for the hero's heroic deeds.

Heroes are forced by circumstance to make critical choices in which they must balance one set of values against competing values. Heroic myths examine the relationship between the individual's desires and his or her responsibilities to society. Often the choice is crucial but uncomplicated: whether or not to risk death to save the community. As the boy becomes a famous doctor, he is challenged by Death to make the right decision. The doctor must choose between obeying his godfather, Death, and the life of his king. As with all men, the doctor looks for a way to outwit Death. His arrogance allows him this one time to win over Death. But Death is never forgiving.

It is the hero who chooses to risk death who acquires honor and lasting fame; the hero who chooses safety is denied both. Individuals achieve heroic stature in part from their accomplishments and in part because they learn to become more sensitive and thoughtful human beings. In spite of their extraordinary abilities, no hero is perfect. Yet their human weaknesses are often as instructive as their heroic qualities. Their imperfections allow ordinary people to identify with them and to like them because everyone has similar conflicts. The doctor is faced once again with risking death or saving his community. He must choose between the love of life or the love of Death. Blinded by his love for a beautiful princess, the hero chooses unwisely, again trying to outwit Death. Though he successfully saves the beautiful princess, life happily ever after is impossible. The hero's death is inevitable.

Many traditions picture the journey of the human soul after death as a descent into the underworld. This journey often involves the search for eternal life. As with other heroes, the doctor enters the realm of the underworld hoping that he too has vanquished Death. After the doctor's fateful decision to save the princess, Death escorts him into an underground cave filled with thousands of lights. In most mythology, light represents life, for everything requires light to live. The life force is represented by the length of each flame, those shining brightest having the greatest life force. Finding his life force ebbing, the doctor asks Death to reignite his flame so that he may become king and marry the beautiful princess. It is here that the hero has lost his way, giving up his mission to heal the sick in order to fulfill his own desires. As with most heroes, those who lose their way are destined to fail.

The cause of human destiny is often put down to the whim of divinities motivated by such apparently human emotions as sexual desire, anger, or jealousy. The doctor's life ends because of Death's need for revenge. It is nature's cruel revenge that for every new life, one must end. Without this continuous cycle, life would cease to exist.

Heroes define themselves by how they relate to external circumstances. They acquire lasting fame by performing deeds of valor, but they acquire even greater heroic stature by winning an inner battle against their desires. Although these heroes lived long ago in cultures very different from our own, they can still serve as models for us. We too want to live in such a way that we are remembered for our good deeds.

Describing
Mrs. Brown

Donald Weinstock

CALIFORNIA STATE UNIVERSITY, LONG BEACH
LONG BEACH, CALIFORNIA

Near the beginning of Nathaniel Hawthorne's "Young Goodman Brown," the protagonist calls his new wife Faith "a blessed angel on earth." Later in the story, "ocular evidence" causes him to exclaim, "My Faith is gone!" When he returns to his village after the horrible events of the previous night, his wife "burst[s] into . . . joy at the sight of him," but he "looked sternly and sadly into her face and passed on without a greeting." Finally, at the story's end, we are told that "he shrank from the bosom of Faith."

WRITING ASSIGNMENT

Discuss the ways that these four changing judgments of Faith (as reflected in the quotations just given) throw light on Hawthorne's story for you.

CONSIDERATIONS FOR WRITING

Nearly all critics say that "Young Goodman Brown" is Hawthorne's response to the guilt he felt over his ancestor's prominent part in prosecuting the Salem Witch Trials. The story, therefore, is about the "Puritan Conscience." We would be foolish to argue with these assertions. What critics don't usually talk about, however, is at least as important and interesting as what they do say.

In your explication of the story, consider carefully the following questions and answer as many of them as you can—support your reading of the story with ample evidence from the text.

- Why does all of the main action in the story occur at night?

- Why is Faith's ribbon pink? Wouldn't you expect it to be white because she's characterized as being pure?

- Why is Brown so certain that what he saw and heard that night was real?

- Why does Brown fail to question any of what he's seen and heard—seeing as it all comes from or through the devil? Would you trust what the devil told and showed you without soliciting a second opinion?

A Clean
Well-Lighted Essay

Diane Gunther
LONG BEACH CITY COLLEGE
LONG BEACH, CALIFORNIA

WRITING ASSIGNMENT

In his short story, "A Clean Well-Lighted Place," Ernest Hemingway shows us an example of the "poverty of empathy." We have discussed the story's events and the lessons to be learned by and from his characters. Now it's your turn.

Write an essay of five paragraphs. First, summarize the story and explain, in your own words, what a "poverty of empathy" means. Next, tell of a real-life situation you know of that shows a poverty of empathy. Finally, give the lesson; tell what the people or person needs to learn or do in order to be a better, more compassionate human being.

Remember to frame the three "parts" with good, clear introductory and concluding paragraphs. Plan ahead. Talk to your friends. Please take thought, care, and pride in this last essay. Shouldn't it look something like this?

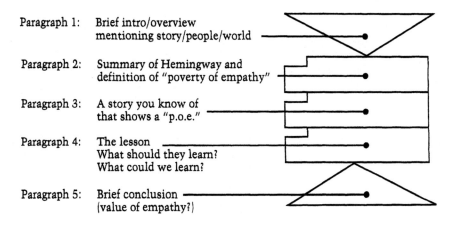

Paragraph 1: Brief intro/overview
mentioning story/people/world

Paragraph 2: Summary of Hemingway and
definition of "poverty of empathy"

Paragraph 3: A story you know of
that shows a "p.o.e."

Paragraph 4: The lesson
What should they learn?
What could we learn?

Paragraph 5: Brief conclusion
(value of empathy?)

Writing about Franz Kafka's *The Metamorphosis*

Alan Jacobs
WHEATON COLLEGE
WHEATON, ILLINOIS

One of the best-known traits of Kafka's stories is their tendency to invite allegorical interpretations. One of the best-known traits of the critics who have written *about* Kafka's stories is their inability to resist such an invitation. Northrop Frye wrote many years ago that many critics dislike allegory because allegory comes with its own commentary, and thereby constricts the interpretive activities of later commentators. But the allegories in Kafka's stories, if they are there at all, are so vague and wispy as to offer no restrictions. One feels encouraged to allegorize but is given few clues about how to do so. And because piecing together an allegory is one of the more pleasurable critical activities, not unlike piecing together a jigsaw puzzle, Kafka's stories have understandably become a critic's playground. *The Metamorphosis* offers innumerable possibilities for this kind of interpretive play. It doesn't take long for people to agree that Gregor Samsa is, to use the favored word, "alienated." But alienated from what and by what? From his father by an Oedipus complex? From bourgeois economic values by a recognition of the moral bankruptcy of capitalism? From bourgeois cultural values by an intellectual or aesthetic awakening? From Christian Europe by an inescapable and unassimilable Jewish identity? ("State the alternative preferred with reasons for your choice.")

This piecing-together activity is something students like to do too, in part because they have been encouraged by high school teachers to hunt for symbols, but in greater part because it is fun. And if professional critics tend not to see the dangers in such an activity, how can students be expected to do so? So what I like to do is give the allegorizing tendency free reign. Before telling my students about any of the standard allegorical interpretations just listed, I ask them to write their own allegorical interpretation of *The Metamorphosis*.

The two desiderata for this assignment are first, that their allegory account for as many details of the narrative as possible, and second, that it be inconsistent with no details of the narrative.

When we go over these allegories in class, it is always surprising and often disconcerting to the students to learn just how many interpretations account more-or-less equally well for the story's features. It is also interesting to see how often they doubt that the standard "professional" allegories of the story are any better supported than their own! This discussion often leads into some ruminations on whether Kafka intended to allow for so many different readings; why he might do such a thing, if indeed he so intended; whether we would have a lower, or perhaps a higher, opinion of the story if we discovered a letter that showed that he had had a very specific allegorical meaning in mind that no one had ever discovered (which is another way of asking how closely we link an author's inferred intentions with our evaluation of a work's literary quality); how we might interpret the story if it is *not* allegorical at all; and so on. Generally, we have a very good time.

Stating the Theme:
D. H. Lawrence's
"The Rocking-Horse Winner"

Jan D. Hodge
MORNINGSIDE COLLEGE
SIOUX CITY, IOWA

Teaching theme can be particularly tricky, especially in light of the current popularity (and excesses) of both deconstructionist theory (which makes it too easy to distrust or even disparage any reading) and reader-response theory (in itself a good thing, but easily inviting an "anything goes" attitude—"It means this because that's what I see in it"). How can one offer a thematic statement without appearing dogmatic or narrowing the range of intelligent interpretations of the story?

First, I review the text discussion of theme, explain the difference between plot summary (what happens in a story), a "moral imperative" (reducing the story to a "Do" or "Don't Do" lesson), and a thematic statement (a sentence stating the controlling idea in or central insight offered by a story; what the story is really about). Next, I discuss possible thematic statements for a few stories we have already read. Then I have the students write (before class) a thematic statement (twenty-five words or less) for Lawrence's "The Rocking-Horse Winner." I ask them to make two copies (one to keep, one to hand in), and then select a few more or less at random to have the class discuss. (Each class will of course generate statements useful to make the important points, and doing it this way frees discussion by preserving anonymity.)

I have found that Lawrence's story lends itself beautifully to exploring exactly the questions raised here, and that a class's collective responses introduce the key questions. The story is of course a fable, characterized by fantasy, its omniscient point of view (including briefly even the dog's), and an explicitly stated moral (thanks to the uncle). Nonetheless, students read it in very different ways—some more appropriate than others.

The fable is an indictment of the excess of a materialistic culture that defines "love" as "money" (or "filthy lucre"), and of what we call "the rat race" for which the rockinghorse is a wonderfully apt symbol. Lawrence was apparently also influenced by Eastern culture and its premise that we can get whatever we want, but that if we want the wrong things, we can never have "enough." Still, though the readings are of course complementary, one gets rather different emphases depending on whether one focuses on Paul or his mother. Many students focus on Paul, arguing that the theme of the story is that children learn their values from their parents, and will often do whatever they think necessary to win a parent's love, even if it hurts them. Focusing on the mother is perhaps more complex; the problem is not that she doesn't love her children but that she seems not to know how to love them, because she has confused love with "luck" (or "money," or things, or "success"), and so can never be satisfied.

Of course, understanding these ideas and their implications is more important than formulating a thematic statement, but the point of the exercise is to teach students to focus on those ideas. Their statements are helpful in discovering both what the story is about and what it is not about. The exercise also offers a good opportunity to wean students from less adequate interpretations. Here to illustrate are a few statements students have offered:

1. *One who has strong feelings about something should follow those feelings through to the end.*

This is an appealing thought, particularly in a culture that preaches "Just Do It" or "Go For It!" and that seems to encourage an "in your face" attitude. But does it work for the story? After all, both the mother and Paul follow their feelings through to the end, with devastating results. Perhaps one should learn to ask if the end is worth it.

2. *One should not gamble, because it can lead to serious problems.*

This is certainly a noble sentiment, and one our society might do well to take seriously. But again, does it apply to the story? Paul is not gambling; his winners (except for one occasion) are a certainty, and the problem isn't caused by "gambling" but by what makes Paul act as he does, so this seems to miss the point of the story.

3. *Some people substitute money for love in an attempt to achieve happiness.*

This is both true and relevant to the story, but it is only the story's premise, and does not address the important consequences dramatized in the story.

4. *When a person loves but feels rejected, he or she will try harder to find acceptance, even if it means death.*

This seems to me a very useful thematic statement, even though it focuses on Paul and therefore gives a different emphasis than that in the uncle's closing words. (It also illustrates flexibility in interpretation—something the class will need to be reminded of after a few statements that seem not to work for the story.)

5. *The price some people pay for "luck" is too high, and it finally costs more than it is worth.*

This too seems helpful. Unlike statement three, it takes into account both premise and consequence, but it could easily be made more useful if it were more specific. What is meant by "luck"? What is—and isn't—it worth?

The next two statements, which try to address the story's complexity more adequately, were formulated collectively by the class after our discussion of the story's theme:

6. *When people are unable to love appropriately because they mistake money or "luck" for love, they may destroy both those they want to love and themselves.*

7. *People who define love as money may cause their children to destroy themselves in an attempt to win approval or acceptance.*

It is important to keep in mind that trying to formulate an adequate thematic statement is only a means to an end, not an end in itself. These last two statements, not surprisingly, are approximate paraphrases of the meaning in the uncle's words (which carry a risk of not having their irony understood), and so the class has come full circle back to the story itself.

Comparing Criteria: O'Connor vs. Oates

Joseph Bathanti

MITCHELL COMMUNITY COLLEGE
STATESVILLE, NORTH CAROLINA

WRITING ASSIGNMENT

Read Flannery O'Connor's "A Good Man Is Hard to Find," as well as her accompanying essay, "The Element of Suspense in 'A Good Man Is Hard to Find.'"

In her essay, O'Connor makes the following observations about "A Good Man Is Hard to Find," observations that she feels can also serve as characteristics of good stories (especially hers) in general:

- There is "a reasonable use of the unreasonable."

- Death is the most "significant position life offers a Christian."

- Some action or gesture by a character that is "both totally right and totally unexpected" indicates "where the real heart of the story lies."

- There is an "intrusion of grace."

- "Violence is strangely capable of returning my characters to reality and preparing them to accept their moment of grace."

- "It is the extreme situation that best reveals what we are essentially."

- "Its way of being serious is a comic one."

O'Connor has also said, "I have found, in short, from reading my own writing, my subject in fiction is the action of grace in territory held largely by the devil."

Go back to "A Good Man Is Hard to Find" and simply rethink the story in light of these observations/characteristics. Can you see them actually playing out in the story and adding an additional dimension? Are they helpful in understanding the story?

How helpful would they be if applied to another's writer's story, say Joyce Carol Oates's "Where Are You Going, Where Have You Been?

There are some very obvious similarities between the two stories. Most obviously, each story has its sociopathic "Misfit" who espouses his own "unique" philosophy and shows up in an automobile. One wears spectacles and the other sunglasses. Both the Grandmother and Connie engage in protracted conversations with their respective Misfits.

I could go on as to their similarities, but I'll stop here, except to quote something Joyce Carol Oates once wrote about her story, which she called a "realistic allegory." What she said was, "Connie is shallow, vain, silly, hopeful, doomed . . . but capable nonetheless of an unexpected gesture of heroism at the story's end." She goes on to say that "The story ends abruptly at the point of her 'crossing over.' We don't know the nature of her sacrifice, only that she is generous enough to make it."

Consider the similarities between the two stories. How can O'Connor's comments be used to establish a basis of comparison? Write a comparison/contrast essay that uses as its point of departure O'Connor's observations about good stories. Remember to keep these "criteria" foremost in your discussion. You must explore their presence, not simply as they exist rhetorically or philosophically, but as they exist in the language employed by the individual authors and in the various turns in the action of their stories.

Character Analysis: Compare and Contrast

Steven Cooper
CALIFORNIA STATE UNIVERSITY, LONG BEACH
LONG BEACH, CALIFORNIA

READING ASSIGNMENT

Read Flannery O'Connor's "A Good Man Is Hard to Find." Read it again a day later. Do the same with Joyce Carol Oates's "Where Are You Going, Where Have You Been?"

Consider the basic similarities between these two stories. Each features a naive and self-centered protagonist who encounters a frightening foil. Chilling consequences ensue.

Now get more specific. Connie, we are told at the beginning of the Oates story, has but "a shadowy vision of herself." By the end of the story that vision has led to an ominous glimpse of the "vast sunlit reaches" of an unidentified land where Connie has never been before, but to which she will now be going—the land of disillusion at least, it would seem, perhaps at worst the land of death.

Similarly, at the beginning of the O'Connor story the Grandmother is all but oblivious to her own shortsightedness and lack of true self-knowledge. In tricking her family to go to see the "old plantation"—evidently a product of her own romantic delusion—she unwittingly leads them all into a much different reality, namely, the hands of a cold-blooded band of mass murderers.

WRITING ASSIGNMENT

Write an essay in which you analyze the respective characters of Connie and the Grandmother, comparing and contrasting the specifics of their development.

Here are some questions that may help you to begin the process of creating a first draft:

- What do the two characters consider important? What do they consider unimportant?

- How do they behave with other members of their families? How do they behave with people to whom they are not related?

- Why is it that for Connie "[e]verything about her had two sides to it"?

- Why does the Grandmother dress as she does?

- How do you think Connie would react if she were to meet the Grandmother? How do you think the Grandmother would respond to Connie?

Think of other questions to ask, applying them where possible to both stories. Remember, you are looking both for similarities and for differences in order to explain your understanding of two parallel but not identical characters. Remember, too, that the best essays include some sense or suggestion of how this understanding matters to the writer—that is, to *you*.

"Where Are You Going, Where Have You Been?" Three Approaches to Enrichment

Jeannette Palmer and Linda C. Rollins
MOTLOW STATE COMMUNITY COLLEGE
TULLAHOMA, TENNESSEE

The following approaches evolved from a passing conversation at the copy machine when Jeannette Palmer was making copies of Bob Dylan's lyrics to "It's All Over Now, Baby Blue" for use with her classes as they studied Joyce Carol Oates's "Where Are You Going, Where Have You Been?" Our conversation centered on trying to make literature relevant and meaningful in the lives of our students who many times complain about having to take literature courses. As we discussed Oates's story, we realized that it contains three essential elements with which we felt our students have a close affinity: everyday people (the types almost everyone knows); music, which is so very much a part of their lives; and events, such as kidnapping and rape, which surround them in their lives and are reported daily in the media. With these ideas in mind, we joined efforts, and over a semester or two of teaching and discussing the story developed these approaches.

THE ARCHETYPE APPROACH

Literature is nothing more than the study of life, a look at life's situations and how we deal with them, a look at how we handle these circumstances and how we interact with those with whom we become involved. Students—traditional and nontraditional as well—readily identify with the circumstances and characters who come alive in Oates's initiation story "Where Are You Going, Where Have You Been?" Whether we are involved with people in everyday life, or with people we encounter through literature, we see archetypes. Such archetypes dominate Oates's story.

Connie, the young protagonist—in one of the rare stories of initiations using a young woman—may be studied as the temptress/femme fatale archetype. She walks a thin line balancing her world at home and "anywhere that was not home." Her youth and beauty are countered by her innocence and lack of experience, completing her duality. Oates strengthens this archetype through numerous descriptions. Examples include:

- "Everything about her had two sides to it, one for home and one for anywhere that was not home: her walk that could be childlike and bobbing, or languid enough to make anyone think that she was hearing music in her head."

- "Connie couldn't do a thing, her mind was all filled with trashy daydreams."

- "Their [Connie and her girlfriend at the mall] faces pleased and expectant."

- "She [Connie] drew her shoulders up and sucked in the breath with the pure pleasure of being alive."

An innocent flirtation draws her into the beginning of the initiation into life when she encounters another of Oates's archetypes, the shadow *(Doppelgänger)* Arnold Friend, who, like Connie, has a dual nature. Connie sees him as "a boy with shaggy black hair, in a convertible jalopy painted gold." This seemingly serendipitous meeting is what Connie perceives as yet one more playful conquest, the game she so likes to play. Unfortunately, her innocence blinds her to his ominous remark: "Gonna get you, baby." This remark begins for Connie, as well as the reader, the unfolding of Arnold's darker side, On that terrifying Sunday when Arnold comes to take her for the final ride into the sunshine, "she could see then that he wasn't a kid—he was much older—thirty, maybe more." Connie realizes that there is no turning back: "'Didn't you see me put my sign in the air when you walked by?'"

Among Oates's other references to Arnold's duality are:

- "His whole face was a mask, she thought wildly."

- "Arnold said, in a gentle-loud voice that was like a stage voice, 'The place where you came from ain't there any more, and where you had in mind to go is cancelled out.'"

Other archetypes in the story include the spinster sister, the detached father, and the resentful but knowing mother. All these archetypes make rich sources for character analyses because to students they are real people.

THE MUSIC APPROACH

A second approach to Oates's story is the use of her numerous references to music. From its opening when Oates dedicates the story to Bob Dylan, a musical prophet of the 1960s, music permeates the world of the characters just as it permeates the world of contemporary students. The following are samples:

- "The music was always in the background like music at a church service, it was something to depend upon."

- ". . . but an idea, a feeling, mixed up with the urgent insistent pounding of the music and humid night air of July."

- "Connie sat with her eyes closed in the sun. . . . how sweet it always was, not the way someone like June would suppose but sweet, gentle, the way it was in movies and promised in song."

- "Connie . . . in a glow of slow-pulsed joy that seemed to rise mysteriously out of the music itself and lay languidly about the airless little room, breathed in and breathed out with each gentle rise and fall of her chest."

- "Connie . . . listening to the music from her radio and the boy's blend together. She stared at Arnold Friend."

- "She recognized all this and also the singsong way he talked, slightly mocking, kidding, but serious and a little melancholy, and she recognized the way he tapped one fist against the other in homage to the perpetual music behind him."

- "Part of those words [Arnold's words] were spoken with a slight rhythmic lilt, and Connie somehow recognized them— the echo of a song from last year, about a girl rushing into her boyfriend's arms and coming home again—"

- "His words were not angry but only part of an incantation. The incantation was kindly."

- " 'My sweet little blue-eyed girl,' he said in a half-sung sigh that had nothing to do with her brown eyes."

The last quote is a direct reference to Bob Dylan's "It's All Over Now Baby Blue," which Oates has stated was an inspiration for her story. Students naturally want to know more about the cryptic reference. After listening to the song and being given a copy of the lyrics, students then do their own analysis of it and its relationship to the story. They may write a detailed comparison of the song and the story or take the many musical references from the story and weave them into a study of music's importance to the atmosphere or characterization. This assignment is also effective when given to a group who can produce a report to be presented to the entire class.

THE MEDIA APPROACH

Another facet of the story is its astonishingly close tie to a real-life event. (The inspiration for using this class exercise comes from Tom Quirk's article, "A Source for 'Where Are You Going, Where Have You Been?'" in the Fall 1981 *Studies in Short Fiction*.) After reading and analyzing the story, students are given a copy of a March 4, 1966, *Life* magazine article, "The Pied Piper of Tucson," by Don Moser, which recounts the terrifying reality of serial murderer Charles "Smitty" Schmid, who targeted blue-eyed, blonde teenage girls. (Quirk asserts in his article that Oates read the *Life* article as well as other accounts in the news magazines.) Students analyze the article for allusions and direct references that Oates uses or adapts in her story, such as the music, Schmid's appearance, Schmid's car, and his modus operandi.

Through this activity, whether done individually or in groups, students begin to see how writers may take actual incidents from print or other media and with their artistic abilities create a piece of literature. Alternate activities can be research projects on short stories and novels that have their bases in actual events, Stephen Crane's "The Open Boat" is a good companion piece. It is a fictionalized version of Crane's own lifeboat experience during the Spanish-American War. Also, other novels that are possible sources include John Steinbeck's *Grapes of Wrath*, based on Steinbeck's reporting during the Great Depression; Truman Capote's *In Cold Blood*, based on a Kansas mass murder by two murderers, which Capote contended was the new novel of the future based on "creative reporting"; Oates's novel *Dark Waters*, which closely parallels the Chappaquiddick Island episode of Senator Edward Kennedy's life; the John Berendt novel *Midnight in the Garden of Good and Evil*, which—by Berendt's own description—is a thinly disguised version of a sensationalized Savannah, Georgia murder; or Thomas Keneally's *Schindler's List*, based on the life of Oskar Schindler and the events of the Holocaust. Another opportunity for writing may involve students choosing a current news story from a local, regional, or national source, from which they write their own short stories based on the ideas that they glean from the source.

We carefully sequence our approach to the story by reading and analyzing *before* introducing any of the three approaches so as to let students become aware of their own insightfulness. After several semesters using these approaches, we have received continuous positive feedback from our students. They, like Connie, discover that literature is more than superficial appearance and, as readers, experience a kind of initiation themselves as they uncover the multiple levels of meaning at which a narrative may be read and appreciated.

REFERENCE

Dylan, Bob. "It's All Over Now, Baby Blue." *Bob Dylan's Greatest Hits*. Vol. II. Columbia Records/CBS.

Moser, Don. "The Pied Piper of Tucson." *Life* (4 March 1966): 18–24ff.

Quirk, Tom. "A Source for 'Where Are You Going, Where Have You Been?'" *Studies in Short Fiction* 18 (Fall 1981): 413–19.

The Faith of Fiction: Symbolism in "A Good Man Is Hard to Find"

Alan Davis
MOORHEAD STATE UNIVERSITY
MOORHEAD, MINNESOTA

Flannery O'Connor is a writer whose luminous ironic vision was lost to us when she died in 1964 at age thirty-nine. Fortunately, she came of age as an artist in her twenties, and "A Good Man Is Hard to Find" is one among a number of her stories that is a small masterpiece. ("Good Country People," "The Artificial Nigger," "The Displaced Person," and "Everything That Rises Must Converge" are other obvious choices.) Dramatically, this story about a petty, prideful grandmother who unintentionally leads her vacationing family into the path of The Misfit, a homicidal maniac who blames his meanness on Jesus, encapsulizes O'Connor's dark Old Testament vision of humankind.

O'Connor is about as far from New Age optimism or secular humanism as it is possible to get without falling off the edge of the earth. As such, she may be particularly appealing to members of the so-called Generation X or to other young adults who are sick to death of moral relativity on the one hand and media flatulence on the other. The Misfit, who believes that Jesus, by raising the dead, had "thrown everything off balance" so that there's "no pleasure but meanness," ends up shooting the whole family, the grandmother last, but not before she reaches out to him and murmurs, "Why you're one of my babies. You're one of my own children!" Such salvation, where the grandmother reaches past her pride to claim kinship with her murderer, is possible for O'Connor's countrified, uneducated Southerners only when extremity forces them to face mortality, the intimation of which contains, paradoxically, the possibility of redemption; with an unerring ear, O'Connor gives life to a landscape and a psychology where people are tested for the seven deadly sins, especially the sin of pride, found to be full to bursting with one or another of those sins, and given a chance to save their souls while they lose everything else, including (possibly) their lives.

Along the way, readers are in for a good deal of fun from a writer who began her creative life as a cartoonist and who never lost touch with the cadences of Southern speech, the idiosyncracies of Southern life, and the moral code of the Old South—an amalgam of the Ten Commandments, *noblesse oblige,* and fundamentalist brimstone that was practiced more in the breach than otherwise. O'Connor's South, as she feared, has become as brand-spanking generic as anywhere else, but her best fictions—which incorporate grotesque violence, racial tension, and religious hypocrisy—are as contemporary as yesterday's headlines. Any reader can open almost any newspaper and find some present-day equivalent of O'Connor's Misfit to consider. Journalists, however, seldom write about grace or redemption. They merely take editorial pleasure in the strange materialistic music of our age, whereas O'Connor's aesthetic integrity is unquestionable. "In good fiction," she has written, "certain of the details will tend to accumulate meaning from the action of the story itself, and when this happens they become symbolic in the way they work."

I want to describe a teaching approach to "A Good Man Is Hard to Find" that begins with small-group readings of the story, readings structured by an O'Connor quotation and by your chosen emphasis, and that ends with each student writing an essay that is both a critical response to group discussion and an appraisal of O'Connor's story. This collaborative approach to reading her fiction keeps students honest and demonstrates that a symbol must be earned by writer and reader alike before it can be claimed. Otherwise, O'Connor's stories, which by today's standards are too well-made, almost slick, create a steel-trap dazzle that ensnares readers into finding symbols like Easter eggs under the shrubbery of every image. Readers can emerge from her stories a little light-headed and lost, sorely tempted to reach for the nearest symbol. My teaching approach has a chance to show students that a symbol, in fiction at least, is an incarnation achieved through technique and not some sleight of hand whereby a writer injects meaning into a story with an image whose cultural symbolism is external to the fictional situation.

Introducing O'Connor, you might let anyone unfamiliar with her work know that she was a devout Catholic and a dyed-in-the-wool Southerner who believed passionately that universal truth could only be tendered in concrete detail, one image following another. Cultural symbols, if they are used, must have fictional context. We cannot assume that our readers, especially inexperienced readers without literary training, will bring any social or cultural context at all to a given fiction. In "The Fiction Writer and His Country," published in *Mystery and Manners*, O'Connor's essential book of occasional essays and lectures published posthumously, she writes, "In the greatest fiction, the writer's moral sense coincides with his dramatic sense, and I see no way for it to do this unless his moral judgment is part of the very act of seeing, and he is free to use it. I have heard it said that belief in Christian dogma is a hindrance to the writer, but I myself have found nothing further from the truth. Actually, it frees the storyteller to observe." In view of this orientation, it also useful for the reader to know that O'Connor's vision is prophetic. As she writes elsewhere in *Mystery and Manners*, "There is the prophetic sense of 'seeing through' reality and there is also the prophetic function of recalling people to known but ignored truths." It is this last sense of prophecy that suggests mystery and requires good manners, for without such manners a reader might very well project anything into a story or its imagery instead of facing what is there, a process that is parallel to the process whereby her characters must face their own lives.

After introducing O'Connor, divide your class into small groups and have each group understand that it will be responsible collectively for presenting its findings, as a sort of panel, to the rest of the class, and responsible individually for writing an essay that responds to the story and to other critical opinions offered in the classroom. Provide each group with an O'Connor quotation, either from the story itself or from the essays in *Mystery and Manners*, and with lead-ins. You may give each group a different quotation and a different emphasis (symbol, character, plot, theme, language, cultural, or social context) or have them all work along the same lines. Each group, for example, can think about the way symbols develop in fiction, and the story can be the common denominator. (It is also possible, given time constraints, to have several groups discussing several stories from the anthology, stories that the class will have all read but only chosen groups will become "expert" on.) In either case, this structured approach, in my experience, keeps inexperienced readers from descending into a mere litany of likes and dislikes, or into a patchwork display of their ignorance, which serves neither O'Connor nor their own sense of literature.

Once the group has had one day to discuss the story and a second day to organize its presentation, it then presents its findings on the third day of the week and responds as well to the insights put forward by other groups. (I am assuming a class that meets three times per week, but this scheme is easily adapted to other configurations.) The papers are written over the weekend and turned in the following week, perhaps after a discussion of rough drafts. (During this discussion and drafting process, you wander from group to group, offering mini-lectures if appropriate but more likely monitoring discussion and kick-starting them as necessary, as well as offering ideas for the panel and for the essays.)

When I teach the story in this fashion, I like to use the following O'Connor quotation (again from *Mystery and Manners*) in combination with quotes from the story: "I suppose the reasons for the use of so much violence in modern fiction will differ with each writer who uses it, but in my own stories I have found that violence is strangely capable of returning my characters to reality and preparing them to accept their moment of grace. Their heads are so hard that almost nothing else will do the work." Inexperienced readers are always shocked at how quickly and (many readers think) how callously O'Connor disposes of the grandmother and her family, despite the fact that the story's first paragraph foreshadows its climax. The story is so well made, in fact, so full of technique and craft in the service of vision and theme, that it sometimes seems to me to be the perfect "teaching" story; the quotation gives students a fulcrum whereby they can open the story, follow its lines of spiritual motion, and trace the concrete details that develop those invisible lines.

The "lead-ins" you provide can direct students to such imagery and detail, to symbolism as a process and an accumulation instead of a definition or a color-by-number procedure. Here are some examples of lead-ins that have worked for me: 1) "Is the Misfit a 'failed prophet,' someone who has seen through the reality of existence but in an unrealistic or delusional way? Analyze his conversation with the grandmother. He may be crazy, but don't just dismiss his statements as nonsense"; 2) "Does the grandmother change at the end? Is it necessary to have her killed? Is she so set in her ways that nothing else will bring her to her senses?"; 3) "Is the violence gratuitous or necessary to the story?"; 4) "A spokesperson is someone who represents the author's views. Is any character a spokesperson for O'Connor? If not, how does the story itself speak for her? Or does it?"

You can certainly find alternatives of your own that will guide your students without controlling their responses or forcing a particular reading or ideology upon them. "A Good Man Is Hard to Find" is profoundly disturbing to many students, as it should be, and allowing them to have their say without allowing them to get away with saying anything makes them think and lets the faith of fiction seep into their bones. O'Connor herself, in *Mystery and Manners*, expresses surprise at the different sorts of readings the story has received over the years. The story, however, no longer belongs to her, even though she wrote it, because it is not a tract but a fully-dramatized fiction, open to interpretation, ambiguity, and dissonance. Still, a symbol is a road map, and it points in the best fiction to real toads in our imaginary gardens; all of us, students and instructors alike, are engaged in learning to be, as the poet Marianne Moore put it, "literalists of the imagination." I am constantly surprised and enlightened by the insights that students who discipline their imaginations come to. Further, I find that the discussions, the panel presentations, and the subsequent essays benefit from a process that replicates the process we use ourselves as we read, discuss, and write about literature.

"The Use of Force" and "I Stand Here Ironing" as Models for Writing Scene and Summary

Lin Enger
MOORHEAD STATE UNIVERSITY
MOORHEAD, MINNESOTA

Many of my introductory composition and creative writing students seem to share a common weakness: the relentless commitment to quick generalization and facile summaries, to easy reliance on any strategy that saves them from having to summon the particular, personal, and distinctive observations necessary to make their work interesting and authentic. Early in every term, I find myself writing the same comments repeatedly in the margins of their papers and stories.

"More"

"Examples needed"

"Be specific, not generic."

"What *exactly* do you mean here?"

Whether from timidity, or from lack of interest, confidence, or instruction, the essay writer in a piece about her confusing relationship with grandparents settles for this hasty accounting of her grandpa: "He is a typical old man who sits and tell stories." But where, I want to know, does he prefer to sit and what sort of stories does he tell? Do people listen to him? Has he lived an interesting life? What about his manner of speech?

Or, take the beginning fiction writer who tacks to the end of his skeletal story a complex explanation of the main character's epiphany. The writer has not taken the time to work though a sequence of fully rendered scenes; and yet he wonders why the story does not carry the emotional weight he intends for it to carry.

Student writers need to learn that the best writing is effective because it bears a strong resemblance to lived life; it rides along on a raft of authentic detail and observation. But effective writing also provides the context within which it can be interpreted and understood. It is not merely a series of details; it is a meaningful series of details. It is both the lumber and the blueprint.

To make this point, I find it helpful to lead students through a two-part writing exercise carried out in parallel to a discussion of two stories representing distinct narrative strategies: scene and summary (or exposition). "The Use of Force" by William Carlos Williams and "I Stand Here Ironing" by Tillie Olsen are an apt pair for this exercise. In both, we witness struggling working-class families. In both, young female characters suffer at the hands of harsh, disinterested forces. In both, adults must confront their own shame at how they've treated these girls. But of course the stories are starkly different from one another. "The Use of Force" is conveyed in a single swift scene, requiring little exposition. In real time the story covers perhaps ten minutes. "I Stand Here Ironing," far more leisurely in pace, is a first-person interior monologue. The narrator, as she irons a dress, reflects on her teenage daughter's life from birth to the present. The six-page story covers nineteen years in real time.

When my students arrive in class (having read the stories overnight), I immediately get them started on the first part of the writing exercises. Without making reference to either story, I ask the students to isolate in their memories a single episode in which their response to a situation was sudden anger, sharp fear, humiliation, or even violence. Their task is to describe not the events leading up to the incident, not their interpretation of it as informed by distance and perspective—but simply the moment itself, the immediate physical and emotional experience. They need to get back there in their memories and, using sensory language, describe what they see and hear and feel in such a way that a reader too will see and hear and feel the same things. A very big job, but that's what writers do.

After fifteen minutes, I have the students stop writing and turn to Williams's story. I ask a series of questions about it. Why does the doctor get angry? How does the nature of his anger change? Why does the girl resist him so violently? Why does the doctor despise the girl's parents? In what sense has the doctor "fallen in love" with the girl? These are questions to which we can usually articulate satisfying answers; to do so, however, we must read with care, for the narrator provides little exposition or direct analysis. We may note, for instance, the narrator's comparison of the girl to a "heifer" and a "savage." We may recognize that midway through the doctor's visit he has begun to "[grind] his teeth" in the fashion of the animals to which he has compared the girl. The point is, Williams manages to create the considerable resonance he does while relying primarily on dramatic devices, on the elements of scene: dialogue, description, and action.

Part two of the writing exercise (which will likely have to wait for the next class meeting) asks students to return to the incidents they described earlier. This time, though, they should avoid any concrete description of the moment itself; rather, they should explain why the experience was important, what factors and forces brought it about, how they feel and think about it in retrospect. Let's say a student has written about the time years ago when she bungled her brief trumpet solo in the middle of a concert performance. She has described the cotton-dry texture of her tongue, the rising panic in her stomach, the pressure of five hundred pairs of eyes all aimed at her, the embarrassing squeak of her instrument. She has successfully re-created her sense of fear and humiliation.

But now she must view the experience from a greater distance and with more careful reflection. She might describe what playing the trumpet meant to her, how powerful it made her feel, sitting as she had in the very center of the orchestra, carrying the melody, attacking those brilliant high notes. She might reflect on how she reacted to her public failure, how she went about renovating her ego. She might suggest in what ways that small failure later prevented her from taking certain risks or shamed her into taking others.

Having tried on this thoughtful, more expository style, students now turn to the Tillie Olsen story, whose narrator takes a long view of things, looking back at her own and her daughter's lives as they have unfolded over two decades. "I Stand Here Ironing" may lack the immediacy and sudden voltage of the Williams story, but it offers its own rewards. Olsen's method allows us to receive the extended and generous insight of an intelligent woman reflecting on universal questions: Have I done well by my children? Have I done well by the people who depend on me? Should I feel regret? This is a story that goes a long way toward answering the questions it asks. It is an emotional piece, but also cerebral. It explains, summarizes, and evaluates; it seems to understand its own significance. In contrast, "The Use of Force," because of its relative lack of exposition, asks the *reader to* create the story's meaning. Williams doesn't want to give it all away.

And that is the practical difference between the strategies of scene and exposition; a scene works by the dramatic force of suggestion, exposition by a more reflective, more thoughtfully analytic power.

Exploring the Mythos
of Man and Woman

Richard J. Jennings
LONG BEACH CITY COLLEGE
LONG BEACH, CALIFORNIA

The difficulties that confront any relationship quickly move beyond the simple conflict of the personalities of the lovers to the perspectives that are inherent in gender differences; that is, in the two quite separate *Weltanschauungen* (worldviews, reality pictures) brought to the bonding process. Of course, these are culturally determined, but the Western tradition of understanding this complex situation begins long before the simplistic categorization of books like *Men Are from Mars, Women Are from Venus*. By the time of Geoffrey Chaucer's *Canterbury Tales* (1385–1400), these ideas were already clearly articulated. Chaucer's psychologically complex Wife of Bath points out that she was born under the equal astrological influences of both planets. In her prologue and tale, the poet has her speak to the essential mystery of the human condition as it involves the relationship between the sexes.

Chaucer's method is to have her establish the contrast between her five marriages, in which there is a continual struggle for mastery (dominance), versus the ideal relationship expressed through the idea of sovereignty, in which the control of the relationship is voluntarily tendered out of grace and love—a love both erotic and platonic. The story she tells is of a knight who rapes a woman and receives the task (from a woman) of finding out what it is that a woman really wants. The knight has a year to return with the answer or face death. The knight fails until, hopeless and returning to his execution, he meets a witchy old hag who offers him the answer—and his life—if he will promise to marry her. With no time left and no other possibilities, he reluctantly agrees to the bargain. His answer delivered and life saved, the old dame gives him a magical choice: He may have her as an old, ugly faithful wife, or a young, beautiful faithless one. (For the answer the knight finds and the solution to his dilemma, you might turn to Chaucer himself, but avoid those sanitized translations into modern

English, which sometimes reduce him to inanity; in fact, you may want to do this to prepare for the writing possibilities to come).

Chaucer's medieval investigation of gender roles is itself an early exploration of a major part of the mystery of the human condition, but culturally speaking, it is by no means the first, or even the most insightful as it is largely based in the "courtly love" tradition. A more modern perspective—either startlingly insightful or frighteningly truthful, or both—comes through the French tradition as it is developed by Georges Bataille's *Death and Sensuality: A Study of Eroticism and the Taboo* (1962).

Early on in the work, Bataille distinguishes between the physical intimacy that is conducive to sexual reproduction and the parallel phenomenon of eroticism, which—though many times absent—is the core of the psychological intimacy necessary to the growth of a relationship, the ability to move beyond the boundaries of self to a real understanding of the needs and beauty of "the other." After defining eroticism and sensuality as necessary human reactions to death, Bataille stresses that the erotic aspect and its exploration is the subject of, and impetus for, most social taboos that concern the relationship of man and woman. These taboos create repression and silence about sexual desire and its connection to beauty and ugliness, violence and death, not just in society but in the real coupling of two people who cherish and desire an emotional and spiritual bond that approaches the ideal.

READING, PREWRITING, AND DRAFTING

Using John Steinbeck's "The Chrysanthemums" as a starting point, examine how the relationship between husband and wife falls victim to this silence and how Eliza's brief relationship with a stranger brings her an ironic recognition of what she will never have at home. Examine her metamorphosis, her transfiguration, into strength and then weakness, making sure to focus on the symbolic value of the flowers.

RESEARCH, READING, PREWRITING, AND DRAFTING

Using either D. H. Lawrence's "Odor of Chrysanthemums" or his "Horse Dealer's Daughter," look for parallel or contrastive development that examines how eroticism is a key to the understanding of another human, to the development of the tolerance, the empathy, and the acceptance of our common lot, our shared experience of the ineluctable mystery of existence.

VISUAL ICONS

Examine *The Joy of Life* by Henri Matisse, or *The Lovers* by Marc Chagall, or *The Kiss* by Auguste Rodin as emblems of the confluence of erotic and spiritual in the ideal human experience of another.

Critical Thinking with "A & P"

Allen Ramsey
CENTRAL MISSOURI STATE UNIVERSITY
WARRENSBURG, MISSOURI

In recent years I have incorporated critical thinking activities into my composition courses. Literature provides innumerable opportunities to take up critical thinking, but one that I especially enjoy is the analysis of humor. After my class has read "A & P," I inquire about its comic effects. My students typically find the story mildly amusing.

The question in this analysis is not, "Is it funny?" but, "If it's funny, why?" As an introduction to the discussion, I provide a handout that has the following newspaper article:

Man Faces Charges in Assaults on Teens

A man accused of knocking down teen-age girls, taking off their shoes and sucking their toes has been arrested.

"It's kind of a humiliating thing. I think emotionally it just degraded them," said St. Louis police Maj. Ronald Henderson. "My main concern was what was next."

Edgar Jones, 28, was charged with assault, indecent exposure and sexual abuse Wednesday in connection with the bizarre crimes, which started occurring in January and continued until two weeks ago.

The eight girls who were victims all identified Jones in a lineup, Henderson said.

"A couple of them broke down," he said.

Jones, a laborer, posed as a jogger in his early morning attacks on the girls, whose ages ranged from 13 to 19, Henderson said.

In the most recent attack, a 13-year-old girl waiting for a school bus was knocked to the ground by a man. He told her he wouldn't hurt her but wanted to suck her toes.

After the girl stopped struggling, the man took off her left shoe and sock and sucked her toes. He did not otherwise harm her, and after a brief time he released her.

In other incidents, "he would run by and touch them and then turn around and come back," Henderson said.

This short statement is provocative because it causes some students to convulse with laughter, some to titter and then clap a hand over their mouth, and some to read solemnly without any expression whatever.

I have asked students to write for ten minutes on this article ("Is this article funny? Why?") before a discussion. The pivotal word is "bizarre," a word that summarizes why some things, at least, are funny. In this case, aberrant behavior is at once preposterous, grotesque, and, for some, offensive. As discussants sort through the curious reactions to the story, the political correctness issue normally emerges: How can you laugh at *victims?* The fact is, practical jokes are comedies of victimization. The practical joke is also a topic of discussion.

Should we laugh at this article? I have never taken a position on this question, and I have never had a class agree. Most interesting to me, though, is seeing a student start to laugh (sometimes uproariously), but then hesitate, choke down the laughter, and then write a solemn essay about those poor girls who were attacked. The question arises: Do we laugh only when it is socially acceptable to do so? Just how inhibited are we by what others think?

In turning to "A & P," we ask if and why this story is funny. Sammy's narrative voice reveals a level of immaturity with his sexuality, his job and his employer, and his coworker Stoksie; his naivete and altruism evoke either amusement or derision (depending on the reader). The analogy to the newspaper article becomes evident: If readers can recognize Sammy's immaturity as immaturity rather than simply chauvinism (chauvinism, as in "chauvinist pig"), the comic elements may emerge. In both cases, the reader must be able to move beyond "How am I supposed to react?" to "Am I human enough to recognize human weakness as part of the human circus?"

There is a final kicker. We are right to ask whether at some point our laughter should become subdued by other emotions, such as compassion, pity, anger, or outrage.

Now that I have talked my way through this pedagogy, it seems to me that this discussion could be useful as a preface to a series of stories: "Gimpel the Fool," "A Good Man Is Hard to Find," "The Catbird Seat," and as a contrast, "Where Are You Going, Where Have You Been?" (the truly unfunny bizarre).

Sample Assignment
for Alice Walker's
"Everyday Use"

Allison M. Cummings
HAMPDEN-SYDNEY COLLEGE
HAMPDEN-SYDNEY, VIRGINIA

At the university where I first taught, most of the freshman composition classes focused on writing either about adolescent change or
about notions of cultural literacy. I tried to combine the two in my
course, by having students write and think about how they interpret
their own lives through narratives. The first assignment was to write
a four-page essay about a turning point in life, or a moment when the
student suddenly became conscious of himself or herself as a
_____ (black, white, latino, Asian, Jewish, Catholic, female,
male, lower-middle class, or any other category that seemed different
from one's general social context). I like to discuss Walker's "Everyday Use" in class before handing out the assignment because it
illustrates with such deft humor how people may invent themselves.
It also hits home with students (and teachers) who are caught in the
midst of debates about multiculturalism: What does it mean? Is race
a matter of the stories you tell yourself, or the stories your family or
culture tells you, or . . . ?

In the story, the mother is pragmatic, unpretentious, but tolerant of her daughter's abrupt changes (which she sees as fairly consistent with Dee's odd personality all along). Dee, a.k.a. Wangero, newly
Afrocentric, suddenly finds the details of her family's roots part of a
cultural narrative about adversity and resourcefulness, from which
she now derives pride. She snaps Polaroids of this house, identical to
the one she perhaps sabotaged as a teen. We discuss why Maggie bears
the burn scars from the house fire Dee may have lit. Although students initially react against Dee/Wangero as a phony, as we talk
about her values and assumptions, it becomes clear that many students share them. We reconsider the difference of the mother's day-
dream of being brought on TV for a reunion with Dee, and her

135

self-description—"who ever knew a Johnson with a quick tongue?"—that now makes her seem like a trickster narrator.

Finally, we talk about the principal opposition the story sets up—between "use" and decoration, which Dee/Wangero refers to, significantly, as "hanging" (paragraph 73). Although the mother seems tolerant of Dee/Wangero's strange values, when Dee claims the quilts that were promised to Maggie, the mother says "something hit me in the head" (paragraph 77), and she snatches the quilts away and throws them and Maggie on the bed. What hits her and why? Why does she hug Maggie, something she never does? How do the mother's and Dee/Wangero's different relations to the quilts (or to the butter churn, the benches, or the house) characterize their relations to each other, to society, and to their own lives?

If there's time left, we talk about why Walker chose to use quilts as the site of mother and daughter struggle, and how quilts encode identity. The bits of Grandma and Big Dee's clothes, plus the tiny piece from their Great Grandpa's Civil War uniform, all silently document the family's past and its role in history. The women's intergenerational work on the quilts and passed-on knowledge of how to make them signifies the self-knowledge that comes from a sense of continuity with and ability to carry forward the past. And the metaphor of quilting, as piecing together bits of clothes, themselves associated with roles and identity, has been used by many feminist writers to connote these multiple relations—of people to identity, to their pasts, to knowledge, creativity and self-expression through everyday objects of art *and* use.

The students generally begin talking about the story sure of who they like and dislike and why. But as we talk more, the story becomes more complicated, particularly if they compare the stance on identity that each character represents to their own stance—is identity derived from what you have and do, or from a story of a legacy, or what? Whether they resolve the story for themselves or not, they get thinking about *what has made them think the way they do about who they are.* Although it is often hard for students to recall a moment when "something hit them" (that realization may be far in the past), they can usually recall small reminders or brief moments when some comment or gesture reminded them: "Oh yeah, I'm female." Students tend to think of moments of differentiation as painful or self-destructive; I encourage them to also think about moments when they felt part of a group and felt good about that differentiation from the larger culture.

I also remind them of how Wangero's interpretation of her heritage seems false, and caution them against relying on abstractions. I urge them to situate their descriptions of themselves in specific images (from pictures, memory, family stories) of before and after—like Dee's relation to the house, before and after her transformation. I tell them to tell a story with two parts, and then to reflect on the difference between them. The paper should clearly contrast the two moments (and comprise about two pages), then switch gears from storytelling to interpretation.

This is the tough part: achieving balance between description and analysis. Most students will do solely one or the other in their first drafts. When they read and critique each other's papers in groups of three—which they do all semester—they see the shortcomings of having only story or only analysis. The summary has no thesis or conclusions (and here is a useful distinction between fiction and analytical papers for them), and the paper has no detailed examples, which every college paper must have. If they have only stories, they develop an analysis through drafts by taking points from the conclusion and putting them first. If they have only abstractions, it isn't hard to point out the need for specific examples. I talk about this kind of draft with the class as a whole, and compare the use of examples to the use of quotations from texts, to give them a sense of the pattern of college papers. This process teaches the students how to work from examples to a thesis and how to reshape their stories or plot summaries into analytical papers.

I think "Everyday Use" is a deceptively simple story that has enormous potential to involve students in heated discussion of complicated issues. We make the story into useful material itself, piecing it into the student's own quiltings of their lives.

A Three-Part Approach to Writing on "Everyday Use"

Peggy Ellsberg
BARNARD COLLEGE
NEW YORK, NEW YORK

Alice Walker's "Everyday Use" is a story that I assign in two classes I teach: one called "Writing Women's Lives" and the other called "Ethnicity and Social Transformation." The story introduces themes applicable to both topics. Both of these courses are designed primarily for first-year students, and my goal in formulating their written exercises is to teach the expository virtues of conciseness, clarity, and focus. I suggest that a paper on "Everyday Use" be two to three pages in length. At least once each semester we rehearse a written exercise together in class.

First, after we have read the story, I ask the students to paraphrase or summarize its plot or content. I write an outline of their statements on the board, compiling them until I reach a consensus that goes something like this: An African American mother, living in simplicity or even poverty in rural Georgia, describes her two daughters. Dee is stylish, confident, and ambitious, has gone to college, and has left home. Maggie is timid and a homebody; soon she will marry a local guy and follow in the footsteps of her forbears as a farmwife. Dee comes back home to visit, arrayed in African garb, accompanied by a comical Black Muslim boyfriend, and the two sisters clash over the divergent values in the respective black cultures that each represents.

Second, I lead my students from a superficial plot summary into a deeper look at the meaning of the story, starting with the special devices and economies of the narrative. I ask them to choose particular sentences, phrases, and words that illuminate the larger meaning of Mama's descriptions: "I am a large, big-boned woman with rough, man-working hands"; "My fat keeps me hot in zero weather"; her comparison of Maggie to a "lame animal"; her recollection of the fire that destroyed their other house and scorched and scarred Maggie. When Dee arrives she is wearing "a dress so loud it hurts my eyes."

Dee has taken an African name, "Wangero Leewanika Keemanjo," discarding the matriarchal ancestral name that Mama gave her. My goal in this part of the exercise is to encourage, to require, students to search for important moments in the narrative and then to fasten every allegation they make about a piece of literature to a proof from the text. By focusing closely on precise details that illuminate the story efficiently, they learn to illustrate their own statements accurately and efficiently.

Finally, the end of the exercise is to analyze or evaluate the message of the story. Having summarized its plot and isolated examples from its special narrative technique, students are now ready to make suggestions (and support them with proof) about the broader meaning of this piece of literature. What polarities in current African American culture do these two sisters represent? How does Mama feel about her two daughters, and how are we expected to feel about Mama's judgments? Does the author respect, or want us to respect, any of these characters more than others? Does this story make a contribution to current debates about Afrocentrism or womanism (black feminism) or about multiculturalism?

In a short explication of a short text—whether a poem, an essay, or a short story—I ask my students to employ a three-part model: 1) paraphrase or summarize; 2) discuss particular literary techniques, especially as they illuminate the meaning of the piece; 3) evaluate or analyze the message. I find that this formula helps to anchor students to an accessible procedure that combines specific observation and creative analysis.

Finding the Point of View

Jim Hauser
WILLIAM PATERSON COLLEGE
WAYNE, NEW JERSEY

I find that Alice Walker's "Everyday Use" is a terrifically rewarding story to teach, at least with the kinds of first-generation college students in my classes at a state college. "Everyday Use" may not have quite the immediate appeal of a story like T. C. Boyle's "Greasy Lake," but it both emotionally and intellectually reaches out to students.

However, while this story appeals to my students and works in the classroom, it is also a story with significant emotional and intellectual problems. But it may well be these problems that finally make "Everyday Use" most valuable for beginning college readers.

Emotionally, many of my students (like myself) are drawn in by the sibling rivalry and by the opportunity to identify with the ugly-duckling child and to participate in the apparently justifiable triumph of this neglected and victimized sister/daughter (as well as the sympathetic, beleaguered mother). In addition, for students who may themselves be caught up in the tension of entering college, and the fear of separation from family which that brings to many of them, the story strikes a powerfully retrogressive emotional chord. It also reaches them in its focus on everyday possessions and on the differing attitudes possible toward material objects and materialism.

Intellectually, too, the story seems very attractive to my students: Its schematically defined oppositions are blessedly free of the thematic murkiness of much of the fiction I assign, and the story affords them a welcome and useful chance to exercise their symbol-reading skills. Few modern fictions afford so clear a study of the ambiguity of symbolic objects. The diverse and conflicting possibilities of meaning that Nathaniel Hawthorne and Herman Melville find in the scarlet letter and the whiteness of the whale, respectively, Walker finds in the quilt and the butter churn. Rarely is it as rewarding as it is here to have students hunt for symbols and define the meanings that different characters attach to them.

Throughout high school, our students have been trained, at best, to identify, and identify with, the point of view of the authors and fictions they've been assigned. If, say, they've read Ken Kesey's *One Flew Over the Cuckoo's Nest* and been offended by its anti-institutional stance, they've been told "that's not what Kesey is saying." "Everyday Use," I believe, provides a fine opportunity for us to teach a more interrogative and adversarial reading strategy: Walker's story seems to beg for what Judith Fetterley calls "the resisting reader."

In defining its opposition between traditional and changing values, this story is as sure of itself as a Rush Limbaugh radio broadcast, and yet it seductively wraps its fears, angers, and biases in a heart-warming sympathy for the neglected Maggie and for the common-sensical, humorous, attractive mother through whom Walker narrates the tale. This story presents an implicit debate about values, but it achieves its lopsided victory for tradition by drawing the character of Dee in a broadly unattractive manner. If we were teaching logic, we would surely want to discuss the nature of *ad hominem* arguments here.

In order to break through the implicit conservatism that this story so beguilingly presents, I want to challenge the students to recognize the ways in which they may be like Dee/Wangero. Their responses vary greatly, and many students can, at most, recognize that situationally they resemble her a bit, for they too have left for college (though, they often protest, going to college does not mean *leaving* family or changing values). However, with the help of either the teacher or, hopefully, their more insightful or more rebellious peers, most students begin to recognize that they have a great deal of Dee within themselves. They too may wish to strike out on their own; somewhere inside them they know that protective parents may be undermining their bids for autonomy; and they may even begin to understand the healthy impulses that underlie changing.

And I believe that if we can get them to identify with Dee, even a little, we can move them toward the interrogatory position that I believe we'd like them to bring to all their reading. In this case, they often need some historical/cultural background as well. We may want to point out that it is not surprising that the mother sees willfulness and cruelty in Dee, for she wishes to maintain her traditional rural position, which involves racial subservience to the whites she knows she could never look directly in the face. This may need some explaining, as may the fact that the assumption of a Muslim name may be a meaningful political action and not merely a whimsically egoistic one.

One way to drive home the point that these characters and this situation may be open to other readings than Walker's is to ask them to rewrite a section of the story from Dee's point of view. I've found that I have to insist that my assignment requires that they experiment with seeing through Dee's eyes, for Walker is very convincing here, and it's often hard for students truly to imagine Dee sympathetically.

I have the students spend a good bit of time in groups working to see Dee/Wangero from perspectives other than Walker's. They discuss specific scenes, looking for what we may broadly call Walker's "biases." Though some surprisingly strong fiction may result from this project in revising a well-known author's writing, it is important to remember that the goal is to use fiction writing in order to train resisting readers.

One student's breakthrough occurred in rewriting sections of the story that depict Dee's attitude toward the objects of "everyday use": in this student's rewriting, Dee was shown as heroically independent—because all quilts, even historically significant ones, do wear out when used at home, Dee's aestheticism was presented as intelligent, necessary, and loving. In discussion, this student suggested that she could imagine someone like Dee someday becoming a museum curator whose goal was to save a disappearing heritage.

The crucial issue here is not that students be led to believe that Walker is in any sense "wrong." Rather, it is important that they be led to recognize that *her* point of view, *any* author's point of view, is *a point of view*, that as intelligent readers they certainly need to identify and understand, but also to explore, question, and resist.

A Useful Videotape
for Both Readers
and Writers

Thomas Carper
UNIVERSITY OF SOUTHERN MAINE
PORTLAND, MAINE

Like many, I try to teach writing in my literature classes and at least some literature in my freshman-level writing classes. For both I have found very useful a half-hour videotaped profile of Eudora Welty (*The Writer in America: Eudora Welty*, Coronet Film and Video, 1975). For literature classes it provides an introduction to a celebrated writer, to her opinions about the role of a woman writer (to be universal and "transcend everything you write"), and to her views about how one discovers a subject. Ms. Welty also gives moving readings from her short stories and her novel *Losing Battles*.

But much of the tape is directly relevant to writing of all kinds, as it focuses illuminatingly on how this writer observes, prepares drafts, and revises. We see her demonstrate her powers of observation as we watch her interpret some of her own early photographs; this helps students understand how any writer must look closely at small details to gain insight into what is happening with the situations or people being observed and analyzed. We hear her speak of how she can write anywhere, when traveling or away from home, but that in her own room she will shape the material, type it out, make it objective—"a physical thing"—look at it, and revise it. "It's adventurous to revise," she says, and it's fun and instructive to watch her take a typescript of several pages, lay it out on a table, cut a paragraph from one sheet and insert it into another, pin it in place—and then report that she will methodically retype the long sheets and, perhaps, revise again.

Today, when most students write their class papers at a computer, it is salutary to be reminded that cutting and pasting on the screen may not be "physical" enough, that the beautiful printout of a first draft may be treacherously easy to produce.

Finally, among many pertinent and insightful remarks, the last one we hear should be meaningful to all who care about their writing: Ms. Welty concludes, "I always respond to my own words."

Poetry

Words Used in Poems

Melinda Barth
EL CAMINO COLLEGE
TORRANCE, CALIFORNIA

WRITING ASSIGNMENT

Select one of the poems that we have read and discussed in class and write an analysis of it that argues that the reader understands the theme if he or she recognizes with what care the poet has chosen to use two or three particular words in the poem. I suggest the following organization for your paper:

Introduction

Give a brief summary of the poem, with title in quotation marks, mention the author's full name, and state what has set this poem into motion, or what has been the occasion for the poem. The introduction does not need to be boring; be creative and complete in your approach.

Thesis

You need a thesis for your paper, an assertion about the word choice that the poet uses. You are writing to convince your reader that your appreciation of the poem and the poet's skill is linked to your understanding of the meaning or multiple meanings of key words that the poet has used in the poem.

You may state the poem's theme in the paragraph with your thesis, creating a deductive argument for your paper, or you may arrive at this "discovery" by an inductive arrangement in your conclusion. Just be *certain* if you want a good grade on this paper that you include a complete expression of a theme, the insights that the poet gives the reader, in at least one place in your paper.

Body

Each paragraph of the body of your paper will argue from an assertion that a particular definition of a word in the poem contributes to an awareness of the poem's theme. Each paragraph will present the specific definition and illustrate how the poet uses the word. You will want to include a quoted line and then analyze its contribution to the poem as a whole. Remember that your analysis may include definition, etymology of the words, connotation, and denotation. Don't settle for a simplistic or superficial analysis. Probe the multiple meanings the poet intends. A sum-up sentence after each part of your analysis will assure the reader of your essay that you understand the theme of the poem as it is advanced by the poet's use of effective words.

Conclusion

You'll probably want to conclude your paper by admitting that a good poet makes sounds that echo the sense of the poem, creates images that are the very threads of which poetry is woven, and chooses words with exquisite care—that is, *all* tools are used to create wonderful poems—but the key to the particular poem that you have chosen to work with is word choice, the feature that you have discussed in your paper.

Title

Write an interesting title—*not* the title the poet has used—unless you want your grade reduced.

Ethos and Imagery

Terry Beers
SANTA CLARA UNIVERSITY
SANTA CLARA, CALIFORNIA

Novice writers become skilled writers only if they want to. Which is not to say that desire is all it takes, just that desire is a necessary ingredient in the overall recipe for writing success. Unfortunately, getting some students to care enough is only a little easier than herding cats. One way to tackle the problem is to help students see that writing does more than advance a thesis, it tells a story about its author. Introduce your students to the Aristotelian concept of rhetorical ethos.

Some students won't need much help with ethos—and its close cousin, persona—but others might, especially if they are used to thinking about the propositional weight of language to the exclusion of its ethical extension. Here is where poetry—especially imagistic poetry with its objectivist bent—comes in handy. Precisely because it is so concise, so firmly rooted in the magic of the moment, readers often overlook how the speakers of imagist poems tell about themselves. Asking students to discern traces of ethos in even the most compact imagistic poems may help convince them to reconsider its importance for their own work.

Begin by defining terms. If students already know something about persona—the "mask" of character that writers assume in their work—they may also be familiar enough with the idea of aesthetic distance that they do not automatically equate such masks with the actual author of a work. If they are not, you can refer them to the section "The Person in the Poem" for a fine discussion of the differences. The concept of ethos, however, brings an additional—and to my mind crucial—dimension to these discussions, because it links our perceptions of character to our judgments about a speaker's good sense, good will, and moral integrity, qualities Aristotle tells us form a powerful appeal to an audience. To consider ethos, then, is to consider the credibility of speakers, to consider the values that they plead—or seem to plead—through their work. And if evidence for these considerations isn't as obvious in poems like Ezra Pound's "In a Station of the Metro" as it is in poems like Robert Browning's "My Last Duchess," that doesn't mean that readers won't notice it and judge the speaker accordingly.

Next, ask your students to apply the concept of ethos to verse. If you think they may not be ready to tackle so concise a poem as Pound's, try something more expansive like Wilfred Owen's "Dulce et Decorum Est," a poem full of disturbing images of war, each one speaking to the authority of the speaker to condemn the bloodshed through a bitter, ironic allusion. Students will probably have little trouble seeing how ethos in this poem works, and class discussion can explore the particulars of how imagery supports the credibility of the speaker and his moral perspective. When you are satisfied with the results, ask students to turn to something more difficult to interpret—that is, in terms of ethos—like William Carlos Williams's "The Red Wheelbarrow," a poem many students like to dismiss as nothing but a pretty picture.

Perceptions of ethos in this poem are likely to feel less grounded and may be harder for students to articulate. Have them ask questions like "Do I trust this speaker?" "Does he speak with authority, with conviction?" "Why do I feel the way I do about this speaker?" As they search for answers to such questions, those students tempted to set this poem aside in frustration may take more notice of the first line, "so much depends," a straightforward statement about the value of the image that follows. However students interpret the significance of that image, they can't dismiss the fact that the speaker links his credibility to the impact of the image he crafts. If you care to introduce an additional complication to the discussion, refer students to the note accompanying "Reading with and without Biography," which tells how the poem reportedly grew from a personal experience of the poet.

Class discussions like these provide a good foundation for writing assignments directing students to explore the concept of ethos in other literary works. (An example appears later.) But you may prefer—as I often do—to turn the fruits of discussion to another purpose, asking students to use ethos as a way to talk about the writing of their peers. During workshop sessions, tell students to swap work in progress and then to ask the same questions about their classmates' work as they asked about Williams's imagist poem. Ask them to share their conclusions. These conclusions—and the evidence that supports them—can surprise those student writers who take for granted that their readers will judge them credible. If they see that their classmates judge otherwise, they have a new incentive to improve their writing. Sometimes, seeing a part of yourself through the eyes of others can be a compelling reason for change.

WRITING ASSIGNMENT: ETHOS AND IMAGERY

Read all the following poems, paying particular attention to how their images help the speakers convince you of their credibility (or lack thereof) and their specific moral perspectives. Ask yourself, "Do I trust these speakers?" "Do they speak with authority, with conviction?" "Why do I feel the way I do about them?" When you have answers to these questions, draft a short essay comparing the credibility of the speakers in any two of these poems:

Taniguchi Buson, "The piercing chill I feel"
H. D. (Hilda Doolittle), "Heat"
John Haines, "Winter News"
T. E. Hulme, "Image"
Ezra Pound, "In a Station of the Metro"
Gary Snyder, "Mid-August at Sourdough Mountain Lookout"
Jean Toomer, "Reapers"

Symbols and Figurative Language

Janis Adams Crowe
FURMAN UNIVERSITY
GREENVILLE, SOUTH CAROLINA

Have the class read the definition of symbol in the chapter "Symbol." Discuss poems that are complex and difficult ("Sailing to Byzantium"), and ones whose meanings are often partly elusive. Discuss language that points us toward conflicting ideas, toward ideas that are hard to pin down—green thoughts. Read X. J. Kennedy's all-time great discussion of figurative language extending meaning by going beyond the literal, and then read Seamus Heaney's "Mother of the Groom" and Cathy Song's "Stamp Collecting." What does the ring symbolize in Heaney's poem? What do the stamps suggest in Song's poem?

WRITING ASSIGNMENT

Take an everyday domestic object you remember from your childhood—something that you loved or found especially interesting—and describe it in conversational prose. Tell your readers what it meant to you explicitly, Then find a metaphor or simile that expresses the value you found in your object by actually using the object, as Heaney and Song do. What happens when you move from explicit statement to figurative suggestion? Which piece of writing needs more words? Why? Is it easier to write about the object in prose or poetry?

Poetry and Song

Victoria Duckworth
SANTA ROSA JUNIOR COLLEGE
SANTA ROSA, CALIFORNIA

Choose both a poem and a song that share the same subject, not necessarily the same theme. For example, both works could be about love although both might say completely different things about this subject. Once you have made your choices, discuss how both are or are not examples of good poetry.

You are doing at least two different (although complementary) things in this assignment. First, you are considering what good poetry is and whether the song you have chosen is, in fact, an example of "good poetry," along with the poem. Second, you are using the terms common to poetry to discuss and evaluate both song and poem.

Try to use any of the poems from our text. The song does not have to be in any specific genre (pop, country, religious, rap), but I will need a copy of the lyrics in order to evaluate your assignment properly. For the sake of efficiency, it would be a good idea to include a copy of the poem attached to the end of your paper.

This assignment is meant to provide you with the opportunity to pull together your ideas of what poetry is and isn't and to consider how our ideas of poetry might be expanding (or at least changing) to include forms like song lyrics. Your grade will be based on the originality of your choices and approach and your ability to respond to the assignment clearly and coherently in writing that is free of major grammar and spelling errors.

What Is Poetry?

Terry Ehret
SANTA ROSA JUNIOR COLLEGE
SANTA ROSA, CALIFORNIA

WRITING ASSIGNMENT

Compose your own answer to the question "What is poetry?" You may want to devise original metaphor(s) to define poetry and then develop your essay with examples and explanations. Select at least one poem from the anthology to illustrate your definition.

Format

Your essay should include an introduction, body, and conclusion. Your introduction should provide the reader with your personal definition of poetry.

The body of your essay should develop this definition either by examining different aspects of the definition, or by exploring different metaphors that help you to define poetry. The body of your essay should also include a close examination of at least one poem that illustrates some aspect of your definition. When you quote from the poem be sure to indicate line breaks with a slash mark, and place the line number(s) in parentheses after the quote. Provide a copy of the complete text of the poem, either as part of the essay if the poem is short, or as an addendum to the end of your essay.

Your conclusion should provide both summary and closure to your essay. It would be a good idea to return to the original definition you offered in the introduction and draw any conclusions you can from this (e.g., a comment on how frustrating it is to define poetry, or how necessary it is to use metaphoric language rather than logical explanations, or the common elements in several different definitions, and the like).

Length: 500–750 words of "reasoned prose." Quotes are not part of the word count.

MLA Works Cited: Please include a standard MLA Works Cited list at the end of the essay.

COMMENTS

I also pass out a list of definitions of poetry with the assignment Some are drawn from the "What Is Poetry?" chapter of *Literature*. Other definitions I include:

"A way to make a reconciliation between the body and the mind."

Octavio Paz

"Poets are like steam valves where feelings can escape and be shown."

Sharon Olds

"Poetry is a kind of listening. Poetry was meant to go into the eye and the heart."

Robert Bly

"Poetry is a great river of possibility swirling around us all the time."

William Stafford

"Poetry is a kind of singing about what it feels like to live on this planet."

Galway Kinnell

Sonnet-writing Assignment

Annie Finch
MIAMI UNIVERSITY
OXFORD, OHIO

After one or two classes devoted to discussion of the sonnet in an Introduction to Literature course, or after some discussion of the form in a basic writing class, I ask the students to write a sonnet themselves. They are often shocked at this; few have written any poetry before, and if they have, it is likely to have been in free verse. I allay any fears by telling them that the exercise is merely a way for them better to understand the structure of the form, and that their effort does not have to be profound or "poetic." Anything they write about will be fine, as long as it is fourteen lines of correctly rhymed iambic pentameter, either Petrarchan or Shakespearean.

By this time, we will have read many of the sonnets in *Literature*. My favorites are those by Michael Drayton, Robert Frost ("The Silken Tent"), Emma Lazarus, Wilfred Owen, Thomas Hardy ("Hap"), John Keats, Elizabeth Barrett Browning ("How Do I Love Thee"), John Donne, and Gwendolyn Brooks. There are also fine sonnets by Weldon Kees, William Wordsworth, Shakespeare, Thomas Carper, R. S. Gwynn, John Milton, Kim Addonizio, and others to choose from. The class has had a chance to discuss the frequency of iambic pentameter in English speech, to listen for the meter in each other's speech, and to discuss its most common metrical variations (anapests to speed things up, spondees to slow things down, trochees to catch attention). Sometimes I let the students memorize a sonnet for extra credit. After a few classes of such preparation, the students generally find writing their sonnet surprisingly easy and feel triumphant that something they feared has been demystified.

The variety of tones and approaches in the finished sonnets is remarkable. The unusual attention to form frees the students from worrying too much about the content of what they are saying, and they can produce very interesting and revealing poems through this exercise. I choose several student sonnets to pass around and discuss during the final class on the sonnet. Before class, I ask the writers if they would enjoy reading their creation aloud, and usually they are glad to do so. Our class discussion of the students' sonnets offers an excellent opportunity to discuss not only the sonnet form but also sentence structure and syntax, diction, verbal connotations, and punctuation. Because this is not a poetry-writing course, I grade the sonnets pass/fail, and I don't worry about how perfectly they scan. The effort is the main thing. I have had several students comment that writing a sonnet was one of the most satisfying exercises in the course.

Student Writing Assignment

Here is a sonnet written for this exercise by a student at the University of Northern Iowa who had never written one before:

POETRY IS VERY AWFUL TO LEARN

Poetry is very awful to learn,
With the meters and meanings invisible.
As your spirits sink with each page you turn,
You feel as though you are an imbecile.
The longer they get the more lost I am,
But even the shorter ones confuse me.
Writing poems is hard, I'd rather eat Spam
And skip the great chance to learn poetry.
I then met a professor, Annie Finch,
Who taught the class, Introduction to Lit.
The guidelines were set, and it was a cinch.
I found out poems don't even hurt a bit.
I now know that writing poems can be fun,
And someday I may write another one.

—Benjamin Havick

Sense and Unsense

John Gery
UNIVERSITY OF NEW ORLEANS
NEW ORLEANS, LOUISIANA

One of the pleasures of teaching poetry, especially the close reading of poems, is that surge of gratification I feel when a student's eyes light up at the moment of understanding the seductiveness in a poem such as John Donne's "The Flea," the pathos in Ezra Pound's "The River Merchant's Wife: A Letter," or the horror in Sylvia Plath's "Lady Lazarus." To watch a student discover his or her intimate feelings of desire, pain, or anger in the language of the lyric fills me with optimism about the ability of poetry to embody and communicate our interior lives.

Often, however, I have learned that a thorough discussion of a poem in class will prompt one or two students afterwards to ask, "Did the poet *really* mean all those things we said? Aren't we just making up our own interpretations?" Or, "I never would have found what other people found in that poem. I myself couldn't make any sense of it all." I reply, of course, that while there is always room for a difference of opinion concerning a poem's sense, we can usually arrive at certain premises the poet must have had in mind, if not while composing, then by the time the poem was completed. Yet the students who ask these questions remain either skeptical about the authority of readers or afraid that they themselves will never understand how poems make meaning.

One exercise that addresses this concept of intentionality, sense and "unsense" is an assignment I have used while reading poems even less accessible than those by Donne, Pound, and Plath—poems such as T. S. Eliot's "The Love Song of J. Alfred Prufrock," E.E. Cummings's "anyone lived in a pretty how town," and the poems of Wallace Stevens, or the syntactically idiosyncratic poems of Emily Dickinson, Dylan Thomas, and John Ashbery. Coming to these difficult poems, I usually start by dissuading students from trying too hard to "make sense" of them. Instead, I emphasize how difficult it is, in fact, for a poet *not* to make sense, or to make "unsense."

The assignment I give is for each student to compose a ten- to twelve-line poem that, if possible, makes absolutely no sense. It is not to write "nonsense," which usually attempts to be funny and therefore has a guiding principle, but to make "unsense," that is, to assemble a series of lines that have no clearly affective qualities or intended meaning. Students may and should use imagery and normal syntax, as well as rhyme and rhythm if they want, rather than just collect words at random (that's another exercise with different goals). If they prefer, they may even write a poem that imitates the syntax of "The Emperor of Ice Cream" or "Fern Hill" exactly, for instance, but that employs wholly different images and words. The challenge is to write a poem in which no image, word, or phrase has any apparent continuity with or ostensible relation to any other, as in Gertrude Stein's line, "Dining is west," or the couplet, "In slipped plates, eels festooned the tunnel's laughter / where tasks, I leapt to note, cringed dully after."

This assignment usually proves far more difficult than it sounds at first, yet most students enjoy trying it, since it liberates them from having to make sense, for a change. After I collect the poems, it is easy to write a few affirmative remarks about their wild effusions in the margins, and more ambitious students will inevitably come up with poems that, on a first reading, sound very much like Wallace Stevens or Dylan Thomas in their creative assemblage of unrelated sounds, images, and diction.

What I do next, with the student's permission, is to reproduce two or three of these "unsense" poems to distribute to the class. We might read them aloud. But without further discussion, I then ask students to choose one and to write a brief (one-page) "explication" of its development and theme. Here again, because students realize that the poem is "not supposed to have meaning," they are encouraged to be as creative in their interpretations as they want, just as long as their essays develop a sustained reading of the poem. In my experience, the results are often surprisingly focused. Because they do not have to worry about the "correct" reading of the poem, they often feel free to read directly from its structure and language and are therefore able to make remarkable connections. Meanwhile, those whose poems are discussed and written about are generally elated that their own inventive words have evoked such cogent and "deep" responses. After this exercise, once we return to the poems in the text, our discussions of meaning tend to take on a more relaxed tone.

The goal of this exercise when it works (and it doesn't always) is threefold: (1) to give students hands-on practice in a nonevaluative manner both in creative writing and analytical writing; (2) to allow them to interact with their peers through a text instead of through discussion alone; and (3) to enhance their awareness of the reading of poetry as part of an interpretive community, in which readers do indeed have the right and power to "make sense" of what they read, tapping both into the intentions of the writer and into the broader cultural ideas each of us brings to poetry. A further result can be that students who at first might approach poetry such as Stevens's or Ashbery's with a suspicion that they are being talked down to (by poets who seem mysteriously privy to what they themselves don't know) might feel less hesitant about offering their interpretations of difficult works, even when they are unsure of the meaning. Once they realize how unfathomable "unsense" actually is, sense itself should seem less sacred and more amenable.

Teaching Grammar with Poetry

Renée Harlow
SOUTHERN CONNECTICUT STATE UNIVERSITY
NEW HAVEN, CONNECTICUT

It is hard to say which puzzles beginning college students more: poems or sentence grammar. I have observed, while introducing students to poetry, that deciphering sentence units in poems presents troubling interpretive problems for many students. In part, the problem is that students do not make connections past the end of a poetic line, but frequently, and more fundamentally, students are insufficiently fluent as punctuation decoders and unskilled as sentence builders. Put bluntly, students often don't know what goes with what in a sentence or a poem, with the result that, for students, poems become sequences of disconnected words. A parallel difficulty, as any teacher of writing can attest, emerges in students' written work. Sentence errors abound and often result from uncertainty about sentence boundaries and patterns.

Some time ago, I began to teach sentence grammar and poetry together. Poems provide limitless possibilities for lessons, as they contain rich examples for discussions about punctuation, sentence building and variety, modifiers, strong verb choices, and the like. Moreover, studying a poem's grammar provides interpretive reasons for caring about choices in sentence structuring, which prevents students from glazing over at the thought of yet another grammar lesson. Following are several of many examples I have used with my students.

SEMICOLONS AND COLONS

Theodore Roethke's poem "My Papa's Waltz" is short and engaging for students. Additionally, it presents compelling uses of punctuation, including semicolons in three of the four stanzas, one of which also includes a colon. After briefly explaining the uses of each punctuation mark, ask students to justify Roethke's choice to link ideas with semicolons rather than separate them with periods. Next, ask students to determine why a comma is used in the fourth stanza. This exercise helps students to distinguish between coordinate and subordinate structures. Finally, ask students how the colon equates the thought in line four to line three.

SENTENCE VARIETY

Reading Emma Lee Warrior's "How I Came to Have a Man's Name" and Henry Taylor's "Riding a One-Eyed Horse" helps students understand how sentence variety makes writing fluid and engaging. The first four lines of Taylor's poem demonstrate the rhythmic impact of alternating short and long sentences. Observing the contrast between the sentence patterns in the second and third stanzas of Warrior's poem emphasizes for students the force of sentence variation. Furthermore, Warrior's first eight lines contain three sentences of various types: one complex sentence and two simple sentences. Additionally, although the second and third sentences are both simple and both include prepositional phrases, they illustrate different rhetorical types: sentence two is periodic, whereas sentence three is cumulative. In Taylor's poem, the effect of using varied functional types of sentences is shown. Though most of the sentences of the poem are declarative, line ten begins an imperative sentence. For practice, have students choose any poem in the anthology to analyze. Have them determine each sentence's grammatical, functional, and rhetorical type. Then ask them to discover differences or similarities in the poet's use of sentence openings and sentence lengths.

THE LONG SENTENCE

Robert Frost's poem "The Silken Tent" and John Keats's "When I have fears that I may cease to be" are marvelous examples of the power of long, elegant sentences. Frost's poem requires careful attention to punctuation and emphasis, so I begin by reading the poem to my students and then asking them to join me in reading aloud again. We then read Keats's poem together. Students often observe that they have to breathe carefully to get through a reading of the poem without gasping. They also notice, especially in Keats's poem, which is usually more immediately understandable and vivid to them than

Frost's, that feeling intensifies throughout each poem and culminates in an emphatic last line. Someone usually observes at this point in our discussion that although each poem has lots of punctuation, neither has a period until the end. We then talk about how the available punctuation controlled the way we read the poem, how it grouped words together and separated them, and how it allowed each poet to extend the sentence. We also examine carefully the structure of each sentence, thinking specifically about connectors and transitions. For practice, I ask students to choose the first sentence of any poem. Then I ask them to expand the sentence by adding phrases, as well as coordinate and subordinate elements. Students enjoy competing with one another to see who can write the longest correct sentence!

PARALLELISM

William Blake's poem "To see a world in a grain of sand" is an elegant example of the verbal power of parallelism. Each line of the poem is parallel in form, balancing an abstract and a concrete noun and containing a noun/prepositional phrase combination as well. The poem also demonstrates the forcefulness of a balanced sentence in which, in this case, ideas are compared.

A FINAL NOTE

Poems are short, vivid linguistic experiences. Using poetry to explore grammatical structures, punctuation, and effective word choices assists the instructor in clarifying the impact of writers' language decisions and engages students in language discovery that affects both their interpretation of poetry and their writing skills. The bonus: Virtually any sentence in any poem is a potential lesson.

WRITING ASSIGNMENT

Have students practice writing elegant and fluent sentences by imitating sentence constructions discussed in any of the poems above. After discussing the grammatical elements of the sentence under consideration, have students copy the sentence's form while making sentences of their own. I also ask student to include and underline at least one example of the sentence pattern in their next writing assignment. Although studies indicate that teaching grammar does not directly affect student writing, it is my experience that when students understand, practice, and implement punctuation and sentence grammar, they begin to think and write like writers: they care about the words and how the words are placed.

"The First Line Exercise"

Robert Phillips
UNIVERSITY OF HOUSTON
HOUSTON, TEXAS

One assignment that has yielded interesting student writing is what I call "The First Line Exercise." I ask students to write on a sheet of paper the first line of any poem with which they are familiar. Then I ask them to write a new poem utilizing that as the first line.

It is difficult not to have something to say after putting down "Nature's first green is gold," or "When you are old and grey and full of sleep," or "I wandered lonely as a cloud." I insist that the students put the borrowed line within quotation marks, to avoid any misunderstandings (or delusions of grandeur) about who wrote what.

The idea isn't to rewrite or paraphrase the original poem. The idea is to create a totally new poem utilizing someone else's first line as a springboard. After the poem is completed, it is handed in together with a copy of the famous poem. In class both are read and analyzed, interpreted, compared, and contrasted. The student poem isn't expected to be "as good" as the other, just different. And in many ways it may be just as interesting and surprising.

The same exercise can work for short fiction as well. Think of the possibilities for taking off after putting to paper, "None of them knew the color of the sky," or "I read about it in the paper, in the subway, on my way to work," or "As Gregor Samsa awoke one morning from uneasy dreams he found himself transformed in his bed into a gigantic insect." Begin in the middle of an arresting situation, and a real story is likely to develop.

Teaching
Poetic Voice

Fred W. Robbins
SOUTHERN ILLINOIS UNIVERSITY
EDWARDSVILLE, ILLINOIS

I find myself fighting the temptation to compare generations of students. However, I do agree with the opinion that current students seem more resistant to and prejudiced against poetry. Some of them insist that poetry matters much less than their pop music lyrics. (Perhaps they merely want to tweak the beard of their ancient professor.) In response, I try to dramatize the voice in poems by reading aloud, hoping to give them a sense that poetry speaks to them, sings to them, much as their pop music does. The hardest part of poetry for many beginning students—and for many more advanced students—is tone of voice. Often they will ask to hear a recording of a poet reading his or her own work. That's fine and it has its place, but at an early point in the course, I don't want the students to get the idea that poetry is only an activity for their entertainment. Many of them are too passive to "get" poetry, anyway. I resist such audiovisual aids and reserve them for relatively advanced students only; students in senior-level courses should be experienced enough to listen, as well as read, critically. But for these freshmen, I dramatize the voice, reading aloud in a moderately melodramatic way.

In introducing the study of the chapter "Listening to a Voice," I will read a poem or two in such an exaggerated manner that the voice becomes a sort of caricature of sententiousness or of sarcasm. Jonson's "To Celia" works pretty well when read aloud one way, then the other—as the conventional courtly love song, then as a complaint and as an assertion of the speaker's boredom with Celia. Richard Lovelace's "To Lucasta" can almost always spark an argument about tone, about degree of irony. Trying to read James Stephens's "A Glass of Beer" without sarcasm is a test for anyone. Reading William Wordsworth's "I Wandered Lonely as a Cloud" with sarcasm is, for me, impossible, yet in straining to do so, I sometimes give the students the sense of voice that must be the foundation for a complete and responsible reading. It probably matters little whether I read aloud well or not, but it does matter that I show the students how one tries to get this sense of voice, working with the extremes of tone—solemnity and sarcasm. I am willing to seem foolish in order to get that across to them.

I always begin the course with poetry, as I am used to introducing the students to critical terminology through the study of verse. The first paper assigned in the semester will be about voice and tone. By the time the paper is due, we will normally have progressed to studying diction and imagery, so the students often make the obvious connections between tone and levels of diction; of course, that is one of the aims of the writing assignment, although not an explicit aim. They are assigned a paper of 500–600 words on a poem in the text; the paper is to be in three parts. Part one interprets the poem straightforwardly and seriously (the "solemn" reading); part two interprets the poem as sarcasm; part three, the meat of the paper, argues for one reading or the other, basing the argument on the diction and figurative language as well as on the sense of voice, the character, the persona in the poem. Often, the students will conclude their papers by admitting that their poems are not wholly solemn or wholly sarcastic, but are a mixture of tones, and they will begin to see how subtle and ephemeral this business of poetic tone can be. If students really demonstrate an understanding of that fact, their papers seem to me to be sound criticism. If the students go on to point out that the language of real people in real situations is often a complex admixture of levels and tones—lovers, men going to war, drunks with grim thirsts, someone struggling to describe an amazing sight such as a locomotive—then they are excellent students and have some talent for language. Most students, the "C" students, will not make these connections, but will just struggle to throw together in a paper some adjectives that describe tone.

If I were to teach this lesson and make this assignment in a literature/composition course, I would certainly help them to plan to mix the comparison structure with the argumentative structure. I would explain the nature of evidence, and talk about the fact that mere assertion does not convince or persuade or offer much insight. A mimeographed handout with a list of the descriptive adjectives commonly applied to tone (such as "joyful," "expectant," "angry") and their synonyms and antonyms is worth a quick tour through a thesaurus. It might keep some students from turning the paper into a struggle and a chore in their minds. Another aid is commenting on the text's discussion of irony, which focuses on the idea of point of view in poetry and makes useful distinctions among several kinds of irony. Another lesson that is worth a few minutes is based on the section "How to Quote a Poem" in the "Writing about Literature" chapter. Most students are completely ignorant about that convention, and such ignorance will inhibit their thinking and keep them from taking care with the more central aspects of composition.

When I began to teach this course in the 1970s, I relied on the obvious expedient of studying a dramatic monologue to reveal the complexities of irony and the manifold possibilities of tonality in verse. Now, such a poem as Robert Browning's "Soliloquy of the Spanish Cloister" seems too complex to begin the course. I reserve such poems with their "unreliable narrators" and tricky points of view until near the end of the poetry unit; that makes a nice transition into the study of fiction or drama. I guess my approach is formal and technical, more or less without ideology, and based on the concerns authors themselves seem to have and the concerns creative writing teachers impart to their students: if the poet can achieve a singular, individual voice, then the poem seems alive. Ideology deadens poems more quickly than it deadens criticism, which is quickly indeed. The life in the poem's voice is worth any number of ideas.

The written assignment sheet for this paper would have the usual directions for a composition, such as length, form, and warnings about conventions and advice about revision and polish. In addition to promoting a three-part organization, I have often specified some works in the "Poems for Further Reading" section that I think they might find most helpful in illustrating tone and voice. I usually require that they choose one poem to write on from such a list as this: Elizabeth Barrett Browning, "How do I love thee? Let me count the ways;" John Donne, "Death be not proud;" Thomas Hardy, "The Convergence of the Twain" and "Hap;" Gerard Manley Hopkins, "Spring and Fall;" A. E. Housman, "Loveliest of Trees" and "To an Athlete Dying Young;" Jonson, "On My First Son;" Pastan, "Ethics." I favor the neoclassical clarity of Housman, and the Hopkins poem is an interesting challenge in its tone. To follow up the initial lesson, I will usually teach, as I noted earlier, a dramatic monologue—Browning's "Soliloquy of the Spanish Cloister" and "My Last Duchess" are both in the book—and then progress to poems of complex tone, such as works by John Keats and Robert Frost ("'Out, Out—'" works well) as well as Marvell's "To His Coy Mistress," a Shakes-

peare sonnet (I favor "That time of year thou may'st in me behold"),
and Henry Reed's marvelous bi-voiced "Naming of Parts." I like to
close this part of the course by talking about William Blake's "The
Tyger" with the class and trying to get them to discuss tone as an
aspect of the poem that perhaps helps us understand the other aspects. That poem is always a challenge to us all.

By the time the class has spent a couple of weeks on voice and
tone and has written once on a poem, I usually move them on to the
units on diction and imagery, which I teach together. Once they have
understood that a poetic voice may seem to say one thing but may
mean another thing altogether, they are more ready for the sometimes surprising workings of imagery and symbolism than they otherwise would have been.

Writing Assignments on W. H. Auden's "Musée des Beaux Arts"

Samuel Maio
SAN JOSE STATE UNIVERSITY
SAN JOSE, CALIFORNIA

One of the more elementary ways to use W. H. Auden's "Musée des Beaux Arts" in order to make a few points about composition is to get students to consider how the poem is structured like a good "theme" paper. This exercise is helpful in reinforcing some of the principal methods of organizing such a paper. The opening lines of the Auden poem can be read as a "thesis statement," even if it is one written with the poet having inverted the usual syntax for rhythmic effect and sound: "About suffering they were never wrong, / The Old Masters . . . " The ensuing lines in the first stanza can be read as the poet's refining his thesis by specifying how the Old Masters variously evoked the broad concept of suffering. The second stanza identifies and explains one specific work by a Master for illustration. Read in this way, the poem becomes the classic paradigm for basic paragraph structure, which, in turn, is the template for structuring any theme, thesis, or argument paper: part one, a statement of thesis or thematic intention or topic; part two, the amplification and further definition of that thesis, theme, or topic; and part three, an example offered as corroboration. The writing exercise should be about two to three pages long. Here are some questions to get students thinking: How would you rearrange the words of the poem's opening lines in order to make a conventionally prosaic thesis statement? How might the poem be read as an essay? What kind of essay would you call it and why? What are the principal methods of organization used in this type of essay?

For segments of a composition course focused more on literature (such as those taught in the University of California system where the introduction to literature course also serves as a freshman-level composition course), a similar exercise can be used. Auden's poem can be regarded as a Petrarchan sonnet, though one not adhering to the form's traditional length, meter, or rhyme schemes. The poem is sonnet-like in its being a brief lyrical meditation on a single theme (suffering). Further, the poem is divided in two parts, moving from the general in the first stanza to the precise in the second. The division between these parts can be viewed as the *volta* (or "turn") found in the Petrarchan sonnet that marks the poem's turn towards its closure, synthesis, or resolution. Some questions to ask students are: What is the poem's rhyme pattern? What effects does this pattern have on the poem? How many times does Auden use the word "how" in the poem and to what effect(s)? How might the poem be read as a sonnet? What type of sonnet would you regard the poem as being, and why? After considering these questions, the student should be asked to compare and contrast, in three to four pages, Auden's poem with a traditional sonnet, such as Thomas Hardy's "Hap," which is a Petrarchan sonnet and is also a meditation on suffering.

Significant Adjectives: W. H. Auden's "The Unknown Citizen"

Donna Haisty Winchell
CLEMSON UNIVERSITY
CLEMSON, SOUTH CAROLINA

Beginning writers often have a great deal of difficulty negotiating the movement between generalizations and specifics. There seems to be the assumption that because the teacher knows the work in question, general statements about it are enough; the teacher can fill in the gaps. In their egocentrism, young writers assume that what is obvious to them is obvious to others, and they don't recognize the need to offer proof. When such young writers read Auden's "The Unknown Citizen," the majority acknowledge that they would not like to live in the sort of society being described. In-class activities that ask them to consider the link between this conclusion and the specific details in the poem that made them feel that way can lead them to practice what James Moffett calls "tracing the history of an idea" before using what they discover to convince readers of the validity of that idea.

WRITING ASSIGNMENT

After you have read "The Unknown Citizen," write down one adjective that in your opinion describes the society in which the Citizen lives. Then list at least five details in the poem that made you come to the conclusion that the adjective is a valid one. After you have completed this prewriting, use your adjective as the basis for a topic sentence stating what the society is like and then use your list of details and any others you think of to write several sentences supporting that topic sentence. You might, for example, start your paragraph, "Life in the society described in Auden's 'The Unknown Citizen' can best be described as. . . . "

RELATED ASSIGNMENT

"The Unknown Citizen" is an easy poem for students compared to Randall Jarrell's "The Death of the Ball Turret Gunner," which also presents a negative view of the State, with a capital *S*. Students can generally approach Auden's poem deductively: They know how they feel about the society being described and work backward in order to pull out the details that made them feel that way to present those details as support in their writing. Jarrell's poem requires more of an inductive approach, a close look at the specifics of word choice and of situation in order to arrive at the generalization about the statement being made about the State. Students generally recognize that the choice of persona here is highly unusual in that the character speaks from beyond the grave. They must be guided more carefully through the subtleties of diction and figurative language. Questions such as these can guide the students toward a topic sentence stating a conclusion they have reached about the view of the State in the poem and can provide the supporting evidence that will later constitute the body of the paragraph: Why might Jarrell have chosen the verb "fell" to describe the character's birth? What effect does Jarrell achieve by his reference to "wet fur" as opposed to wet skin? Why the reference to the fur's freezing? How are our normal assumptions about waking and sleeping reversed? What attitude toward the character is suggested by the way his remains are disposed of?

A Two-Step Imitation: Elizabeth Bishop's "The Fish"

Lee Upton
LAFAYETTE COLLEGE
EASTON, PENNSYLVANIA

Elizabeth Bishop's "The Fish"—so beautifully bent on the effects of re-envisioning—makes its own subtle argument for the sort of serious revision that we ask of our students. In working with "The Fish," it may be useful to ask students to write both an imitation of the poem and a revision of their first imitation, noting that they will revise their first imitation after we discuss Bishop's poem in some depth in class. First, they are to create an exploratory, generative imitation; that is, they must compose an imitation as a means for studying Bishop's poem and preparing for an in-depth classroom discussion of it. After our classroom discussion, they are to compose a second draft (or an entirely new imitation of "The Fish," should they wish) accompanied by a description (at least one page in length) of their processes in which they explain the decisions they made as they sought to duplicate Bishop's effects. For this exercise not only imitations but parodies are allowed ("And I ate the fish whole").

In the first draft of the imitation students are to pay special attention to the range of images that Bishop employs. They may begin by dramatically changing the tone of the original, perhaps by substituting another subject for Bishop's. To gain an initial sense of the poem's shape, students may find it helpful to count the syllables in each line of Bishop's poem. They might also want to note the ratio of monosyllabic to polysyllabic words. They should note the poem's particular sound effects and the use of simile and metaphor and the intervals between them. They might also be encouraged to pay attention to Bishop's punctuation, particularly her use of dashes, as these mark the fisher's attempts to focus more precisely on her catch.

To be sure, some first drafts are quite wonderful ("And I let the certified public accountant go"; "And I let my husband/wife go"). But a piece of writing that imitates some of the sophisticated visual adventures of the original, that allows for psychological and imagistic complexity, is called for in a revision. The second attempt—written after we have discussed as a group both the students' imitations and Bishop's poem—may make it possible for students to change their imitations dramatically.

After the first imitations are completed and read aloud in class, we discuss Bishop's poem in depth. At this point, some students already tend to have a laudable sense of partial ownership of "The Fish," of having participated from the inside out with the poem's dynamics. By creating an imitation, students have read and written with intensity, and, as a result, our classroom discussion of the poem's challenges and idiosyncracies may be more specific and more closely textured. In particular, students have had an opportunity through this sort of combination of emulation and active study to gain a greater awareness of the working of images, not simply as accumulations of details but as conceptual and emotional acts.

Just as the poem is devoted to moments of re-envisioning and requestioning initial perceptions, so too during class discussion should we focus on taking another look at Bishop's poem. We might explore, for instance, the progression in meaning that Bishop's images make possible and that first drafts generally cannot accommodate. That is, together, we examine the fisher's peculiar manner of seeing as it affects her understanding.

Any somewhat close imitation of "The Fish" must hinge on a reversal of original intention, a moment of discovery that is revealed through the speaker's newly dazzled vision and her culminating action: "And I let the fish go." We must ask ourselves what images have led toward such an epiphanic moment. During discussion we focus on the ways in which the poem is more than a catalogue of details. Images of the fish inform us of the fisher's own identity, and of her way of seeing and of orienting herself in the world. Initially the fisher sees the fish as an object, focusing on its external appearance with a penetrating attention that overcomes revulsion as she notes the fish's "tiny white sea-lice." We then follow her movement inward, a nearly surgical invasiveness as she imagines the fish's interior, "the coarse white flesh / packed in like feathers" and "the pink swim-bladder / like a big peony." We note the distancing elements of her images, her focus on dissimilarity. For much of the poem she forgoes any note of similarity between herself and the fish. The fish's eyes do not "return" her "stare"; the fish's jaw works by means of a "mechanism." The speaker's distanced observation is only disrupted when she notes the fishhooks embedded in the fish's "lower lip." We may then plot out the fisher's remarkable shift in attitude as her descriptiveness makes the fish, in a dramatic turnabout, a source of complex wonder.

As students explore this turning point of the poem, it can be useful to ask them to write in class a response to the question: What motivates the speaker's perception of a "victory"? I have found it fruitful to ask students to overread, putting forward many potential answers. Some students might speculate, for instance, that the fisher's victory amounts to a celebration of her sportsmanship, of having bested the fish and other fishers. More frequently, students suggest that her vision is transformed (here we meet the most commonly accepted reading) by her awe in recognition of the fish as a valiant survivor and fighter. If we have spent class time with elements of Bishop's biography, responses might take another turn. It is a critical commonplace to think of Bishop as a poet preoccupied with questions about the nature of home. Essentially parentless, she was what her biographer, Brett C. Millier, calls "a chronically displaced person." Students might ask if the fish in this, her most anthologized poem, would seem to be mysteriously allied with the issue of home: the fish is described as "homely," and, early on, it is cast in domestic terms that link it to the faded walls of a home:

> his brown skin hung in strips
> like ancient wall-paper,
> and its pattern of darker brown
> was like wall-paper:
> shapes like full-blown roses
> stained and lost through age.

Students might ask if the fish represents a repressed desire for home, a desire that must now be "let go" by a speaker who is herself precariously poised, self-consciously out of her element in her "rented boat." Is the poem the release of a desire or an acknowledgment of a desire?

Certainly there is much else to discuss when working with "The Fish," and there's much else besides discussion that one can do during a class session devoted to "The Fish." Students might be asked to list images in the poem and categorize them according to the reference areas from which they emerge and the associations they evoke.

Students can isolate "I" statements ("I caught"; "I thought"; "I looked"; "I admired"; "I saw"; "I stared and stared"; "And I let the fish go") and discuss the pattern of meaning that is created through them. They can experiment with revising the poem into the second or third person and writing an in-class response about the shifts in meaning and psychological distance that such changes impose.

As we closely examine Bishop's poem, students gain a new entry point into it, and the second stage of their assignment—writing a revision of their original imitation—creates a further challenge, for their revisions should attempt to accommodate some of the descriptive daring and psychological complexity of Bishop's poem.

Even though simply assigning one draft of an imitation can work quite well, there are advantages to the sort of two-step imitation that I am proposing. Students initially learn about the poem independently by attempting to copy some of its elements. At times unselfconscious acts of bold mimicry occur. Students may find that an imitation offers them both structure and within that structure the freedom of discovery. In turn, some students assume that a poem must come to the poet "whole" and immediately or not at all, and they are intrigued by the exhilarating discipline that revision requires. Their second revision or version of an imitation may create a more sophisticated sensory response to their subject. And because the assignment works especially well as we study imagery, students may find that through their own revisions they gain a greater sense of the power of images and the associations to which images give rise.

Gathering: Elizabeth Bishop's "Sestina"

Terri Witek
STETSON UNIVERSITY
DE LAND, FLORIDA

To appreciate the mysteriousness and beauty of this poem, have the class read "Sestina" at home and ask that each person bring in an object that holds some sort of personal significance. They should not discuss their choices, and when they arrive in class with their objects, they may not explain them, offer their histories, or even tell what they are, and no one may ask any questions. The objects should be gathered in the middle of the room where everyone can see them. When everyone has settled, ask each student to silently choose six objects and write a brief paragraph in which all six appear. Allot ten minutes to the task.

When everyone is finished, and rustling around in a self-congratulatory way, ask them to write a second, different paragraph in which the objects appear again. Allot ten more minutes.

Then poll the room. Who chose which objects and why? Often the whole class will have found one or two objects so compelling that everyone uses them: What is it that has made that snow dome and that pencil sharpener seem essential? What objects didn't they choose? The discussion often elicits the point that Bishop's poem makes: that the most homely of objects (and note that she uses all nouns) are transformed into something rich and strange when they are put into the same space—the space of the room, the space of the poem. The sacredness of simple objects amounts to a belief system in the poetry of the last half of the twentieth century, you may point out. And add that because the endless recombination of such objects is one way of making of the everyday world a magic space, a sestina is a perfect example of the way this belief is matched with a form. What happened, for example, when they were forced into new combinations in their second paragraphs?

Now ask the students to read Bishop's poem aloud, a new voice for each stanza. Discuss the poem in light of what they have learned from their own experiments. Which, for example, are Bishop's most mysterious end words? Which are the hardest to reuse? What is the most amazing recombination? Which of her objects would they most like to have in our pile?

End class by having the students each read one of their own paragraphs out loud, one after another, so that their texts can hook together in their own mysterious logic. Then each student collects an object and moves off into the rest of the day.

Composing Wedding Vows

Brian Anderson

CENTRAL PIEDMONT COMMUNITY COLLEGE
CHARLOTTE, NORTH CAROLINA

WRITING ASSIGNMENT

In recent years it has become fashionable for couples to compose their own wedding vows. The pair customizes the wedding ceremony, making promises and proclamations of love, that are unique to their own personalities, their own tastes, their own values. For this essay, choose the narrator of one of the dramatic monologue poems we studied (e.g., "The Love Song of J. Alfred Prufrock" by T. S. Eliot, "My Last Duchess" by Robert Browning, or "The Farmer's Bride" by Charlotte Mew) and then:

1. Explain the circumstances of the character's wedding. Is the Duke marrying the first duchess or the second?

2. Compose wedding vows (about one page, maybe a little less) that you think are appropriate to that character. Remember that vows are just that: a series of promises and expectations. What do you think Prufrock would be able to promise, and how would he frame his promise?

3. Finally, compose an argumentative essay (about three pages) in which you explain, defend, and analyze those vows. What promise would your characters likely make? What would be their attitudes toward their spouse? *Remember to support your assertion using evidence from the poem.*

COMMENTARY

The best reason to use this assignment is to drive home those poetry lessons about voice and narration. Students are likely to assume that Robert Frost is speaking out of his own direct experience of mending walls or stopping by woods. If that's the case, then Edgar Allan Poe must really have had the tense conversation with a raven.

And Emily Dickinson's career must have been even more posthumous than we ever knew! But when students go about the business of composing wedding vows for J. Alfred Prufrock or Mew's farmer, they're performing the same act that the poets themselves did: They're inventing conversation, and by extension, developing character. This process helps them better understand how to separate the poem from the poet, and they realize that poetry isn't necessarily autobiography.

The assignment also forces careful analytical reading. The main part of the assignment, the essay, should emphasize the poem more than the vows. Instead of an extra-textual "what if" sort of assignment, students should be able to use the language and details of the poetry to support their assertions about the narrator. Sometimes students want to write the woman's vows also. I let them do so as long as the main goal is to illuminate the speaker.

I have had success with this exercise as a regular writing assignment. It also fits nicely in a three-hour final exam period.

Student Essay

The Duke's Vows
to His First Bride

Trey Montgomery
CENTRAL PIEDMONT COMMUNITY COLLEGE
CHARLOTTE, NORTH CAROLINA

THE DUKE'S VOWS

My soon to be Duchess,

Out of all the women I could have chosen to be my bride (and there were many), I have chosen you. I have and will always hold you on a pedestal in my heart. I expect you to hold me in your heart the same way. After all, I am the Duke and you are going to be my Duchess.

It pleases me when I see you. You make my heart soar to the heavens, and I know that seeing me pleases you. You unknowingly show it through that spot of joy on your cheek. And I do love to see it. One day I should have a painting done of you so that spot of joy can last forever. And though I don't see why I should worry about such a thing, I feel I must warn you: I shall be the only thing to summon that spot of joy. But I know that such talk is not needed. After all, you are going to be my Duchess.

I will please you in every way possible. I will bestow upon you anything your little heart desires, though I can't imagine what could be better than the nine-hundred-years-old name I am giving you now. But I'm sure I don't need to bother with such warnings. After all, you are about to become my Duchess.

Oh! There's one other thing. It is true that you will be the Duchess. And as the Duchess, you will have certain status and power. People will look up to you and admire you. People will serve you and even die for you. But never forget that you are *my* duchess. When the people look to you and admire you, they will be looking at me and admiring me. When the people serve you and even die for you, they are serving me. They are dying for me. You will have power, but only the power I allow you to have.

If you obey these things I have demanded of you, then we will live long happy lives with each other. If not, well . . .

THE DUKE'S WARNING

The vows I have written for the Duke are appropriate for his character. They portray him as the pompous, stuck-up rich boy that he is. They clearly explain what his idea of a "duchess" is and even warn his future bride what he expects from her. His vows display a very pompous attitude and should be read with the same type of accent as the guy from "Life Styles of the Rich and Famous."

The vows start with the Duke telling his bride that out of all the women he could have chosen for his bride, he chose her. He even says "there were many." This admission begins the poem with his arrogant attitude. Even while saying his wedding vows, the most romantic time for a man to talk, he brags about himself. The next line reinforces that attitude when he expects her to put him on a "pedestal." The best thing that illustrates this pompous attitude of the Duke's comes at the end of the poem. He tells his companion to "notice Neptune, taming a sea horse." Neptune is the Roman god of the sea, one of the most powerful and respected gods. He is comparing himself to Neptune. He actually considers himself a god among men. But maybe he's right. After all, he is the Duke, and what could be more majestic than a Duke?

The next vow speaks of "that spot of joy" on the Duchess' cheek. In the poem, the Duke explains that:

> twas not
> Her husband's presence only, called that spot
> Of joy into the Duchess' cheek . . . (13–15)

In his vow, he tried to explain to her that he wants to be the "only thing to summon that spot of joy." Of course, he says it in the same pompous way with which he began. He would be surprised that anything else could please her in the same manner that he does. After all, he is the Duke, a god in his own right.

In his vows, he explains that he knows he doesn't need to tell her that he should be "the only one to please her." This is where you start to realize that he has a specific idea in his mind of what she should be like. To him, no matter what she was like before, once she becomes royalty, she should be just the way he would like her to be. She should know automatically how to act. That is basically what the poem is about. He is telling the servant of the father of his second bride what he expects a Duchess to be. He wants the servant to go back to his master and tell him what his daughter needs to learn to live successfully with the Duke. Of course, if you were to ask the Duke, he would say that "such talk is not needed, after all, she is going to be a Duchess."

One thing the Duke expects of his bride is not to be "too easily impressed." We find out in the poem that his "last Duchess" behaved just that way. She "liked whate'er she looked on." The smallest gifts would bring a smile from her—whether it was the Duke's "favor at her breast, / the dropping of the daylight in the West," or even the "white mule / She rode with round the terrace." He doesn't understand that most humans enjoy these things. Oh! Wait a second. I forgot. She isn't human; she's a Duchess. According to the poem and his vows, the only thing that should matter to her is the gift of his "nine-hundred-years-old name." After all, she is "going to be a Duchess."

The Duke then becomes even more arrogant, showing his need for power. He tells his bride about the "power" and "status" that she will have as the Duchess. He tells her that people will "look up to [her] and admire [her]." The Duke tells her that the only reason she'll have status is because he does. He says that the only power she will have is the power that he will allow her to have. In fact, he is using his power on her while he is doing this. It is obvious that the Duke feels he needs to use power in the poem. This need is manifested in the curtain hiding the painting. He makes sure that he is the only one to open it. And he makes sure that the servant he is speaking with knows this:

> The depth and passion of its earnest glance,
> But to myself they turned (since none puts by
> the curtain I have drawn for you, but I.)

This feeling of power is also evident in the statue of Neptune he points out to the servant. He is comparing himself to an all-powerful god who is depicted "taming a sea horse." Indeed, the Duchess was to be his sea horse.

I believe that the vows I have written for the Duke aptly portray his pompous attitude. They show his feelings and beliefs about the Duchess and his expectations about what a Duchess should be like. They also portray his need for power. If these vows are (or were) followed, there shouldn't be a problem. After all, he is a Duke, and she is "going to be a Duchess."

Understanding Parody: Persian Versions

Joyce S. Brown
JOHNS HOPKINS UNIVERSITY
BALTIMORE, MARYLAND

> "Truth, 'tis supposed, may bear all lights; and one of those principal lights or natural mediums by which things are to be viewed in order to a thorough recognition [*sic*] is ridicule itself."
>
> Anthony Cooper, 3rd Earl of Shaftesbury (1671–1713),
> *Essay on the Freedom of Wit and Humour, Sect. I*

PREPARATION

Assign the selections from Edward FitzGerald's 1859–79 translations of *The Rubaiyat of Omar Khayyam* found in *Literature* (or better still, assign all 101 stanzas) along with Wendy Cope's parody "*From* Strugnell's *Rubáiyát*," found in the same chapter. Students might need or want to know that a *rubai* is a quatrain of iambic pentameter lines rhyming *aaba*. *Rubaiyat* is the plural Arabic word for quatrain.

To get started, give the class a few definitions of humor (see the preceding quote for one), then ask students to discuss their responses, or their own ideas of what constitutes humor. Explain that Mr. Jason Strugnell is a creation of Wendy Cope's imagination. He is an exceptionally bad poet. One of Strugnell's haiku reads as follows:

The cherry blossom
In my neighbor's garden — Oh!
It looks really nice.

Students will not fail to catch this humor, as most of them are familiar with the "rules" of haiku: a Japanese form of three unrhymed lines of 5, 7, and 5 syllables that states or implies a season and a spiritual insight (see Kennedy/Gioia's *Literature* for further definitions).

The critical paper should start with a discussion of parody, a work that burlesques another work, usually a serious one. Kennedy and Gioia define *parody* as a work in which "one writer imitates another writer or another work for the purpose of poking fun." Holman and Harmon's *A Handbook to Literature* says a parody may humorously ridicule or criticize the content or style of an author, or "may imply a flattering tribute to the original writer. . . . The parody is in literature what the caricature and the cartoon are in art. . . . Parody makes fun of some familiar style, typically by keeping the style more or less constant while markedly lowering or debasing the subject." These editors use a parody (unattributed) to Emily Dickinson as an example:

> *Dickinson:*
> The Soul selects her own Society—
> Then—shuts the Door—
>
> *Parody:*
> The Soul selects her own Sorority—
> Then—shuts the Dorm—

WRITING ASSIGNMENT

Students should consider what Cope has done in creating Strugnell's "art."

Why are his stanzas funny? In what ways is Cope having fun with poetry? From appreciating what is bad, through the kindness of a good poet who is creating a fictitious and humorously bad one, students will grasp by indirection what makes a good poem.

The paper ideally would work itself out like an informal essay, again, as defined by Holman and Harmon, as follows, "Qualities that make an essay informal, include the personal element . . . humor, graceful style, rambling structure, unconventionality or novelty of theme, freshness of form, freedom from stiffness and affectation, incomplete or tentative treatment of topic."

Updating Prufrock

Mark Royden Winchell
CLEMSON UNIVERSITY
CLEMSON, SOUTH CAROLINA

T. S. Eliot's "The Love Song of J. Alfred Prufrock" is surely one of the most frequently anthologized and frequently taught poems in the English language. Prufrock may not be quite an Everyman, but he is a familiar figure to us all. (Who has not known an individual plagued by self-doubt and sexual timidity?) In fact, most people have had a little bit of Prufrock in them at some point in their lives. This is particularly true of college students, who are often still wrestling with the uncertainties of adolescence.

Unfortunately, the social milieu that Prufrock inhabits is so different from that in which our students live that they sometimes fail to understand and appreciate the universality of Eliot's great poem. For better or worse, American undergraduates don't ordinarily feast on tea and crumpets or spend their spare time in art museums talking about Michelangelo. What is needed is a writing assignment that will force them to put Prufrock into their world.

WRITING ASSIGNMENT

The student is asked to write a story or poem in which a character like Prufrock lives in the present-day United States, preferably in their own community. Their Prufrock, like Eliot's, should experience the tension between an inhibited waking life and a rich dream life. As an example I offer the opening sections of a parody that I wrote in 1985. This poem was inspired by a friend and colleague who frequented country and western singers' bars in a futile search for the girl of his dreams.

A few topical references may need to be explained to students who are unfamiliar with country music and mid-1980s popular culture.

188

- First, Merle Haggard is one of the great singer-songwriters in the history of country music. (One critic called him "America's foremost proletarian poet.")
- Second, David Allan Coe is a less-well-known country artist, whose songs include "Divers Do It Deeper," "This Long Hair Don't Cover Up My Red Neck," and "Take This Job and Shove It."
- Third, "Are you lucky, punk?" evokes a line spoken by Clint Eastwood's character Dirty Harry Callahan when apprehending criminals. (The protagonist of this poem might do well to heed another Dirty Harry admonition: "A man has got to know his limitations.")

Following are the opening sections of my parody.

Prufrock in South Carolina

for Merle Haggard, *il miglior fabbro*

Let us go then you and I,
With happy hour nigh,
Like a cowboy riding from a stable.
We will drive on secondary roads
And the darkened inner states
Of boredom and bravado,
As if in Colorado,
Not this cursed palmetto state!

In the bars the women come and go
Talking of David Allan Coe.

The smoke at 4 A. M. rises from the billiard tables,
Like a junkyard dog—erect and on the prowl.
Snorting and drooling, it struts across the room,
Leaps upon the band in desperation,
Falls back into the crowd,
And seeing that its passion's spent,
Lift a leg to piss,
Curls once around the jukebox and passes out.

And indeed there will be time—
To wonder "What the hell" and "Should I tell
This redneck what makes them stand in line?"
(I dream of consummation
And a bimbo that is mine.)
My cowboy shirt and white bandana wound around the chin,
My Stetson hat, so macho, above a horny grin,
(They will say: "I hope he has a twin!")
Do I dare to do the two-step
Or ask that slut to dance?

But I have lost them all, blown all my chances.
I have made obscene advances, sought casual romances,
And been left to curse the darkness of my home.
The bedroom door ajar,
Invites the music of a farther bar.

I have known the stares already, known them all—
The glares that stop me in my tracks
And push me back like rewound film,
Through all the butt-end daze of celluloid and cigarellos,
Until, my day, unmade, I ask:
"Are you lucky, punk?"

                                        Mark Royden Winchell, 1985

Mapping "Desert Places": The Value of an Outline

David Peck

CALIFORNIA STATE UNIVERSITY, LONG BEACH
LONG BEACH, CALIFORNIA

Writing a brief outline can help students organize their thoughts. I sometimes assign a writing exercise in two stages. I ask them first to prepare a brief outline. Then they should develop the outline into a short paper. This approach can work on most literary texts, but I have had especially good results assigning Robert Frost's "Desert Places."

WRITING ASSIGNMENT

What is the meaning of Robert Frost's "Desert Places"? How do the different poetic devices of the poem—word choice, imagery, rime, rhythm, metaphor, and so on—help achieve that meaning?

Prepare your paper in two stages. First, spend some time organizing your thoughts in a brief outline. Then use your outline to write a short, coherent paper (approximately 500 words) focused on your own central ideas.

Student Essay

"Desert Places"
Outline and Essay

Anya Kim
CALIFORNIA STATE UNIVERSITY, LONG BEACH
LONG BEACH, CALIFORNIA

OUTLINE

I. Meaning: the Loneliness of an Empty Soul
II. Poetic Devices Used
   A. Strong Images
      1. Coldness of Ground Covered with Snow
      2. Vastness of Space/Universe
   B. Connotations
      1. Desert—Loneliness
   C. Rimes
      1. Use of End/Internal Rimes
   D. Repetition of Words

LONELINESS IN "DESERT PLACES"

In his poem, "Desert Places," Robert Frost writes about the loneliness of an empty soul. He writes that the loneliness he feels from within is greater—and stronger—than the loneliness one feels as an individual in this great vast world and universe.

Frost uses various poetic devices to achieve this meaning. First of all, Frost uses strong images. The reader feels the coldness of the falling snow and the blackness of the falling night in the poem's first stanza. Then Frost goes on to present the vastness of outer space by talking about "the empty spaces / Between stars" (13–14). All these strong images lead the reader to feel a sense of loneliness in a big place like (the title suggests) a desert.

Frost also repeats words like "lonely" and "loneliness" to em-

192

phasize his point. He feels "the loneliness" in the snow-covered woods; "and lonely as it is, that loneliness / Will be more lonely ere it will be less" (9–10). This feeling comes while looking at the vast snow-covered ground.

Frost's decision to title his poem "Desert Places" also helps convey the theme of loneliness. The word "desert" has connotations of a great, empty geographical area where few people choose to live. When one thinks of the desert, one often associates loneliness with it. Therefore, when Frost says he has his own desert places (in his soul), the reader can understand and feel that Frost means he is lonely because of the deserted places in his soul. Frost's use of rime makes the poem more rhythmic and easier to read. It also helps achieve his meaning. For instance, in the last stanza, Frost ends a line with the words "empty spaces" and rimes it in the next line with "human race is" (13, 14). This pairing has the reader associate "empty space" with "human race." Humans can experience emptiness (empty space) in their souls.

Multiple Meanings: Robert Frost's "Nothing Gold Can Stay"

Melinda Barth
EL CAMINO COLLEGE
TORRANCE, CALIFORNIA

After we have read and discussed four or five poems in class, early in the "Writing about Literature" (post–freshman composition) course, I ask students to write a short paper to convince a reader that knowing the multiple denotative meanings of particular words in a poem is vital to the reader's understanding the theme of the poem. One choice is Robert Frost's "Nothing Gold Can Stay," with the suggested key words "gold," "green," and "flower."

One goal in the assignment is to encourage the students to use a dictionary when they read, and especially when they read poetry, because the poem is such a condensed form that every word counts. I also want the students to see the multiple definitions of the key words, beyond the denotative meaning of the word that they may already know, so that they can admire how clever poets are in their choice of words.

Students feel clever, too, when they make the discovery of the second or third definition of a word they thought they knew and see how it can be applied to understanding the poem. The paper is non-threatening and short, about three pages. I provide the thesis: The reader's understanding of the theme of the poem is linked to understanding the multiple denotative definitions of key words in the poem. The organization is apparent: Each section of the paper develops from one of the definitions of a key word and the interpretation of the line of the poem with the particular definition applied.

For example, the line "Her early leaf's a flower" is paradoxical, contradictory, or incomprehensible unless the reader knows that the fourth definition of "flower" is "the best period of a person or thing; time of flourishing." With that definition in mind, the reader of the poem understands that this line means that Nature's first growth, or "early" leaf, like her "first green" is her best or most flourishing time. Students will discover that this line reiterates Frost's theme: that perfection, or "the best period," is at the beginning and that perfection is ephemeral.

George D. Gopen argues in "Rhyme and Reason: Why the Study of Poetry Is the Best Preparation for the Study of Law" (*College English*, April 1984) that the study of poetry teaches that words are not often "fungible" or replaceable. Because I want my students to carry with them—long after they have completed the humanities requirements for general education—the idea that poets carefully choose words, this writing exercise is a favorite of mine.

Can We Improve on Robert Frost?

Len Krisak
NORTHEASTERN UNIVERSITY
BOSTON, MASSACHUSETTS

Robert Frost's "Stopping by Woods on a Snowy Evening" is one of the most famous poems ever written by an American. Surely, a work so well known (and by now almost eighty years old)—a poem written about by many famous critics and memorized by countless students and lovers of verse—should have yielded up by now all its possible meanings and secrets. And just as surely, a paraphrase—a line-by-line summary of "what the poet is trying to say" written in plain prose language—should exhaust its riches.

But poems exist not for the "meanings" alone, but also for the beauties, pleasures, and playfulness of their language. Frost was especially fond of the idea of the poem as both a performance and a great occasion for sheer verbal enjoyment—on the part of the listener *and* the poet.

If you are not convinced of this modest proposal, here is an exercise you can do that might help you come to some new conclusions about verbal artistry and "meaning."

WRITING ASSIGNMENT

Using the same number of syllables per line, rewrite Frost's poem, line-for-line. Be sure to keep the same total number of lines and the same number of stanzas (each of your new stanzas should end with a period, showing a complete grammatical thought).

You need only substitute new nouns, verbs, and adjectives if you like, but try finding new prepositions as well, if you can ("until I rest" for "before I sleep"?). If you need to, you can keep small words like *a*, *and*, and *the* the same.

If "the meaning is all," then you should be able to come up with synonyms for almost every word in the poem (*forests* for *woods*?) and still convey exactly what it is Frost is trying to communicate.

Oh, and in case I forgot, be sure your version of this poem rhymes (and in exactly the same places Frost's does).

QUESTIONS

1. What kinds of difficulties did you run into on your excursion into the world of writing poetry?

2. Did you find the exercise hard or easy?

3. If you decided to substitute words like *forests* for *woods*, what happened to the requirement that your line have the same number of syllables as Frost's?

4. Frost's poem takes place on the "darkest evening of the year." That would seem to indicate that the speaker of the poem has stopped on the night of December 21. What happened to your "exact" paraphrase if you chose some other word, like *coldest* or *shortest*? Or does Frost mean something more than just seasonal by his use of *darkest*?

5. Were you able to come up with synonyms for *deep, keep,* and *sleep* that also rhyme? Why not?

6. Since you only had to repeat your next-to-last line, that part of the exercise should have been easy. Were you happy with the results of your choice? Did you end up saying what you thought Frost was trying to say? Why or why not?

Writing Assignment for Gary Gildner's "First Practice"

Mark Sanders
COLLEGE OF THE MAINLAND
TEXAS CITY, TEXAS

A BRIEF OVERVIEW

We might read Gary Gildner's "First Practice" as a coming-of-age poem. Under the bullying guidance of Clifford Hill, a man who once served in the military and "killed / for his country," boys are not only taught how to play football and win the championship, but they are taught also that "dogs / ate dogs," and that when scrimmage lines form so does hate among friends. Anyone not agreeing with Clifford Hill's philosophy is a girl, not a man.

TOPICS FOR WRITING ASSIGNMENTS

1. Characterize Clifford Hill, examining how his attitude toward football and boys is shaped by extreme chauvinistic and militaristic attitudes. Having done this, compare or contrast Coach Hill to a coach you may have encountered during your schooling. Make an assessment of both coaches; that is, would you care to play for either one? Explain.

2. Philosophically, do you believe that Coach Hill's methods are appropriate for the training of young athletes? Describe what you might anticipate in a standard practice with Coach Hill, and discuss whether you think such a practice is beneficial for learning to play a particular sport.

3. In "First Practice," Gary Gildner describes the location for the practice as "under the grade school, / where we went in case of attack / or storm." These particular lines bear far more importance than might first be noted, but when we consider the connotations attached to the description, we discover that the gym is an underground shelter. Discuss

what a shelter's purpose is and the irony of Hill's abuse—his "attack / or storm"—in such a location. Can you think of other shelters children have that ironically place them in abusive situations? Explain.

4. Frequently in American literature, the building has been used as a model for the psyche. Generally and simply speaking, the upstairs portions of buildings represent the activities or impulses of the ego; what transpires on the staircases or elevators is a representation of superego activities or impulses; and, what takes place beneath ground level, in the basement or cellar, is representative of id activities or impulses. If we regard the grade school's basement as a psychological model of the id, the children have been drawn to asocial and amoral depths in the very institution that pedagogically seeks to train them in superego and ego responses to daily living. Metaphorically, the children are taken to the basement to be trained in the dark impulses of humanity. Discuss what these dark impulses are as illustrated in the poem and how these do not align to morality and reason as taught in school.

Two Michigan Fathers

Will Clemens
UNIVERSITY OF CINCINNATI
CINCINNATI, OHIO

How can an image of a father's hands speak to his career or to his social class? To what extent can form be indicative of a writer's education or ethnicity? Is it necessary to completely understand the setting of a poem about a poet's childhood? Theodore Roethke's "My Papa's Waltz" (1948) and Robert Hayden's "Those Winter Sundays" (1962) provide an excellent opportunity to discuss the pros and cons of reading a text without knowing much about who wrote it. To further discussion, ask students if they can glean from these poems what sorts of jobs the fathers hold. Can they tell where the poems take place? In a brief essay, journal entry, list, or outline, have students compare and contrast the personality of the father in Roethke's poem with that of the father in Hayden's. Ask for volunteers to read or share the similarities and differences they found.

Next offer at least the following background information: both Roethke (1908–1963) and Hayden (1913–1980) grew up in eastern Michigan in the early 1900s: Roethke in a town on Saginaw Bay where his father operated a greenhouse; Hayden in a ghetto on the east side of Detroit where his foster father was a day laborer. Now have students write a short essay, journal entry, list, or outline comparing and contrasting Roethke's relationship with his Saginaw father to Hayden's relationship with his Detroit foster father. Ask students to read or share some of their key points of comparison and contrast. Discuss how even a brief biography enhances or diminishes one's sense of a poem. As a final step, ask if the poems themselves would be better or worse with more biographical or geographical detail.

"The Purpose of Poetry Is to Tell Us about Life"

Ron Rash
TRI-COUNTY TECHNICAL COLLEGE
PENDLETON, SOUTH CAROLINA

In his chapbook *Fugue State,* Indiana poet Jared Carter states, "The purpose of poetry is to tell us about life." A poem that supports Carter's comment especially well is Robert Hayden's "Those Winter Sundays," and I have found this poem to be one that makes the connection between art and life clear to my freshman composition students. After discussing the child's indifference to his father's labors of love, I ask my students to recall similar moments from their own childhoods, moments when they were indifferent or only aware years later of "love's austere and lonely offices." Because some of my students have not grown up in a traditional family setting, I emphasize to my students that the adult does not have to be their biological father or mother; it can be anyone who raised or helped raise them. Almost always my students are quick to respond with examples from their own lives. The one time when no immediate personal anecdotes were forthcoming, I offered an example from my own life. When I finished my anecdote, I again asked the class for some examples, and several hands went up.

I have never had a class in which every student offers an example from his or her life. Some students are too shy or are uncomfortable discussing personal aspects of their lives in a classroom setting. For others, an example does not come immediately to mind. However, hearing examples from other students' lives triggers similar memories for the students who do not speak up in class. Furthermore, I offer to help students after class if they are still having trouble finding an example from their own lives. Perhaps I have been lucky, but I have never had a student who could not compare an event in his or her life to Hayden's poem.

At the end of the class period I give the actual assignment: an essay in which the student compares an experience in his or her own life to "Those Winter Sundays." Because there is sometimes a tendency for students to forget that the assignment is a comparison of a work of art to an event in their lives, not just an autobiographical essay, I emphasize that the body of the essay should discuss both the event in their lives *and* its similarity to the poem.

After completing this assignment, I believe my students have a better understanding of Jared Carter's comment.

Student Essay

A Father's Love

Susan Huggins
TRI-COUNTY TECHNICAL COLLEGE
PENDLETON, SOUTH CAROLINA

The moment I read Robert Hayden's "Those Winter Sundays," my mind went back to my own childhood. I remember well the bone-chilling winters in Detroit. I remember the snow and the joy I had playing in that winter wonderland. I also remember that even though my childhood was happy, there seemed to be a coldness in the home atmosphere as well. There was not a great deal of affection given. My father, in particular, seemed to be unable to show me the kind of affection and love that I needed. My young heart was unable to comprehend that Daddy was demonstrating his love for me by his sacrificial acts of kindness.

In my remembering, I cannot recall ever getting up on a frigid winter morning and finding the house cold. Just as Hayden's father rose early to stoke the fire, my father also got up well before the rest of the family. The furnace that had been turned down to a chilly fifty-five degrees during the night was turned back up to a comfortable seventy degrees by the time I got out of bed.

I do not remember ever thanking my father for performing that act of kindness. It was a sacrifice for him because he hates the cold. He is extremely thin, and the cold goes right to his bones. Even so, he was willing to get up in the cold so the rest of us could be warm. Daddy told me that he enjoyed rising early. He said he liked the quiet and the solitude. As a six-year-old would, I believed him. Now, as an adult, I see that excuse as another proof of his love. He did not want me to feel sorry for him. He wanted to remove any feelings of guilt that I might have for not being thankful.

Hayden also mentions that his good shoes were polished for Sunday. I, too, often found my Sunday shoes shined and ready for me to wear to church. Daddy's hands, tired and painful from welding burns, carefully and lovingly cleaned my shoes. I was longing for hugs and kisses and silly times because that was the way all the daddies in the storybooks acted. However, all I usually received was a quick kiss on the forehead at bedtime. Today I treasure the memory of those little kisses because I know how difficult it was for Daddy to show affection.

Now that I am forty-two and Daddy is seventy-two, I realize those little sacrifices were his way of saying, "I love you, Curly." Not long ago Daddy came to visit for a few days. Each morning he slept in until well after nine o'clock! At first I thought he must be sick, but then it dawned on me. My husband had risen early, turned up the heat pump, and had a warm crackling fire in the fireplace. Daddy did not have to sacrifice for me anymore. He had passed that torch to my husband many years ago. Now he can sleep in until the house is warm. He can warm those loving hands by the fire anytime. At the end of "Those Winter Sundays," Hayden laments, "What did I know, what did I know of love's austere and lonely offices?" I, too, can cry out, I did not know." But now I know, and it is not too late to tell him.

Fathers and Children: Theodore Roethke vs. Robert Hayden

Donna Haisty Winchell
CLEMSON UNIVERSITY
CLEMSON, SOUTH CAROLINA

The assumptions one makes about tone are critical to any reading of Theodore Roethke's "My Papa's Waltz." Without guidance, students reach vastly different conclusions regarding how the narrator felt about being danced about the kitchen by his drunken father. Some try to argue that the poem is an indictment of child abuse. Much that they offer in support of such a reading clearly violates the words that are on the printed page. The belt buckle that scrapes the young boy's ear during the waltz becomes an instrument of abuse. Their leap is to the indignant belief that the boy is being beaten with the buckle end of the belt. In such a reading, the father's scraped knuckle clearly came as a result of swinging a fist at his son. The father's belting out time on the boy's head easily becomes further evidence that the child is being beaten by his father.

After students have read the poem, as an in-class informal writing assignment they can be asked to explain how they think the boy felt about his father and what specifically in the poem made them feel that way. Some will advance the child abuse argument; others will feel that the boy enjoys the wild, drunken dance. Members of each group—and those who don't have a clue about tone—must be forced to consider the evidence for either reading that the poem offers. The challenge is to determine what can reasonably and fairly be inferred, because the narrator never reveals directly what his attitude toward his father was. In preparation for writing more formally about the poem, students can be asked to consider what specific choices made by Roethke reveal tone, starting with the use of "my papa" in the poem's title and ending with the boy's being waltzed off to bed by his father at the end.

A productive writing assignment can ask students to link the attitude toward his father that the narrator has in Roethke's poem to the attitude toward a father held by the narrator in Robert Hayden's "Those Winter Sundays." (Having been warned against gender bias and against assuming that author and persona are one and the same, they tend to avoid declaring the speaker here a male.)

WRITING ASSIGNMENT

Both Theodore Roethke in "My Papa's Waltz" and Robert Hayden in "Those Winter Sundays" deal with a father/child relationship. Compare the tone in the two poems. To do so, consider each speaker's attitude toward his (or her) father. Is the attitude toward the father the same in each case? If so, make clear in your thesis statement how both speakers felt (or feel) about their fathers and use specific words from or references to the poems to support your opinion. If not, make clear in your thesis how the tone of the two poems differ and use specific words from or references to the poems to explain the difference.

Dramatic Situation and the Uses of Induction

R.S. Gwynn
LAMAR UNIVERSITY
BEAUMONT, TEXAS

We hear a great deal these days about such matters as the "indeterminacy" of poems and the error of instructors' attempting to impose their own interpretations on literary texts. I do not wish to get into arguments about the uses and abuses of current literary theory in the classroom, but I must assert that occasionally it is the instructor's responsibility to exercise his or her authority as a trained reader of poems and to reject some of the readings students come up with. A poem should not be turned into a *tabula rasa* on which students are allowed to scrawl purely subjective responses that have little or nothing to do with the text at hand. In student writing, gross misreadings of poems may occur if students have not been taught to ask basic questions about a poem's dramatic situation and to determine the answers to this question: *"Who is saying what to whom under what circumstances?"* Because students must work with tiny hints and clues in the poems, they must apply the inductive method to establish the basis upon which all other matters of interpretation must rest.

For a writing assignment on poetry, I favor using three or four short poems, each usually under ten lines, for an assignment that is usually titled something like "Different Types of Dramatic Situation." I usually select several poems from *Literature* and distribute copies of others from the public domain. Some of my favorites include A. E. Housman's "Eight O'Clock," Walter Savage Landor's "Mother, I Cannot Mind My Wheel," Robert Louis Stevenson's "Requiem," Countee Cullen's "Incident" or "For a Lady I Know," and Sarah Cleghorn's "The Golf Links." These are all traditional poems written in simple language, and the list contains examples of lyric, narrative, and dramatic poetry, In some of them the speaker seems to be the poet; in others, an invented character or omniscient narrator. Landor's poem has a named auditor. "Eight O'Clock" and "The Golf Links," to mention two, have clearly defined settings, and time is important in both Housman's poem and Cullen's "Incident." Of course, there are many other poems that may be used for this assignment, even longer ones, but the instructor should take care to select poems with a variety of speakers, auditors, and sets of circumstances.

Practice on similar poems, and a day or so of in-class preparation (discussion groups are especially valuable here) are useful for this assignment. It is important to stress that some matters of interpretation (if we can call them that) are really not open to much debate. "Eight O'Clock," for example, is not about a harried businessman who is troubled by a too-tight seatbelt while stuck in a traffic jam on the way to his downtown office; it is about a convicted man with a noose around his neck—no more, no less. It is true that we do not know the exact nature of his crime or even whether he feels any remorse about it—these things *are* debatable and may be legitimately asked. For example, does "cursed his luck" mean that the criminal remains unrepentant? In writing about these poems, students who do not look carefully at virtually every word in each poem will go astray; many have glossed over the crucial "noosed" in "Eight O'Clock" and, thus, do not recognize the impending execution. In Countee Cullen's "For a Lady I Know," misdefining "class" might lead them to assume that the title character is a schoolteacher when, in fact, Cullen means "class" in the social sense. Not thinking of the historical meaning of "wheel" in Landor's little masterpiece can also result in misidentifying the setting, and failure to look closely at the verb tenses in the same poem might result in students' not understanding that the young woman's love has proven inconstant. If students can master techniques here, in fairly accessible poems that can be discussed in compact paragraphs, then they should be able to apply the same inductive methods of reading to the more complicated poems and interpretive matters that they will encounter later in the course.

Using "Theme for English B" to Develop Awareness of the Author/Audience Relationship

William L. Scurrah
PIMA COMMUNITY COLLEGE
TUCSON, ARIZONA

Composition instructors often confront students who are reluctant, even afraid, to write. When such students say that they know what they want to say but don't know how to say it or that they suffer from writer's block, what they may in fact be telling us is that they don't know how to say what they want to say *to us*. Helping students to see their instructors as an audience, not just as judges, will open up the writing experience for them in new and creative ways. Langston Hughes's poem "Theme for English B" is the perfect vehicle for developing such awareness in our composition students, for in it he confronts the same dilemmas as they do whenever they are assigned to write an essay.

The poem begins with the assignment: "Go home and write / a page tonight. / And let that page come out of you— / Then, it will be true." These are fairly typical instructions, and to an instructor, seemingly not only innocuous, but open-ended, encouraging the students to a degree of freedom. But as Hughes goes on to itemize, the assignment is fraught with dangers; it raises two kinds of questions in the student's mind: 1) What does "come out of you" mean? Is it really what the instructor wants? Do I really want to reveal so much of myself to a stranger? 2) How safe is it to be truthful? What is "truth" in this situation? How do I state my truth so that my instructor understands and accepts it *as* true? No wonder Hughes says, "I wonder if it's that simple?," and no wonder we get students crowding around us after class, asking for more specific guidance: What should we write about? Is it all right to do this? Or that? Should I write about current events? Can I write about my dog? And so on.

Students are aware that the assignment is not "that simple" and that their grade depends upon how they answer the questions the assignment raises. Fortunately, Hughes's poem provides some answers having to do with the crucial author/audience relationship. A reading and class discussion of the poem should therefore help students address and resolve the conflicts they confront whenever they have to write a college essay.

The poem may be assigned for overnight reading or presented unannounced in class the day you plan to assign an essay (the personal essay would work best for this, although the principles apply to any). Read the poem aloud and then invite general response. Because this poem deals directly with an immediate concern of the students, responses are likely to be numerous and varied; of course, they will include comments of Hughes's dilemmas as a black student with a white instructor and on how he attempts to resolve that conflict by claiming their shared Americanness, but as discussion progresses and is prompted by the instructor, students will also begin to reveal their identification with the poet's experience as an English student like themselves. The discussion can then be directed toward discovering how Hughes resolved the problems inherent in the assignment.

First, Hughes gives a bare-bones biography, where he lives, how old he is, and so forth, establishing the physical distance or difference between himself and his instructor. Thus he demonstrates that where one comes from acts as a point of beginning for the essay: "I take the elevator / up to my room, sit down, and write this page:". The colon at the end of the stanza signals a beginning, a beginning from a physical reality of age, ethnicity, neighborhood, economic circumstance, etc. He is not a disembodied ideal student but has a real, experienced, describable existence—as do each of our students in our classes. (To facilitate students' use of personal biography as the starting point for thinking about the author/audience dialogue, the instructor might present a brief oral autobiography, thus beginning the process of making the students think about him/her as a human being who can be addressed, as an audience not as a judge.) Then, Hughes attempts to itemize the points of connection and measure the areas of difference between himself and his instructor: "You, me, talk on this page" about age, place, race, tastes, relative freedom, and so forth. When he says "Sometimes perhaps you don't want to be a part of me. / Nor do I often want to be a part of you," he may resonate with students who often do not want to be in an English class and do not know why they have to be there, and when he says, "But we are, that's true!" he underlines that through the writing of an essay, a student can establish a connection with his/her audience.

After general class discussion, assign students to write an essay of about five hundred words modeled after or inspired by Hughes's poem in which they address the issues he raises from their own points of view: How do they approach writing assignments? How do they resolve the conflicts any college writing assignment creates? What authorial stance do they take vis-à-vis their instructor? What do they assume an instructor wants and how do they reconcile that with what they want to write? Follow description of the assignment with a short period (twenty minutes) of small groups during which students can discuss among themselves their experiences and fears of writing, especially in terms of author/audience relationships.

The purpose of this exercise is to cultivate in students a consciousness of the dynamics involved in the relationship between an author and his/her audience, especially to help them realize the value of establishing their identities in their essay writing and not to lose themselves behind a facade of artificial objectivity sometimes so extreme that their essays seem written by "Anonymous." Offering Hughes's poem as a model will help students see themselves in a new way, as authors with something to say to an audience: "As I learn from you, / I guess you learn from me."

Teaching War Poems— in the Traditional Classroom and in Cyberspace

John K. Swensson
DE ANZA COLLEGE
CUPERTINO, CALIFORNIA

Poetry is my first love, and teaching argumentation is what I do best—a holdover from three years teaching Plebe English at West Point in the early 1970s. But teaching poetry and teaching argumentation work together, and they work especially well if you have a good selection of poems to work from. Here are three exercises built on poems that share a common subject, modern warfare. These poems almost always work well with my students. I use each poem to teach a different aspect of argumentation. Each exercise employs a different type of composition—in art, in performance, and in imagery.

WRITING WITH ART: "THE DEATH OF THE BALL TURRET GUNNER"

If a student can draw a picture of a poem, and explain the picture, she or he probably has made a good start toward understanding the poem. If the student provides an incorrect or culturally influenced picture, then we have a point of departure to find new meanings, correct meanings, or fun meanings. I often start with a short poem that is laden with images, such as Randall Jarrell's "The Death of the Ball Turret Gunner."

The Death of the Ball Turret Gunner

From my mother's sleep I fell into the State
And I hunched in its belly till my wet fur froze.
Six miles from earth, loosed from its dream of life,
I woke to black flak and the nightmare fighters.
When I died they washed me out of the turret with a hose.

I prefer to start without Jarrell's own footnote, which explains what a ball turret is on a World War II B-17 bomber. The assignment is to read the poem aloud at home and draw a picture of what they hear.

I allow students to use any medium. I don't grade the artwork, just how many ideas they can capture from the poem. I tell students if they really get stuck to try drawing a line at a time, and I draw a stick figure on the board to show them that I cannot draw either. I tell them that abstract art is OK if they can relate their picture to the poem. In class I may have them go to the board in groups with their pictures and draw a composite group picture. Each group must be prepared to defend its picture. This makes for wonderful collaboration.

One of the reasons I do not like Jarrell's footnote is that I have a large number of Asian students, particularly Vietnamese. I have often seen them look up the word *turret*, and then they draw a turreted castle in a setting that looks like their homeland. I applaud their selection of turret and we talk about context. Or I may find helicopters in their pictures in place of airplanes. The helicopter was the warship they knew in their parents' war. We learn more from mistakes, and other cultures. I want the students to take chances, and I generally have the groups with the most outlandish pictures go last after we have established what is in the poem with the tamer pictures. Today I am starting to get a lot of computer art, or *anime* in the drawings. I welcome the use of technology. Recently a group of students was supposed to draw a picture of E. A. Robinson's masterful "The Mill," which laments the death of the trades in the nineteenth century. I suggested to the students that they might want to take my digital camera to the old Los Gatos Mill/Museum. They did much better. One of their members was a film major, and he made a wonderful video keyed to the lines in the poem.

WRITING FOR PERFORMANCE: "DULCE ET DECORUM EST"

Another war poem lends itself to a play—Wilfred Owen's "Dulce et Decorum Est"—because it has so much loud music, coughing, and gagging in it, a discovery that I owe to seeing it done one Saturday morning on public TV.

Gas! Gas! Quick, boys! . . .

. . . .

In all my dreams, before my helpless sight,
He plunges at me, guttering, choking, drowning.

This year I asked two students to do it as a play the next morning in lieu of drawing a picture. This was week one, and I wanted students to take some risks in class. These two students—both from the Philippines—put on a play that was not to be believed. They were in costume with the woman dragging the gassed man, both of them in costume. They also played a computer disc that had a WAV sound file. I thought we were hearing professional readers, but it was a recording of the two of them reading the poem to which they had added combat sounds downloaded from the Web. They did this all in about four hours; it would have taken me four days and technical training.

COLLABORATIVE WRITING WITH PLAY AND PICTURE: "NAMING OF PARTS"

After we have done the earlier exercises, I up the ante to Henry Reed's incredible balance and blending of imagery, sound, and structure in "Naming of Parts." I have group assignments that deal with each of those three elements as we wrestle with John Ciardi's wonderful question, "How Does a Poem Mean?" I tell students that if you can answer Ciardi's question, you are developing an argument, and it might even be organized argument. The beauty of Reed's poem is in the balance. Is it sheer coincidence that the same harsh consonants in the first stanza in line one are muted or their sounds disappear in line five?

Today we have naming of parts. Yesterday,
We had daily cleaning. And tomorrow morning,
We shall have what to do after firing. But today,
Today we have naming of parts. Japonica
Glistens like coral in all of the neighboring gardens,
And today we have naming of parts.

One group draws a picture of the setting of the poem. At minimum I had better see trainees and a sergeant and some neighboring trees and some bees and some flowers (later stanzas). We are getting to some understanding if we have this much. Because the group is going to explain its picture to the class publicly, the heat is on. This is one of the few times when I do not have the Sound group go first. The group that has to deal with sound and meaning then reads the poem aloud, often with two readers in each stanza. We then go to another group, which had to research and draw the parts of the rifle with its various swivels. Plenty of those pictures are on the Internet.

The imagery group has specific questions about the imagery. I suggest they deal with the sexual imagery by starting with the bees and working backwards. I may have another group read and explicate Reed's companion poem "Judging Distances," or I may read that aloud and point out similarities. As long as we get to the message of the poem—make love, not war—I am happy, and the students have a lot of fun along the way. They are also much better prepared to write about the poems.

POETRY IN CYBERSPACE

I teach both in the classroom and through distanced learning. The online material I have developed may interest some instructors. My Freshman Composition Reading List (which uses a lot of poetry) is at <http://saturn.fhda.edu/instructor/swensson/index.html.> There are no passwords required, and I invite you to visit. I used the Inference Search Engine to find Web pages about the poets and the poems. In many cases the texts of poems are on the Web, but you need to be very careful about checking the layout and typography. The indentations in "My Last Duchess," for example, are difficult to replicate on the Web—and your own browser may confuse things as well. Be that as it may, there are wonderful pages about Robinson, Jarrell, Frost, Faulkner, and your favorite poet, on the Web. Students can interact with other students, write poems, have poems edited, all on the Web. Ask your students to post their favorite poem on a class Web page—or put it on a Bulletin Board (BBS) using INTERACTION or other software. I have students write their interpretations of poems for all to see on my BBS. I also encourage students to send their favorite poems around via listserv, so that we all may share in their preferences.

Examining Alliteration and Assonance in Open-Form Poems

Joseph Green
LOWER COLUMBIA COLLEGE
LONGVIEW, WASHINGTON

Because they've grown up with it and continue to live with it in popular music, whether they enjoy reading poetry or not, my students never have any trouble recognizing exact rhyme, especially end rhyme; however, they sometimes resist the notion of slant rhyme and find all but the most obvious use of alliteration and assonance downright elusive. In the chapter "Sound," the examples that X. J. Kennedy and Dana Gioia use to illustrate assonance and alliteration are mainly closed-form poems with rhymed line endings. Though they do comment further on sound in their chapter "Open Form," they don't give it much analysis there.

To observe the repetition of sounds in a poem, I always have to say the words aloud, feel them, polish them on the tongue. For me, this is one of the great pleasures of reading poetry, and the rewards are especially satisfying when they surprise me, when sound effects are not reinforced by an obvious rhyme scheme or rhythmical pattern. Consequently, the first objective of this assignment is to draw students directly into that same experience: reading open-form poems aloud for the sake of their sound.

For example, take a look at the first four lines of "Men at Forty," by Donald Justice:

Men at forty
Learn to close softly
The doors to rooms they will not be
Coming back to.

If you read the lines aloud, pacing them, pronouncing the words roundly, you'll *feel* the sounds as much as hear them. "Learn" recalls "Men." "Doors" recalls "forty," and in a different manner, perhaps

216

somewhat less obviously, "close." At the end of the second and third lines, "not be" rhymes with "softly." And at the end of the fourth line, "to" calls back to "rooms." The sounds of consonants and vowels braid the lines together.

The rest of the poem is equally rich in sound, sometimes with obvious effect—"stair" mirroring "rest" in the first line of the next stanza, and later "lather" echoing "father"—and sometimes more subtly. By the time you reach the end of the poem, you're ready for the last word, "houses," to close (softly, of course) with a recollection of "sound" from the first line of the final stanza and "now" from the stanza before.

When students follow this process, reading aloud, examining the repetition of consonant vowel sounds, they very quickly reach an understanding of alliteration and assonance, and they start to feel the music of language in open-form poems, where they may have thought before that it was missing. Still, a poem like "Men at Forty" is much more than a collection of sounds, so the assignment's second objective is to move students toward analyzing the connection between sound, structure, and sense.

I usually provide a list of poems, good candidates for aural analysis. This limits the potential difficulties somewhat, keeps the discussion focused on open-form poems, and creates automatic working groups among students. I select different poems from time to time, just to keep myself fresh, but some favorites include Robert Hayden's "Those Winter Sundays," Theodore Roethke's "Root Cellar," Alice Fulton's "What I Like," and, of course, Donald Justice's "Men at Forty."

Students read all the poems on the list, and then select one to examine in a short essay. They practice saying the poem they have chosen, trying to feel it as they speak, writing down the sounds and the words that connect them, more or less in the manner that I moved through the first stanza of "Men at Forty." The next step—making a statement about the use of sound, the effect of it in the poem—can be the hardest part for some students, but because it forms a thesis for the essay, it is a crucial step. I like to have students work in small groups at this point, helping one another to hear the poems, raising questions, and offering suggestions, until they have a sense of what they want to say in their essays. Often they discover various ways in which sound can reinforce imagery or meaning in a poem. Then they're really onto something.

I generally ask students to present their papers, saying the poems aloud and sharing their ideas with the whole class in a round-table discussion before they attempt their final drafts. This allows them to say things that aren't quite safe or completely tested, and it gives them an opportunity to ask questions of their audience. Many essays go through dramatic changes as a result of these sessions. Final drafts, typed and double-spaced, are usually about three pages long.

This assignment has worked especially well for me in introductory poetry classes, but it can also be effective in composition courses. I like to introduce it with this quote from Richard Hugo: "When I was a young poet, I set an arbitrary rule that when I made a sound I felt was strong, a sound I liked specially [sic], I'd make a similar sound three to eight syllables later. Of course it would often be a slant rhyme. Why three to eight? Don't ask. You have to be silly to write poems at all" (*The Triggering Town.* New York: Norton, 1979). By the end of the assignment, students will usually have a sense of why Hugo would set such a rule for himself—and most of them don't think it's silly.

Letting Go:
Robert Lowell's "Skunk Hour"

Terri Witek
STETSON UNIVERSITY
DE LAND, FLORIDA

Teach this poem directly after Elizabeth Bishop's "Sestina," pointing out ahead of time that Lowell and Bishop were very good friends and admired each other's work. Tell the class that in several earlier versions of "Skunk Hour" the poem was not only dedicated to Bishop, but that she seemed to be riding around in one of the "love cars" with him, and in one version they seem to have a crying baby. In another version the persona addresses the man in the moon. The point is that a lot of things that used to be gathered in the drafts of "Skunk Hour" have disappeared in the final version.

Ask the students to read the poem, then come to class with two paragraphs in which they have written a story that includes a specific setting, several minor characters, a relationship between the narrator and someone else, at least two pieces of overheard language, and at least two declarative statements. In class, ask them to eliminate at least half of what they've brought in by crossing out sentences. Then they should cross out inessential words in the sentences. Now ask them to line up what remains on a new sheet of paper, rearranging the elements if they wish. When they feel they are finished, tell them they must take one object from the last class and confront it in at least two new lines at the end. Now read the Lowell poem aloud and ask the students what their own work has taught them about it.

The beginning of this exercise demonstrates that making objects disappear from a space can be as mysteriously productive as gathering them: Bishop and Lowell use quite different techniques to similar ends in "Sestina" and "Skunk Hour." Oddly enough, both poems offer worlds that are filled with objects and yet from which things seem to be missing: Not only the objects but the spaces between them, then, resonate with meaning. What the students have taken out of their writing is as important as the repressed histories and explanations of the objects they brought into class during the "Sestina" discussion. This suggests that, to latter-day twentieth-century poets like Lowell and Bishop, both what fills a space and what it lacks are ways of telling the story of the essential mysteriousness of the world.

Of course the most perverse part of the exercise is what happens at the end, when the students are forced to include an object from another place. But that's what Lowell did by adding in a skunk after all his deletions, and it's the final triumph of his poem. (It's also a way of dedicating our efforts to Bishop, too.) The move reminds us that one new element has the power to alter a space forever: Each new object invades our domesticated landscapes much like Lowell's mother skunk invades his garbage pail. Though there is something scary about this, there is something wonderful in the world's determination to break into even our most protected spaces. Have the students read their revised work aloud and prove the point: Inevitably, they like the last parts best.

Giving Form to Loss

Angie Estes
CALIFORNIA POLYTECHNIC STATE UNIVERSITY
SAN LUIS OBISPO, CALIFORNIA

Primary text:
Edna St. Vincent Millay, "What lips my lips have kissed, and where, and why"

Related texts for teaching:
Elizabeth Bishop, "One Art"
Ezra Pound, "The River-Merchant's Wife: a Letter"
Ernest Hemingway, "A Clean Well-Lighted Place"

WRITING ASSIGNMENT

Write an essay about the loss of someone in your life. Your essay should show the reader how and why this person was (or still is) significant for you. It should also convey to the reader your experience of loss. Following the examples of Millay, Bishop, Pound, and Hemingway in the works we have discussed, use specific detail and descriptive language to evoke a sense of who this person was and what the person meant to you. Finally, using the metaphor in the sestet of Millay's poem as an example, incorporate into your essay a central metaphor that gives shape to your sense of loss.

Remember that your essay should not only explain and describe, it should also persuade. In other words, one of your goals in the essay is to get the reader to enter into this experience of loss as do Millay, Bishop, Pound, and Hemingway—and to understand the loss and its significance.

TEACHING STRATEGIES

All four of the works on which this assignment is based attempt to deal with loss through the shaping power of language. In class, I focus discussion and analysis on the poems of Millay and Bishop, both of whom use tight, formal structures—the sonnet for Millay and the villanelle for Bishop—to shape and convey their experience of loss. In addition to examining the images, metaphors, and deceptive language

221

employed by these poets in their overall structuring of the poem, we look specifically at how Millay and Bishop use the technique of repetition—in syntax, rhythm, and sound. This provides students the opportunity to begin to discover the ways in which these techniques can be used to achieve emphasis in their own writing.

Hemingway's story, of course, makes a nice bridge between poetry and prose, demonstrating how the techniques of poetry and prose can overlap. His repetition of syntax, as well as his use of metaphor and descriptive language, help students to understand how to incorporate those strategies into their own writing. (Although it is not included in the anthology, I usually also bring in Hemingway's "Big Two-Hearted River" as an additional excellent example.) Pound's poem is a useful model, clearly, for the striking images of loss it provides: the monkeys making "sorrowful noise overhead"; the mosses at the gate "too deep to clear them away"; and the "paired butterflies" that are "already yellow with August."

Students inevitably find the most challenging—and ultimately the most rewarding—part of this assignment to be the discovery of a central metaphor that will give shape to and convey their sense of loss. A close examination, however, of Millay's moving and complex metaphor developed in the brilliant sestet at the end of her sonnet—a metaphor in which the speaker is a winter tree that has lost the song/summer of birds/lovers—convinces students of the possibilities and power of shaped language. Likewise, Bishop's linking of everyday details and diction with the "disaster" of irrevocable loss, by means of the shaping force of her villanelle, exemplifies for students the power of language to shape and express their lives.

Finally, this assignment works particularly well towards the middle or end of the term. It requires students to use several forms of expository writing—narration, description, explanation—while at the same time introducing them to persuasive writing. I find the assignment especially useful, in fact, in helping students to understand that *all* successful writing is persuasive writing. The assignment can also introduce students to more sophisticated elements of writing—such as style and voice—by asking them to incorporate figurative language, as well as perhaps the stylistic technique of repetition into their essays. In addition, if you are teaching a course in which you discuss literary periods or movements, these poems provide the opportunity to introduce students to some of the major writing strategies—and themes—of Modernist authors.

Making Decisions
about Values and Ethics

David McCracken
COKER COLLEGE
HARTSVILLE, SOUTH CAROLINA

During the semesters that I have taught English: Introduction to Literature, one assignment seems to evoke more energetic, insightful, personal responses from students than any other, and although it relates to more than one poem, the exercise asks students to focus on one question that is pertinent to their study of literature.

When I assign students to read the chapter "Listening to a Voice," I ask them to pay special attention to several of the canonical works such as Williams's "The Red Wheelbarrow," Auden's "The Unknown Citizen," Owen's "Dulce et Decorum Est," and Blake's "The Chimney Sweeper." Most of the students in the class have taken AP English courses during high school and have read the poems; however, almost none of them have been exposed to Bettie Sellers's "In the Counselor's Waiting Room." As a result, I ask my students to be prepared to discuss Sellers's poem and also Linda Pastan's "Ethics," and then to write a response in their journals to this question: "Without extensively experiencing the world outside of the classroom, are people well prepared enough to make effective decisions about values or ethics?"

My teaching objectives in an introductory literature course are to expose students to the various genres, to help them to understand literary techniques, and to show them how to unveil the deeper meanings in the texts. I stress writing as well as reading during the course, and besides several short essays and an exam, I ask students to keep a journal in which they react personally to the literature. Sometimes I tell the students that we will discuss their entries during class and not to be afraid to bring their own frames of reference to bear upon the literature. Doing this often creates interpretations with which I nor your editors agree. When explicating Roethke's "My Papa's Waltz," I agree with Kennedy that the poem's rhythm is "rollicking" and I visualize a touching scene affectionately remembered by the speaker, but when students interpret the work as the persona's recollection of an alcoholic father and a codependant mother, I will not say that their interpretation is wrong if they are thorough in their discussion. (I once gave this poem to a physician who coordinated an alcohol and drug rehabilitation program and spent hours refuting his interpretation that the poem is about substance abuse.)

When I teach the chapter about voice, I select one of the assigned poems and demonstrate how an analysis of the speaker's tone helps us to understand the overall meaning of the text. When students begin to discuss "In the Counselor's Waiting Room," they usually summarize that there is a young woman attending a psychology course whose mother has asked her to see one of the college counselors because she has begun to reject her parents' values, especially concerning family and home. When they begin to investigate how irony illuminates the poem's meaning, several students interpret the poem as your editors do in the instructor's manual, that it is ironic that the earthy "terra cotta girl," product of her "home soil," does not appear to have the same proclivity for procreation as the previous generations of women in her family. However, after this, the discussion may take several turns. Several students will often question the irony of the farm girl attending college and reading about existentialism, some will defend that the enlightened girl has a right to make her own decisions, others will argue that one psychology class does not provide enough worldly knowledge for the girl to disobey her family. At some point, students question what is meant by "finds no ease there / from the guilt of loving / the quiet girl down the hall." Contrary to what your editors consider as perhaps reading too much into the poem, many students interpret the work as one about sexual repression. They may begin questioning Sellers's selections of "existentialism," "psychology," and "Baptist," and when they do, I write on the board their connotations of each word and I keep a dictionary handy so that we can compare them to their denotations.

This progression of events has occurred in each of the introduction to literature classes that I have taught, and when students begin to examine the social implications of the poem, I ask them to explain to me the relationship between the "terra cotta girl" and her mother and to determine the conflicting values between them. This is usually when the quietest students in the class express themselves. They may argue that the "home soil" has no right to ask the girl to visit the counselor, that the poem illustrates the negative stereotype of women as only breeder, and that the girl should be able to make her own sexual and social decisions. If the discussion has reached this point, I ask the class to shift to "Ethics." On the board, I list their perceptions of ethics and then offer them a standard definition, usually citing that it is a code of morals of a particular person, religion, group, or profession. I then ask the students to describe the speaker's tone in the first part of the poem, and I particularly listen to how they respond to the academic setting in which Linda replies that the woman should make the decision whether or not to be saved.

When we discuss the second section of the work, I ask the students if there is a tone shift and what perhaps has caused the change. I then ask them to notice how the last six and a half lines relate to some of the descriptions in Sellers's poem. I point out "the browns of the earth" that the now elderly speaker sees in the painting and how she now realizes that the "woman / and painting and season are almost one / and all beyond saving by children" corresponds to the earth images and the young woman, redirecting the students back to their initial journal question: "Without extensively experiencing the world outside of the classroom, are people well prepared enough to make effective decisions about values or ethics?"

Obviously, each class is different, and students will respond in other ways than the ones that I have mentioned. If there is not enough class time to complete this exercise, I will go over "Tone" and "In the Counselor's Waiting Room," and because most of the journal entries will react to "Ethics," I will respond to their impressions through my comments.

Connecting Images in Sylvia Plath's "Metaphors"

Grant Hier
UNIVERSITY OF CALIFORNIA, IRVINE
IRVINE, CALIFORNIA

One tightrope we walk as writing instructors is the line between teaching cohesive and structured writing and challenging students to be original and take risks. In stressing organizational techniques, our assignments can lean toward the preconceived "Grecian urn" models with the "compare and contrast" essay and the overused get-the-students-to-care-by-writing-about-themselves "personal experience" essay. The current pedagogical paradigm stresses "process" over "product," but canned assignments to specific forms and formulas can communicate just the opposite message (no matter how much we might have students practice revision).

In the art world, modern painters—abstract expressionists in particular—challenged similar restrictions. Rather than seek to produce a polished, expected finished "picture," artists unabashedly let the very "process" of their exploration and discovery stand as the work.

Similarly, this assignment uses a poem that deals in abstract, figurative language and simply asks students to show the "process" of their investigation. Instructors should be sure to stress that solving the poem's riddle in discovering what these metaphors are referring to is of little importance here. If they happen to solve it, great, but it is not expected. Tell students that the only thing you want them to do is reveal their thought processes: Communicate the connections they make, and show the "why" in their investigation. Such exploratory writing gives students a taste of sophisticated writing and its most difficult yet rewarding aspects. By design, it forces the author to take risks; de-centers the self as author; deeply engages the material in exploring and challenging its content; admits complexity and a degree of uncertainty; and encourages voice and originality.

Students will see that the direction their essays take is not linear, but neither is the writing process. Bee-line attacks usually result in mediocre (albeit logical) essays. How much more engaging and fresh the writing that explores, challenges, and concedes ambiguities than that of the author who heads for only one thesis and hits his points along the way in order, like driving nails. Or, to use a more appropriate metaphor, how much more compelling to look at an artist's self-portrait than some paint-by-number clown face.

The most common weaknesses in freshman composition papers are the lack of any real development of ideas, the vague and nonspecific language, and the high degree of overgeneralization. On the other hand, by asking students to reveal their thought process as the assignment itself, it forces students to show their reasoning and logic, support their claims, and provide specific details and examples along the way.

WRITING ASSIGNMENT

Part I

All on one page, make a drawing of each image that Plath mentions in "Metaphors." Don't worry about the level of your artistic skills, just scratch out some sort of visual representation of each image. Begin to look for similarities between the drawings, both in physical characteristics (shapes, sizes, and weights) and in their more abstract concepts and underlying ideas (functions). On another sheet make an informal list of every connection you can see, no matter how outrageous or absurd. Consider EVERY word Plath uses in the poem.

[**Note to Instructors:** Before assigning Part II of this assignment, be sure to introduce (or review) a lesson on figurative language and metaphor. This helps students to get in the mind-set of abstract thinking required for this assignment. Also, conduct a brief group workshop with the entire class discussing a few of the connections made thus far. This preparation helps students who might be struggling, but be sure to tell the class NOT to reveal what they think the "answer" is at this point. Merely discuss some of the more obvious connections (e.g., a "purse" and a "bag" each are designed to hold something smaller inside).]

Part II

In writing, articulate the connections you can discern between these images and ideas. Explore the various ways these images might be related. Don't panic if your connections seem to be reaching or if your conclusions differ from someone else's. That is inevitable. Just make sure that you support each claim. Don't worry if you seem to be rambling. A stream-of-consciousness exploration is acceptable here. The main goal is for you to show your reasoning and logic along the way. Be specific, providing details and examples whenever possible.

[**Note to Instructors:** Conduct another group workshop with the entire class where everyone brainstorms on the connections and makes guesses until the answer is found. If no one is close, focus on the word choice "nine." Have them count the number of lines in the poem and the number of syllables in each line. What things are associated with the number nine? If they're still lost, ask them how one would feel and look after eating an entire bag of green apples. Who else looks and feels like that? Once everyone sees that the poem is about being pregnant, you might want to consider the following third assignment to stress the concepts of revision, of a single piece of text metamorphosing into other forms, and of writing as a process.]

Part III

Now that the answer to the riddle is known, write an essay where you reshape all the previous exploration and analysis into a formal analysis of Plath's methods.

Metaphor and Shades of Meaning

April Lindner
WITTENBERG UNIVERSITY
SPRINGFIELD, OHIO

Have the class read Sylvia Plath's "Metaphors." Begin by asking the answer to the riddle posed by the poem to ensure that each student realizes that the poem is a series of metaphors describing pregnancy. Next, ask the class to consider whether the poem is simply an intellectual puzzle. Does it call up any emotion in the reader? Does it reveal anything about the speaker's attitudes? By way of answering this question, have each student choose a line from the poem and freewrite for a couple of minutes about the metaphor or metaphors therein. What associations does the line call up in the student's mind? What is the emotional content of the line? In other words, what does each metaphor say about the speaker's attitude toward her pregnancy? For example, a line like "This loaf's big with its yeasty rising" might call up more positive responses than "I'm a means, a stage, a cow in calf."

Reconvene the class and, working from the beginning of the poem to the end, have students volunteer their responses to each individual line. You might list the various emotions on the board as a way of illustrating the speaker's ambivalence toward her pregnancy. You might also ask the class whether or not there is a progression in the poem from a particular emotion toward a different emotion. Can the class find a plot, of sorts, within the poem? Next, have your students do an informal freewrite. Students should recall a pivotal event from long ago or the recent past (for example, losing a baby tooth or leaving home for college) about which they had conflicting feelings. Have students list their various feelings about the event. Then have them rewrite the passage using a metaphor to describe each feeling as accurately as possible. Finally, have them write a bit about the difference metaphor makes. Do they feel that the rewritten passage conveys their feelings more accurately than the initial list? If so, why? If not, why not?

This exercise should provide an object lesson on the uses of metaphor—how it can convey the nuances of emotion and shifts in attitude, and how students, as writers, can use metaphor to lend impact to their own ideas.

Revision and Meaning: Ezra Pound's "In a Station of the Metro"

David J. Rothman
CRESTED BUTTE ACADEMY
CRESTED BUTTE, COLORADO

The French poet Paul Valéry once made a comment to the effect that poems are never finished, only abandoned. We tend to think that this abandoning happens when a poet publishes his or her work—but that is not always the case. Many of the most powerful poems have been revised—sometimes repeatedly—after they have already been published, and they exist in several public versions. Among others, Walt Whitman and W. H. Auden are particularly well-known for having revised work that had already appeared; to cite another kind of example, there are more than fifty manuscripts of William Langland's fourteenth-century poem *Piers Plowman,* many of which were heavily edited by scribes over a long period of time, and which are very different from each other.

We know that when Ezra Pound was working on "In a Station of the Metro" in the early 1910s, he was experimenting with different techniques in an attempt to create a truly modern poetry. What most readers don't realize is that this famous poem, which is often taken as a breakthrough to the techniques of Imagism and High Modernism, looked quite different in later, book versions than when it first appeared in *Poetry* magazine in 1913. In later versions, the poem looks like this:

> The apparition of these faces in the crowd;
> Petals on a wet, black bough.

But in the *Poetry* version, the one first published, the poem looks something like this:

> The apparition   of these faces   in the crowd   :
> Petals   on a wet, black   bough

Pound's revisions are particularly fascinating, as they involve not a single change to any word in the poem—yet when we look at the two versions, they seem quite different, in a number of ways.

In your essay, describe the changes that Pound made to his poem, then speculate as to why he might have made them. What is added to the poem by the changes? What is lost? What remains unchanged (if anything)? Do Pound's changes indicate different cues for performance, or do they have significance in and of themselves as unperformable qualities of the poem's meaning? (How does one perform the extra space before a period in the original version, for example?) Or can the revision involve both of these kinds of changes at the same time? On a larger level—why, in his search for what is "modern," do you think Pound might have revised his little poem to look more conventional on the page? Which version do you think is more successful (if either)?

Remember, as you write, that well-organized speculation is as powerful as any conclusion you might reach. This question of poetic craft is profound and confusing: Entertain the possibilities.

Beyond Binary Thinking: "My Papa's Waltz" by Theodore Roethke

Grant Hier
UNIVERSITY OF CALIFORNIA, IRVINE
IRVINE, CALIFORNIA

Students first introduced to poetry often tend to seek strictly literal interpretations. The fact that there can be numerous levels of abstraction and multiple levels of meaning in poetry—indeed, in all language—is troublesome for some. Many students look for a singular, quantifiable answer, as if a poem were a mathematical equation. Likewise, composition students often tend to reduce their arguments to either/or propositions: "Here is my opinion. Here is an example of why it is right. All else is wrong." This type of writing, of course, contains no real development of ideas, no divergent thinking, no risk. Upon first reading, most students accept a rather simplistic interpretation of "My Papa's Waltz." Closer analysis, however, can reveal opposite, yet equally valid interpretations. This assignment helps students to get beyond binary thinking as they learn to analyze and find evidence to support their claims.

As a pre-assignment activity, don't let them know the title of the poem beforehand; either give them a copy of the poem, *sans* title, or write just the body of the poem on the board and workshop it as a group from there. Don't let them know that the poem is in their book. Read the poem aloud and immediately ask for a one-word description of the tone of the poem: "What is the mood here?" The most common words that come up, in my experience, have been "fear," "anger," "bitterness," and "resentfulness." Write these on the board.

Next, ask the students what they think the poem is about. Have the whole class quickly formulate with you a one-sentence summary on the board: "This is a small boy's recollection of a drunken father who abused him." Take a poll and ask how many see the poem as unhappy or negative. The majority, if not all, will.

Now ask for words or phrases found within the poem to

support this negative interpretation. LET THE STUDENTS FIND THESE THEMSELVES! Write these on the board (better yet, have students get out of their seats and do it). They should come up with "dizzy," "death," "not easy," "unfrown," "battered," "scraped," "beat," et al.

Now paraphrase an argument aloud that analyzes the text, elaborating on these found examples: "The first thing we're told is that the booze on the father's breath is so strong it makes the boy dizzy. The dad's probably an alcoholic. The speaker says outright it's 'not easy,' that he has to hang on 'like death,' and that the mother can't 'unfrown' her face. There is nothing joyful about this. Clearly it's a story of abuse. The father is holding the boy's wrist, a blatant act of dominance. His knuckle is battered, implying that it has struck something before. He 'beat' him on the head with symbolically dirty hands. Furthermore, 'to bed' could even have sexual overtones; is it significant that the boy's ear is waist high? When the dad finally swings him into the bedroom, the boy is hanging on for dear life. Dismal, right?" Nods will abound.

Now, here is where you get them to move beyond binary thinking and into deeper analytical process. Point out to your class that the title of a poem is the primary indicator of the author's intent, then write the title on the board. Ask them to look closely at word choice. "My" claims possession. "Papa" is a warm, loving term of affection. A "waltz" is never negative or violent; quite the opposite, it implies light-heartedness and grace. Thus, the title seems to indicate that this is a positive experience! After all, Roethke did not title it "The Old Man's Stomp" or "Drunken Dad in a Mosh Pit."

Now ask if they can dig in and cite evidence to support a happier tone. If they get stuck, help them out. Well, the word "romped" certainly implies play. What "romps" in life? Puppies! Paraphrase the poem now so as to emphasize a strictly positive reading: "Did you ever pillow fight or jump up and down on the bed or 'romp' until things fell? This is a happy story of a boy fondly remembering bonding with his 'Papa.' Is everyone with the smell of liquor on their breath necessarily an alcoholic? No. We can see here a family provider who, after working hard all day, comes home to have a drink, unwind, and play with his son. The word 'We' in 'We waltzed' means that both parties participated in the act. Not only does the author use the word 'waltz' in the title, but he refers to it twice more in the poem—a joyful dance." Continue the positive analysis, ending with "The boy hung on, never wanting it to end."

Now we have the two extremes on the table for discussion. Ask which one is right. A show of hands, strictly positive, then strictly negative. There will be a split now. Still processing this new evidence, many will not have raised their hands for either. "So, then, perhaps the answer lies somewhere between." Use this as an opportunity to point out the value in research and gathering evidence from outside sources. Tell them that if they investigate the history of Roethke, they would find out that his father was a gardener. This explains the "palms caked hard by dirt" and supports the happier, "hard working provider" interpretation. But they might also discover that Roethke's dad was an alcoholic, and so you could lead them back and forth in considering opposing viewpoints and finer and finer distinctions between shades of gray. This very process of delving deeper—of discovering additional strata of interpretation beyond the surface-level and bipolar observations made at the start—will no doubt parallel our students' experiences as they progress with their own essays of analysis.

WRITING ASSIGNMENTS

1. Turn to the one-word descriptions of the tone of the poem found earlier ("fear," "anger"). For each one-word description, cite specific words or phrases within the poem that support such a feeling. Write a paragraph for each of the citings explaining how it helps to establish such a tone.

2. Now focus on those individual words and phrases cited as evidence to support first a negative, then a positive interpretation. Address each and explain, in writing, why the specific word or phrase carries either negative or positive weight. Compose a sentence where each word or phrase, used in another context, carries similar negative or positive connotations ("The puppies romped across the lawn.").

Writing Assignment for Anne Sexton's "Her Kind"

Mark Sanders
COLLEGE OF THE MAINLAND
TEXAS CITY, TEXAS

A BRIEF OVERVIEW

Anne Sexton's "Her Kind" is a bitter examination of womanhood. The poem illustrates a sisterhood of women who are "possessed" witches, "braver at night," and "dreaming evil." Sexton describes a woman as a "lonely thing, twelve-fingered, out of mind," "not a woman, quite." Suburban homes are "warm caves in the woods," and husbands and children are worms and elves. Additionally, Sexton alludes to lovers as being like Pluto, the Greek god of the underworld. Abducted and seduced, the woman as Persephone waves good-bye to villages along "the last bright routes," is consumed and bitten by Pluto's hellish passions, and is ultimately crushed under his wheels. Consequently, "a woman like that is not ashamed to die."

TOPICS FOR WRITING ASSIGNMENT

1. "Her Kind" shows the disparity between actual womanhood and ideal womanhood. A woman, as described by Sexton, is "not a woman, quite." Contrast Sexton's illustration of womanhood to what you perceive as ideal womanhood. In other words, what will it take to make a woman a woman?

2. Trying to overlook Sexton's own suicide, concentrate on the last two lines. The poem's apparent nihilism suggests that death is sometimes a preferred alternative to life. What in the poem illustrates that life is so unsatisfactory to women that they should not feel shame in choosing death? Additionally, while this may be a disquieting thought, what in your own existence would make death a preferred alternative to life?

Or, what in even the most unhappy of existences keeps life sacred?

3. Think about women you know. How well do they fit Sexton's descriptions? Do you know a woman who is "out of mind"? How did she get that way? Do you know a woman who is "braver at night"? What necessitates her inhibitions? Look at each of Sexton's descriptions and draw parallels to women you know.

4. If "Her Kind" depicts womanhood, it also depicts manhood. According to Sexton's implications, what are men like? How arc they worms and devils; what, along with their elfish children, do they whine about and "disalign"; how do they make women lonely? How do they make women want to die?

For Tennyson's "Ulysses"

Fred Dings
WICHITA STATE UNIVERSITY
WICHITA, KANSAS

COMPOSITION WRITING ASSIGNMENT

Write an essay that examines and compares the version or "reading" of Ulysses in Tennyson's poem to an earlier or more recent depiction. Be sure to discuss the similarities and differences of each version and explain how the versions are representative of the time in which they were written. In all cases, you might want to consider to what extent Tennyson's Ulysses is or is not representative of our time. Be sure to compare, analyze, and argue in your paper.

POETRY WRITING ASSIGNMENT

Write a poem in the first person or third person in which you feature Ulysses or any other figure from classical mythology, such as Greek, Roman, or Judeo-Christian. Use a contemporary voice, and make decisions about rhythm, rhyme, diction, texture, images, and metaphors within the context of this particular project. In other words, try to make the form and content of your poem mutually responsive. You might consider the figure in some new situation, a contemporary one, or in a particular attitude, mood, or predisposition. Your poem might reveal some new way of thinking about the figure or our times.

COMMENTARY

One of the advantages of using Tennyson's poem as a focal point is not only its kinship with our modern sensibility, but its revisionary relationship to a literary tradition about which most students know little. Because we are working with poetry, a lecture including the versions of Ulysses found in Homer, Dante, Tennyson, and, possibly, Wallace Stevens can provide an overview of a tradition in less than one hour, even with students who have read none of the poems. This can be done entirely by lecture with a reading of selected passages in class or else with advanced reading of selected passages placed on reserve in the library. An assignment of this nature increases students' sense of their relationship to literary tradition and requires them to think and write comparatively.

In preparation for this assignment, I always spend time discussing the tradition of poetry featuring Ulysses, how Tennyson's poem fits into and adds to this tradition, and why this type of poem continues to be written. The extent to which I discuss these things depends on the level and nature of the course.

To begin, I review the characterization of Ulysses in Homer and Dante. First, I highlight the different characterizations we get of Odysseus (Ulysses) even in Homer, depending on whether we are reading the *Iliad* or the *Odyssey*, two texts that offer competing traditions. In particular, I focus on certain passages in each text. In Book IX of the *Iliad*, we find Odysseus acting as an emissary to Akhilleus to rejoin the battle and save the ships from burning. Odysseus is known for his cleverness and craft in this tradition; because the text is celebrating the physical prowess and force of Akhilleus in competition with the craft of Odysseus. Odysseus is featured as a supplicant and told by Akhilleus to go and *think* of a way to save the ships without the power of Akhilleus, a power that of course becomes vitally necessary. In the *Odyssey*, Odysseus' talents are stressed over those of Akhilleus. In Book XI, we find Odysseus summoning the underworld and talking to the shade of Akhilleus. Here, in this competing tradition, we hear Akhilleus pronounce his own error in sacrificing his life for immortal fame, tacitly acknowledging Odysseus' way as that best virtue which defeats death. Unless I am teaching a literature course, I seldom develop the discussion further than this.

Next, if there is time, I briefly discuss the characterization of Ulysses (Odysseus) in Virgil as a "man of iron" and how Aeneas himself is in part an Ulyssean figure. Normally, however, I move directly on to Dante's placement of Ulysses in the eighth level of hell for being a fraudulent counselor, for convincing his men to pursue knowledge and new experiences in the world instead of pursuing knowledge of Christian love. In Canto XXVI, we find Ulysses portrayed as one "horn" of a two-horned flame; the flame is described as "a tongue that tried to speak" (Mandelbaum 1. 89). The flame, figured as both a horn and a tongue, is also then the language of Ulysses that goaded others along with himself to eternal damnation. (This is a good time to further underscore the value and working of the poetic image.)

I now lead directly into Tennyson's poem and discuss how Ulysses' heroic quest for knowledge is not only redeemed but redemptive as he copes with declining powers in old age. The meter, blank verse, is of course the meter of such English epics as John Milton's *Paradise Lost* and William Wordsworth's *The Prelude*. The connections here with the tradition should be apparent, but they might be stressed anyway. As a class, we already will have read and discussed the overall poem, but now I will focus on the heroic quest for knowledge featured in lines such as 6–7, 31–32, 50–54, and 65–70. The main point to make here in terms of the tradition is how Tennyson takes the figure of Ulysses and features him as an exemplar of modern "scientific" man. In a time when orthodox Christianity is less influential as a worldview than it once might have been, Tennyson's *reading* of Ulysses revises Dante's and reflects the dominant values and attitudes of our time just as Dante's reading reflected the dominant Christian worldview of his time. In addition, the tradition and character of Ulysses helps us read ourselves and our relationship to the part in some new way, This, you might stress, is one of the great values of being knowledgeable of our literary traditions.

At this point, a thoughtful student might suggest that Tennyson's view of Ulysses is no longer of our time. This would be an ideal time to encourage that student to write an essay that argues that point. If I have enough time, I include a reading of Stevens's "The Sail of Ulysses" and a few contemporary poems to bring the discussion to the nearly literal present. I also point out that this sort of chronological reading can be done with several major mythological figures. Also, because one problem that sometimes occurs in the poetry writing assignment is a student's too-loose identification with Tennyson's voice, I will bring in Louise Glück's "Aphrodite" or Mark Strand's "Orpheus Alone" as examples of other voices and interpretations of other mythological figures.

In closing, reading and writing in conscious relationship to our literary traditions is something that, among other things, I encourage. In a composition class, the organization, articulation, and analysis of ideas can in this case also lead to a greater appreciation of our poetic and mythological traditions.

Details:
A Writing Assignment

Madeleine Mysko
JOHNS HOPKINS UNIVERSITY
BALTIMORE, MARYLAND

I have used the following writing assignment to reinforce the lesson that strong writing is characterized by the efficient handling of details. In preparation, I choose a character the class has encountered in the assigned readings. Particularly useful for this writing assignment are characters who have a "history" in the community or family, and whose changes over time have been observed (as opposed to revealed omnisciently or through that character's own first-person narration)—in fiction, for example, William Faulkner's Miss Emily ("A Rose for Emily") and James Baldwin's Sonny ("Sonny's Blues"); in poetry, Edwin Arlington Robinson's "Miniver Cheevy," and John Updike's Flick Webb ("Ex-Basketball Player").

I then write, and duplicate as a handout, a rather boring (but blessedly short) paragraph about that character, keeping the paragraph well above its subject, padding liberally with generalizations or abstractions, and avoiding particulars. For an example I have chosen Updike's Flick Webb:

> Flick Webb, who is employed at a local garage, is a familiar character in town. Although he has a lot of athletic potential and was once a promising member of his high school basketball team, Flick now appears to be unmotivated. When he is not at the garage, Flick seeks his relaxation in a nearby restaurant. He is a disappointment to those who remember his former accomplishments.

For this writing assignment I find I need a full class period, devoted half to discussion and half to in-class writing exercise. I begin the discussion by reading "Ex-Basketball Player," followed by the paragraph I wrote about Flick. I point out the obvious: that while my paragraph presents the same Flick Webb, the picture isn't sharp at all, not only because clichés like "athletic potential" are always fuzzy, but also because details have been stripped from the exposition. By returning to the poem the class can then (either in small groups, or as a whole with someone recording at the blackboard) compile a list of specific details Updike provides. The list looks something like this:

- names of people and places ("Pearl Avenue" and "Mae")

- setting: the exact location of Berth's Garage, even the direction it faces; description of the pumps; description of Mae's luncheonette

- Flick's exact record: 390 points

- description of Flick's hands

- the names of real things: *lugwrench, inner tube, pinball, Necco Wafers*

The list could be much longer, of course.

Once, I attempted a short, in-class writing exercise in which students were to write a coherent paragraph or two from the above details. I found, alas, that the exercise was not so easy. The students were writing at a distance from their subject—a character about whom they had only second-hand information and feelings. Moreover, it proved defeating: After all, everybody could see before we started that a paragraph about Flick Webb couldn't hold a candle to Updike's poem, so why bother?

But listing details about Flick Webb, on the blackboard or in small-group discussion, does provide an excellent example of the sort of list-making one might do before writing the personal essay. Thus, during the remaining class time, I now ask my students to take a few minutes to choose a character they know well, but not intimately, as the speaker of "Ex-Basketball Player" knows Flick well, but not intimately. Some suggestions are:

- an elderly relative

- someone your age, not necessarily a friend, whom you remember from school

- someone in your community you would describe as a "character," such as the mail carrier who likes to chat, the Little League coach with the red face, the beloved parish priest who left the church to get married, the neighborhood busybody.

Then I have them take a few more minutes to list as many specific details about that character they can call up. Once they have their own lists in front of them, we discuss the downside of these wonderfully revealing details: They have to be managed. If one or two students share their lists of details, the class can readily devise a means to organize them. Details about the neighborhood busybody can, for example, be divided as follows: physical description, location of his house on the street, his tactics in garnering gossip, specific incidents.

Beyond paragraph organization, the in-class portion of this assignment is also useful in demonstrating unity of purpose. Before I send my students off to actually begin writing their essays, I return to "Ex-Basketball Player." I point out that the underpinning of all good writing—fiction, poetry, expository writing—is unity of purpose. Updike's title is the point beyond which most folks in Flick's town probably don't venture: "Flick is an ex-basketball player"—enough said. But the writer takes a closer look, gathers details, and presents them with a purpose: to reveal what it means that Flick is an ex-basketball player. He is an ex-basketball player, and he'll never be anything else.

I have a tendency to wax poetic about that strong relationship between writer and audience that flourishes wherever unity of purpose prevails, so it is just as well I've about run out of class time when I get to this point. I suggest that my students try to determine for themselves the purpose of their essay by writing a one-line "thesis" caption to go with the mental picture of the character they've chosen to write about. The purpose may be, for example, to reveal that "Mr. Jones, the neighborhood busybody, is a real pain in the neck," or it may be to reveal that "Mr. Jones, the neighborhood busybody, retired too soon," or that "Mr. Jones, the neighborhood busybody, is a lonely old man." Whatever that caption may be, it will determine not only which details are chosen, but also the order in which they are presented, and the tone of voice the reader ultimately hears.

The Specific Gravity of Words: Richard Wilbur's "The Writer"

David Mason
COLORADO COLLEGE
COLORADO SPRINGS, COLORADO

As a child of scientists, I was always aware of the oddity of metaphorical reading. In my thinking, which baffled my parents, nothing was itself, everything figured something else. Marianne Moore's "literalists of the imagination" were creatures I recognized from the moment I met them. Yet Moore could also be a simple literalist, an accurate observer of the world, and it is perhaps too easy for wanderers in imaginary gardens to stray from their literal paths.

Now that I have taught poetry for several years, I can understand my parents' bemusement at their imaginatively wayward son. Indeed, one of my mild frustrations with that species of thinker known as the English major is that he or she is too eager to leap to symbolic interpretations of every poem, failing to see the literal sense, the felt life in lines of verse. I'm not sure how or when it happened, but many of my students assume that poets never mean what they say, that some lofty, abstracted pot o'gold lies at the end of every poem's rainbow. This can be carried to absurd lengths—symbols of Christ or the grim reaper hidden in every leaf, blossom, or bole.

Though I sometimes pretend that poems have no "hidden meanings," I do not wish to deny the importance of symbolic or metaphorical structures. But students can too easily trick themselves into abstraction, expecting professors to praise their intellectuality, before they have enjoyed the pleasurable relation of words to the world. I call this relation "specific gravity," which literally refers to the ratio of a solid or liquid mass to the mass of an equal volume of distilled water at 4 degrees Celsius. My sense of the heft of words is meant to correspond to the world they represent. But diction is not the only problem my students face; there is also the matter of grammar and rhetoric. A complex and passionate poet like William Butler Yeats is, with surprising frequency, coldly syllogistic in the stanzaic outline of his argument. Too frequently I will ask students what he could mean by a given passage, only to discover that, perhaps under the spell of his powerful meters, they have failed to hear the logical sense of a subject, verb, and predicate. When these fundamental derailings take place, the last refuge of inexperienced minds is abstraction; they go symbol hunting and reduce poems to formulaic equations.

If English majors can fall victim to their own symbolic thinking—supercharged trains flying off the rails of the poem—perhaps freshman have it worse. Somehow they have been taught that poetry is always difficult, always symbolic before it is anything else. No wonder they sometimes think it has no relation to the real world!

Metaphors and symbols must make literal sense before their figurative values can be understood. In both class discussion and writing assignments, I will often outlaw hidden meanings: Frost's scythe in "Mowing" is a literal scythe, and the poem celebrates real work for its balance of fact and dream. Again, my point is not to pretend that language is other than it is, but to let my students feel the world's weight in words before they drown in exaggerated interpretations.

The assignment I have devised for freshman or introductory students emphasizes two things: literal meaning and the transformative value of poetry. My usual procedure is never to assign a particular poem to all of my students; they are always free to find any poem in the book that is attractive to them. I am convinced that their effort to identify these poems for themselves is beneficial. In this case, however, I might choose several poems for specific qualities, especially a balance of literal and figurative meanings. For the sake of clarity, let's say that I have assigned Richard Wilbur's poem "The Writer."

WRITING ASSIGNMENT

The assignment has two parts. In Part One, students are to write a paraphrase of the poem. I recommend that they break it into sentences and translate the poem into their own prose statements: "My daughter is in her room writing a story, etc." The room is just a room; it is not a symbol for the mind or anything else.

Part Two is an essay stressing the differences between paraphrase and poem. Two of the differences they might assert are Wilbur's figurative language and the accuracy of diction. The "prow of the house" suggests that the child's room, like her mind in the act of creation, voyages to some unknown destination, a metaphor Wilbur extends through three stanzas, then questions in the fourth when he notices that his daughter has paused—his mind lovingly attentive to her typing. The second figure is the "dazed starling" they once saw trapped in the room, in a panic to escape—another metaphor for writing and so much more. These two figures lend the poem its rhetorical structure, but they hardly explain its precision and tenderness. Students should be attentive to the poet's vivid appeals to our senses: "a commotion of typewriter keys / like a chain hauled over a gunwale, " or the way "A stillness greatens." Why "greatens" and not the prosaic "enlarges"? Why should father and daughter try not to "affright" the starling? Why does it "Batter against the brilliance" and not merely against the glass? Why "drop like a glove" and not a light, feathery thing with wings? Simple accuracy of description takes on figurative meaning, suggesting Wilbur's powerful correspondences between matter and spirit. But accuracy comes first.

Attentiveness to literal meaning in a highly figurative poem should help students appreciate the astonishing precision and care with which Wilbur expresses his love. The "starling" becomes his "darling," and like all parents, he finds that there is precious little he can do for her on her flight.

This assignment can be modified to emphasize other elements of poetry such as meter or tone. But the point is always the same: to catch students before they run off into the never-never land of abstraction and help them pay close attention to the specific gravity of words.

Why Is It Poetry? Reading "The Red Wheelbarrow"

Peter Fortunato
ITHACA COLLEGE
ITHACA, NEW YORK

It's remarkable, isn't it, that after almost three-quarters of a century readers have not exhausted their delight and fascination with the workings of William Carlos Williams's "The Red Wheelbarrow." Certainly, much of this brief poem's appeal is its accessibility: simple language arranged somewhat unusually on the page, and content that anyone can see. But you'd expect we might be bored with these sixteen words by now: You'd expect that what isn't already self-apparent has probably been discussed to death.

What typically happens with a poem, or any work of art as well known as this one, is that when it is brought up, discussion moves quickly away from the piece itself to a critical context woven about it. To some extent, that's what the continuity of culture is: the weaving that continues; for example, relating "The Red Wheelbarrow" to Modernism, or Imagism or literature in the American idiom, and so on. I love this poem, however, not because of its abstract "importance": in its particulars, the poem stays fresh for me. It's true that teaching it to new readers helps keep it fresh, but there's more. If poetry is news that stays news, then that red wheelbarrow of Bill Williams keeps delivering it.

How it does what it does is the question I love to pose to myself and my students—who might think on first reading that the simplicity of the content and some cleverness with mechanics are all there is to it. I might need to point out to them that the poem is fundamentally a machinery of words and asks to be read with attention to the line and stanza breaks, that it has a distinct rhythm, which when vocalized is part of its charm. It's true that the simplicity is a delight, of course, and many students will readily compare this poem to haiku, if only because of its brevity.

After having assigned a reading of it, the first thing I do in teaching this work is to write it out on the blackboard without its first two lines, and then ask if there is enough left to qualify as a complete poem. This in itself can be an interesting writing assignment or source of classroom discussion. Most students will eventually see that description is not enough to make a poem, nor is typography, because without the opening, "so much depends / upon," we will want to ask, "Well, *what about* that wet, red wheelbarrow and those white chickens? Why should we pay attention to them?"

Indeed, that question is introduced by the opening lines. "What do you think depends upon the things Williams is pointing out? Why is he pointing them out?" I ask my students. I have found that they are likely to write or talk about many subjects here, ranging from the joys of a simple, rural life (and nostalgia for it) to all kinds of social and ecological dimensions that might surround the scene. It's amazing how much that red wheelbarrow can carry, and it can be fun to ask a class to particularize through playful, free association what they can imagine loaded into the wheelbarrow.

A few students will probably arrive independently at what I consider to be the most important dimension of the poem, and if they don't bring it up, I will ask, is it just the wheelbarrow and this particular context, or is he writing about a way to apprehend any everyday experience? The fact that the poem directs our attention so completely to such homely things as a red wheelbarrow, white chickens, and rain water is its accomplishment. It deftly "glazes" the ordinary so that it can be perceived as *extraordinary*. (In this way, the poem is most akin to Japanese haiku, though I don't know that Williams himself was interested in that comparison.) The poem is an example of the sort of perceptiveness that can make anything in our lives, even if only for an instant, a complete focus. In my reading of the poem, *everything* depends upon this moment, because it opens into an activity, a way of being alive that is rich beyond limitation. Poetry speaks to that richness. I want my students to see that.

And it has so much to do with the first two lines, so much depends upon *them*. That the simple act of calling our attention to a wheelbarrow and chickens opens up into poetry is also quite humorous, I think.

William Carlos Williams's "The Red Wheelbarrow"

Roy Scheele
DOANE COLLEGE
CRETE, NEBRASKA

Over the years, I have found this little masterpiece to be very useful both in literature and composition classes, regardless of whether the subject under discussion is poetry or prose, because the poem provides an easy point of entry into a consideration of the virtues of compression. In addition, discussing the poem often leads students who are not habitual readers of poetry to overturn some of their inhibitions and misconceptions about the art, while usually holding some discovery even for those students who are "into" poetry.

I start by printing the poem on the board, then adding the poet's name beneath and finally adding the title. Those students who have read little or no modern poetry are typically skeptical as to whether the specimen just produced is a poem at all; many of them equate poetry with rhyme and simple narrative, something more along the lines of "Casey at the Bat" or "The Face on the Barroom Floor."

As we begin to discuss the Williams poem, I try to draw them out by asking whether it reminds them of anything, what it is like. We talk about the poem's images (wheelbarrow, rain water, chickens) and colors (red and white, yes, but also the colors implied in the prisms of the raindrops, and in the things not named that might be expected to be there: grass, gravel, house or barn or fence nearby, and the like). Someone inevitably compares the poem to a color snapshot, and we discuss the poem's photographic qualities for a while. I now turn to a consideration of the poem as a flat assertion. What is the "so much," I ask, that "depends upon" this simple array of wheelbarrow, rain water, and chickens? The students normally view the statement as a species of nonsense. The images seem unimportant in themselves; what in the world is the "so much" said to depend upon this little tableau?

Almost without exception the students take "depends upon" not in its literal but in its idiomatic sense, so I suggest that we look at the etymology of the word "depend": from the Latin *de + pendere*, "to hang down," and they see that what literally "depends upon" the red wheelbarrow is the raindrops. If we now put the literal sense beside the idiomatic sense of "relies on," the poem's images constellate into a meaning: the wheelbarrow, rain, and chickens become part of a larger whole. We are in the realm of symbol and metaphor.

At this level of consideration the wheelbarrow can be seen to represent human labor (and the artifice that makes tools useful to that labor). The rain is symbolic of the renewal and sustaining of life, and the chickens of all the things man raises and eats for his own sustenance. Thus the poem can be viewed as a miniature essay on the interconnectedness of all life, human and nonhuman, in nature, and the poem's assertion becomes not an overstatement but an understatement: That "so much" is *everything*—all life depends on the water that nurtures it.

As a final step, I like to get the students to think about the poem's form. I point out that it is written in unrhymed syllabic couplets, four of them, each first line having either three or four syllables and each second line, two; this syllabically regular second line, steadily recurring, replaces the regular metrics and rhyme of the traditional couplet. I try to show how each second line sets up an expectation of two syllables, an expectation that the poem continually fulfills, and how this contributes to the poem's playfulness: breaking "depends upon" into two units in the first couplet, "wheelbarrow" into two units in the second, "rainwater" into two units in the third, and separating epithet from noun ("white" from "chickens") in the last couplet. I suggest that, in terms of the poem's form, what "depends upon" the statement of the opening couplet is the succeeding three couplets. Form follows statement, as it were.

If one wishes to pursue the matter of form, I have found Robert Frost's "Dust of Snow" to be excellent for comparison, having the same number of lines and a comparable brilliance of imagery while being written in rhymed quatrains and having a very different tone and rhetorical structure.

The Frivolous Profundity
of Poetic Music

David J. Rothman
CRESTED BUTTE ACADEMY
CRESTED BUTTE, COLORADO

One of the strange things about literature—and particularly poetry—
is the way that questions that seem either pointless or obvious can
yield surprisingly fertile results for critical thinking. For if one function of poetry is, as Alexander Pope wrote, to say "What oft was
thought, but ne'er so well express'd," then it is the simplest things
that often embody the most powerful forces in a poem.

William Butler Yeats's "The Lake Isle of Innisfree" is a mysterious poem in this sense, for though it appears to be just a simple song
of longing for peace and quiet, it is filled with little specifics that
shimmer with a symbolic power that is difficult to describe. These
little things are worth meditating on at length, not only for what they
can tell us about the poem, but because they help us to see what the
poem is trying to say about an attitude towards life. One way to ask
this question more specifically is to wonder why Yeats has written,
in the third line of the first stanza, "Nine bean-rows will I have
there." Why nine? The number may be irrelevant, and it may have a
private or occult significance; but are there other ways to answer this
question?

Without worrying too much about the particular number
nine, for example, we might ask why Yeats picks any specific
number. After all, he does not indicate how many wattles (poles
intertwined with twigs, reeds, and branches) he is going to construct in building his cabin—why count bean-rows instead of
wattles, or wattle-poles?

Remember that the point of this kind of an essay is not to hunt
down the symbolic significance of the number "9," although such
information, and the way that Yeats understood it, may well be
meaningful and helpful in reading the poem. Instead it is to explore
why this specificity, this simple detail, is important to Yeats's imagination, at least in this poem. This is one of Yeats's deservedly
most famous lyrics, and if we can discover some of the imaginative

relations among the many simple words in the poem (go, clay, nine, alone, peace, slow, night, day), we can begin to articulate the feeling that flows from it. In the end, the purpose is to describe how such simple mysterious words like "nine" are just as important in this poem as the more obviously important words like "alone" and "peace."

Writing Exercise for W. B. Yeats's "Leda and the Swan"

Mark Sanders
COLLEGE OF THE MAINLAND
TEXAS CITY, TEXAS

A BRIEF OVERVIEW

When we think about Yeats's "Leda and the Swan," our curiosity might be teased by his occultism, the automatic script, his gyres, his swan symbolism, or the myth to which the poem alludes. However, we might make the poem more intimately accessible and contemporary if we also view the poem as follows: One of the principles of Yeats's gyres is that the future is dependent upon the present; frequently enough, the bridge between the two makes way for the destruction of longstanding personal, cultural, or societal systems. Status quo is rocked, ceremonies dissolve, and new orders take tyrannical charge—but not without cost.

We do not live insular, private lives. Every act—large or small—produces innumerable effects. Certainly, we do not ascertain readily all the effects, and we sometimes choose or fail to look beyond the immediacy of an act. If we throw a rock into a pond, we take pleasure in the explosion we created; however, we may overlook the remaining subsequent actions: the leaves that ride the waves, the concentric ripples, the splashing and gurgling of water upon the reedy bank. And what of the deep effects? What did we disturb in the muddy depths? What, besides the peace of calm water, did we destroy?

We are taught that we are created in God's image. God is the Creator, and, because we are like God, we create too. Yet how often do we perceive God as Destroyer? In "Leda and the Swan," God transforms into a swan, a creature both beautiful and beastly. When God rapes Leda, his act of willful aggression, his assertion of power, it is a god-act. Ironically, the act is resultant from a creative energy that destroys Leda's peace and calm. We are made to wonder, then, about our own place in the world. Leda's world is our world; it is the quiet pond. And someone, perhaps ourselves, is preparing to throw a rock. A god-act is about to happen.

Let us not, however, minimize "Leda and the Swan" as merely a cause-effect poem. In the last two lines, "did she put on his knowledge with his power / Before the indifferent beak could let her drop?" Yeats burdens Leda with a moral dilemma that all humans must share. To be human is to possess knowledge. We claim superiority over all other beasts because we think and know beyond instinct. To be created in God's image is to share not just physical characteristics but to reflect God's knowledge. Because Leda has had intimate contact with God, she should have acquired a greater portion of God's knowledge and power. Mythologically, she has "married" God and is privy to all that God has. If God is omnipotent and can change and create, then Leda—as well as all of us—is able to know and to change and create.

But what does Leda know? How does she choose to handle the burden of knowledge? She must know that passion is not necessarily an unthinking emotion. She must know the miracle that has occurred to her, that God, despite his violence, has shown her favor. Because she possesses God's omnipotence, she must know the outcome of aggression and passion. Metaphorically, what she conceives is "the broken wall, the burning roof and tower / And Agamemnon dead," not the twin daughters who, in their times of passion and aggression, bring these images of destruction to pass. Leda is not just the mother of Helen and Clytemnestra, she is also the mother of the end of a civilization. She knows this. If she possesses God's power to change and to create, as Yeats questions, she faces a tremendous moral crisis. If she is able to change history, to keep her children from their future violence, why does she not? Why does she allow the violence to occur? Perhaps she chooses to worship her daughters rather than see the destruction that will arise from their birth. However, does this blind love constitute misuse of knowledge and power?

TOPICS FOR WRITING ASSIGNMENTS

1. What would you do if you were in Leda's place? You have been blessed and cursed with omniscience, and in your godly knowledge you see that a child of yours is going to be responsible for future destruction. A son will climb to the top of a bell tower on a university campus and kill a hundred people

with a high-powered rifle. This act will cause chaos and fear on campuses across the country, cost millions in litigation, produce fathomless grief for hundreds, and prompt related acts of violence. A daughter will poison the drinks of our government's leaders at a special fund-raiser, and all will die. The country will fall apart, and nationwide riots will ensue as the worst, filled with "passionate intensity" (Yeats, "The Second Coming"), maneuver for power. Another child will become a genius specializing in nuclear science, but he sells vital information and materials to terrorists who consequently blow up New York, Los Angeles, Tokyo, and Hong Kong. Millions die immediately, and the nuclear fallout and radiation will kill millions more. You see all this and know that without your intervention these events will occur. Just as you have godly knowledge, you also have godly power. You can change things. What will you do? Will you act against your unconditional love for your children or against the sanctity of your world? Explain your position.

2. Leda is not the only human to whom God showed favor. Her case, certainly, is a violent example, but other examples exist in New Testament stories. As described in Luke 1:27–38, the Virgin Mary is impregnated by the Holy Spirit. The visiting angel tells her that the child will be the Son of God and the savior of humanity. Mary has God's wisdom imparted to her, and she seems almost complacent with the knowledge. "I am the Lord's servant," Mary tells the angel. "May it be to me as you have said."

   However, she also understands the sacrifices involved. Prophecies she has heard speak of the Messiah's self-sacrifice for the sins of humankind, and Mary will live to see her own son crucified. If she had power, as we might suppose she did if Leda's example is parallel, she may have found a way to save Jesus from his death while still allowing him to absolve us from our sins. After all, others to whom God had appeared received power to change and to create. For example, in the Old Testament, God tells Noah about the impending destruction of the earth to divest it of evil humanity. In yet another example, God gives Moses the burden of freeing Israel. Both Noah and

Moses are given godly powers: Noah creates an ark that will not only hold all species of animals but withstand an earth-destroying storm; Moses parts the Red Sea, makes the heavens rain bread, and causes a variety of plagues to afflict Egypt. In the fifteenth century, God directed Joan of Arc to lead her army against the enemy despite her gender, societal norms, and limited military strength. The Oglala Sioux warrior Crazy Horse had a godly vision, too, enabling him to wage a successful countercampaign against the white cavalry. So long as he complies to vision's dictates, white men's bullets cannot harm him. Factually, the only harm he ever encountered was through the hands of his own people: Once, he was shot by a tribe member over a domestic matter; and, when he died at Fort Robinson, Indian guards held him while a white soldier bayoneted him.

Thus, if God remains present among us, either directly or indirectly in visions or dreams, we have access to a greater portion of God's knowledge and power. Sometimes, we are told that we have divine purposes on this earth, that we are called into God's service. Thinking about what you have seen in your own dreams or visions, or remembering what you have heard from the voices in your head (call these the voices of conscience, if you desire), what is your divine purpose in this world? If you have power to complete this purpose or to alter it, will you? How?

3. Let us say you have not been visited by God, that you have no inside, pragmatic knowledge of Leda's dilemma or of the burdens Mary, Noah, Moses, Joan of Arc, or Crazy Horse carried. However, your turn is coming. Let us say God will visit you, and God will favor you with knowledge and power. Like these other people, you will bear the cost of such knowledge and power, and you will have to sacrifice something valuable because God has favored you. You will lose your freedom, your family, your son or daughter, your respect from others, or your life. You can see the long-range effects, and this sacrifice will benefit many. Will you allow the sacrifice to occur or exercise the power to keep things as they are? If the sacrifice

only benefits a few people, will you allow the sacrifice to occur then?

4. If "Leda and the Swan" illustrates how private acts of violence create a wider spread of violence, consider this phenomenon in contemporary times. Argue these two points: One, do private acts of violence at home, as in cases of domestic abuse, create larger acts of violence in society?; two, if violence creates greater violence, and each subsequent violent act creates additional violence, how can we ever bring our world to peace?

5. Let us consider the sensuality of the poem. Passion is both frightening and tender, as Yeats suggests through the poem's language. Consider, too, the disparity between female and male sensibilities; once the passionate act is completed, the female wonders about the experience whereas the male is indifferent. Sensual experience does not have to be limited to sexuality, however; any experience that produces both frightening and pleasurable intense feeling is a sensual experience. Write about a number of specific sensual experiences that you have had, and perhaps consider the distinction of how women and men respond to those experiences.

Drama

Creating a Tragic Character

Mary Piering Hiltbrand
UNIVERSITY OF SOUTHERN COLORADO
PUEBLO, COLORADO

WRITING ASSIGNMENT

Choose a figure from contemporary life. This person may be someone from the world of entertainment, politics, athletics, performing arts, science, or academia. (No characters from literary works, please.) Write a thorough, well-organized, interesting essay in which you argue that this figure constitutes a tragic hero/heroine. Support any assertions that you make about this person with concrete examples of his or her actions or activities.

This assignment requires that students compose a definition/criteria match essay. I usually suggest that they construct paragraphs around each of the criteria for a tragic hero.

Students often pose the question, "How can I prove that this person is someone of high standing?" to which I respond, for example, "What is their status in the world of professional basketball?" Off they go to the library to look up some sports statistics. Without realizing it, they are performing two important academic skills: research and backing up assertions with proof.

The assignment also often leads to discussions of proximate versus more remote causes to identify what is the real tragic flaw. For example, is the promiscuous behavior of a certain professional athlete his tragic flaw, or is the underlying personality trait that causes that behavior the real flaw? This leads students to see that sometimes we must look further back to locate the real cause of a behavior and that oftentimes certain behaviors are simply symptoms of a bigger problem. (This is certainly a valuable and necessary skill in any discussion of contemporary social problems and thus has applicability to other disciplines.)

The assignment also reveals the importance of definitions. Though a rodeo rider who is now paralyzed as a result of a bull-riding accident may be deemed "tragic" by those about him, he probably doesn't meet the criteria of a tragic hero. (This can often be illustrated by pointing out recent high-profile legal cases [sexual harassment and police brutality] whose outcomes have depended upon just such clear application of specific legal criteria.)

Finally, students sometimes ask, "How does this person's behavior affect anyone but himself or herself?" I usually ask the student how he or she feels about this person. Frequently, the student replies that he or she no longer admires the athlete or actor, or whomever. Discussions of possible cause-effect relationships between the tawdry behavior of certain public figures and the pervasive climate of cynicism often ensue, sometimes leading students to decide that the behaviors of contemporary public figures, no matter how remote, may in fact still have some effect on ordinary people.

This assignment leads to lively class discussions whenever I share students' choices for tragic heroes/heroines. The choices are often unexpected and cause us to think about people in ways that we hadn't before. I, for example, have some difficulty in regarding Tonya Harding as a tragic heroine, but as one student commented, "Willy Loman isn't exactly a very attractive guy either!"

Breaking into
the Classics

Francie Kisko
SKAGIT VALLEY COMMUNITY COLLEGE,
SAN JUAN CENTER
FRIDAY HARBOR, WASHINGTON

An easy way to break students into the classics is to have them read the plays by Sophocles and Shakespeare aloud in class—with each student taking an active part. Those students who do not play an individual character might join in the role of the "chorus," or read stage directions. After the reading, a class discussion could lead to the basis for a term paper.

Sophocles' *Oedipus the King* and *Antigone*, for example, lend themselves nicely to development of either a compare-and-contrast essay or a cause-and-effect essay. Focusing in on Aristotle's *Poetics* and the fatal or "tragic flaw" theme, have the students write either a compare-and-contrast essay, comparing the steps that led to the reversal of fortune for King Oedipus and King Creon, or a cause-and-effect essay, again tracing the causes that led to either king's *peripeteia* (effect). This exercise could be expanded to include short fiction, such as Jack London's "To Build a Fire," or possibly John Cheever's "The Five-Forty-Eight." The students could even include an example from contemporary society—someone who has undergone a similar reversal of fortune due to his or her "tragic flaw."

In the case of the compare-and-contrast essay, the student would be working with more than one piece of literature, which would give the student practical experience at documenting more than one source and blending the ideas of different authors. For example, the student could write a point-by-point essay about *Oedipus the King* and "To Build a Fire" by comparing Oedipus' pride in his justice with "the man's" pride in his ability to withstand the cold, showing the steps by which each proceeded to his downfall. Each character receives warnings along the way (Oedipus from the chorus, and London's protagonist from the "old-timer"), which are great transitional pieces between each step. Or the student could write a block essay, telling first all the steps that led to Oedipus' downfall, followed by all the steps that led to "the man's" downfall, then concluding how the two stories were similar and how they were different.

Henrik Ibsen's *A Doll's House* is an example of a modern play that might be compared and contrasted with short fiction, such as William Faulkner's "Barn Burning." In each case, the protagonist goes through a rite of passage by stepping out of an old way of life into a new, unknown future.

Shakespeare's *Othello* is an especially effective piece when dealing with students of mixed ethnic backgrounds. It is the perfect springboard for launching into discussion and essays on prejudice (between sexes, economic classes, and the like, as well as races). The O. J. Simpson tragedy could be a contemporary example that could be used as a compare-and-contrast or cause-and-effect basis for an essay.

For a cause-and-effect essay, the student could trace the steps by which Othello's jealousy led him to the murder of his faithful wife, followed by a conclusion showing how jealousies and prejudices (between races, sexes, economic classes, and so on) can hurt innocent people. Likewise, the student could trace the causes for Nora's walking out on her husband and family in Ibsen's *A Doll's House*, that threshold decision (the effect), which could develop into an interesting essay. This could lead into a general discussion of how we tend to conform to other people's expectations of us. In each case, the student is exposed to some wonderful literature while learning the mechanics of college essay writing.

Writing Assignments on Plays

Argumentative Paper on *A Doll's House*

Al Capovilla
FOLSOM LAKE CENTER
FOLSOM, CALIFORNIA

GENERAL INFORMATION

You have been the family lawyer for the Helmers. In fact, you graduated from the same law school as Torvald. You have been a close family friend as long as Doctor Rank has been.

Torvald has come to you with a request. He tells you he wants to continue as bank manager in the small community, but he is fearful of gossip and scandal. Since Nora has left him, he had made up a story that she has simply gone out of town to take care of a sick aunt. He made up this lie to save his reputation.

Now, he wants you to contact Nora and have her come to your office so that he can try one more time to "talk" with her. He wants you to listen and to decide for him whether to file for legal divorce (charging Nora with child neglect and abandonment) or to try one more time for reconciliation by having Nora move back into the house. He will abide by your *written decision.*

You persuade Nora to come to your office. You listen as Nora and Torvald try to "talk" things out.

NORA AND TORVALD'S "TALK"

Torvald, you have never seriously communicated with me. You
leave me out of decisions. You don't
share your office problems with
me.

I don't think a husband should
constantly discuss the office problems with his wife. [You couldn't
possibly help me.]*

My father and you, Torvald,
have never let me express my opinions. Both of you treated me as a
doll. [I've lived by doing tricks for
you, Torvald. But that's the way
you wanted it. You and Daddy did
me a great wrong.]

It's an exaggeration, Nora!
[You loved me as a wife should love
her husband. It was simply that you
didn't have the experience to judge
what was the best way of going
about things. But do you think I
love you any the less for that; just
because you don't know how to act
on your own responsibility? No, no,
you just lean on me, I shall give you
all the advice and guidance you
need. I wouldn't be a proper man if I
didn't find a woman doubly attractive for being so obviously helpless.]

Note: * [indicates lines taken verbatim from play]

Give me a chance, Torvald! [If I'm ever to reach any understanding of myself and the things around me, I must learn to stand alone. That's why I can't stay here with you any longer.] I'm going to lean on my inner self for once!

Inner self? You are going to [leave your home, your husband, and your children? Don't you care what people will say?]

[Listen, Torvald, from what I've heard, when a wife leaves her husband's house as I am doing now, he is absolved by law of all responsibility for her. I can free you from all responsibility . . . There must be full freedom on both sides.]

Your definition of freedom doesn't fit mine, Nora. [This is outrageous! You are betraying your most sacred duty.] Have you forgotten your marriage duties as a wife and mother! [Surely you are clear about your position in your own home? Haven't you an infallible guide in questions like these? Haven't you your religion?]

Torvald, don't drag religion into this. [I have another duty equally sacred. . . . My duty to myself . . . I am an individual, just as much as you are or at least I'm going to try to be.]

YOUR TASK

You have heard both sides of the "talk." In a way the format is like an argumentative paper.

Now, it is your task to write a short decision. Use the format of an argumentative paper. You may select words from Nora and Torvald's "talk" and any other significant lines from the play to support your decision paper. Show both sides of the argument.

Conclude your paper with your recommendation. What do you recommend under the circumstances—legal divorce or a try at reconciliation?

Spatial Imagery in Ibsen's *A Doll's House;* or, Nora in a Box

Beverly E. Schneller
MILLERSVILLE UNIVERSITY
MILLERSVILLE, PENNSYLVANIA

One of the more interesting aspects of Henrik Ibsen's drama is his use of spatial imagery. When I teach *A Doll's House*, I focus a large measure of the class discussion on stage movement, props and scenery, and the symbolic uses of space in the play. In the first class period, discussion of the drama is concentrated on the rich opening stage description of the house decorated for Christmas and the several doors that Ibsen mentions as common, of course, to city houses. In particular, there is the door to Torvald's study that serves to symbolically separate him from the family's main rooms, from Nora, and from the life of the house itself. With Helmer in his study for large parts of the play, Ibsen underscores his isolation from his family and the theme of the failure of communication between spouses. As the class continues to discuss *A Doll's House*, we look for images of boxes and doors and other kinds of barriers that divide the characters. We also watch scenes from the Jane Fonda and Claire Bloom videotaped productions and discuss the details of set decoration. At this point, because the students see that the play has been slightly altered for film (especially in the Fonda version wherein a new scene is added at the beginning about Nora and Mrs. Linde's past), I also have the opportunity to discuss the work of the dramaturge.

After we have begun discussion of the play, which takes usually a little more than a week, the students write their first papers on the use of spatial imagery using the following diagram:

Dr. Rank	Nora Helmer	T. Helmer
Mr. Krogstad		Mrs. Linde

I write this on the board and ask them to develop a thesis and discussion around this spatial representation of the characters' relationships to one another. Students who might be familiar with *Hedda Gabler* may note the similarity in character relations between the two plays, as Ibsen also places Hedda in a boxed-in situation that she, of course, cannot escape.

In addition to looking for images of enclosure in *A Doll's House*, we also search the text for images of freedom; students then go on to discuss in small groups their responses to Nora's decision to strike out on her own at the end of the play. I again direct their attention to Ibsen's use of imagery and add to that a concentration on his language, asking students if Ibsen creates different voices for each character. In their second writing assignment of *A Doll's House*, students are asked to compare and contrast the character of Nora with another character from the play focusing on plot lines, dialogue, images that surround them, and their stage movements.

Responses to the spatial relations paper are generally quite thorough, and students seem surprised at how many images of enclosure they locate: the doors, the windows, the letters, the letter box (with its lid enclosing the fateful letters), for instance. Some student writers also contrast the squareness of the house with the spinning of Nora in the tarantella to describe her as something like a projectile going through the roof. Usually the students see the confinement of Nora extending through the appearance of the house and its architecture, onto her associations in the play, and into the language itself; for, it is not until the climax of the play that she and Torvald actually communicate, and their communication results in their final separation.

At the end of the drama unit (which also includes the reading of *Oedipus, Othello,* and *Hamlet*), I test the students comprehensively. Among the essay questions I have developed on *A Doll's House* are: If Nora returns, what do you see happening in the Helmer household?

How realistic does the action of the play seem to you, that is, could you see yourself or someone you know experiencing a similar situation? Would it be possible for *A Doll's House* to occur in any other setting or at any other time? Or, I ask a compare-and-contrast question involving Ibsen's debt to classical drama to Shakespeare in his use of the tragic plot.

Questions to Help Community College Students Read *A Doll's House*

Karen Locke
LANE COMMUNITY COLLEGE
EUGENE, OREGON

Our literature courses at Lane Community College are writing-intensive. I apply this method by assigning essays, short or long, in addition to exams. I also require a journal that is written primarily out of class; the students may also add or revise entries after class discussion. For the journal, I provide questions that are designed to enhance critical thinking as well as reading, studying, and class discussion; some journal entries may simply be immediate reactions to the play. Depending on my whim in any particular term, the following questions may be used by the students individually for their journals, in small group work before the general discussion begins, or for general discussion. These questions may be assigned individually or as part of a list of several.

- In what ways does *A Doll's House* seem to apply to life today?

- Is it in any way dated?

- Is the play valuable only as it depicts life in the nineteenth century in Norway, or does it still tell us something about life today?

- Could there be a Nora or a Torvald in the United States today? (The possibilities for this one are probably obvious: the students immediately offer true-to-life Noras and Torvalds right here in Eugene.)

I am interested in feminist criticism, and I teach a course titled Images of Women and Men in Literature, which explores the links among social roles, stereotypes, and literary images; *A Doll's House* fits well into this course. I tend to teach *A Doll's House* from the same viewpoint when I use the play in my Introduction to Drama class as well. We talk about Ibsen's statement that the play is not about women's rights but rather is about human rights. We try to determine whether or not there can be any difference between the two. I ask the students to look up three terms: feminist, humanist, and egalitarian. This exercise can be quite enlightening for some students.

We also explore the historical and cultural aspects of the play, which naturally leads to the expected roles of the era and social position of the characters. In this vein, we try to determine whether or not Torvald is a sympathetic character, and we discuss how realistically Nora is portrayed. Students tend to have more sympathy for Nora, of course; but there are those who find her to be so scatterbrained that they doubt her transformation, and these same students sometimes believe Torvald is misunderstood and unduly rejected at the end. A reminder of willing suspension of disbelief and of the convention of larger-than-life character fits in well at this point in the discussion.

Character in
A Doll's House

Cindy Milwe
SANTA MONICA HIGH SCHOOL
SANTA MONICA, CALIFORNIA

When *A Doll's House* debuted in 1879, audiences were shocked by Nora's traumatic awakening. When I first taught the play in 1992, I was shocked that my fourteen-year-olds so easily connected to its rather adult themes. Obviously, high school students can't yet speak of marriage from experience, but they do understand the nature of power (or a perceived lack thereof), and the ways in which we are supposed to act, based on familial or societal conventions.

Nora's issues are the issues of any young person in the process of becoming an independent adult, which makes the play appropriate for students of all ages. I have taught *A Doll's House* to high school freshmen and seniors, and know it would work just as well in any "Introduction to Literature," "Writing about Literature," or "Critical Thinking and Writing" class on the college level.

Teenagers relate to the idea of feeling trapped (in their case, within the confines of home and/or school) and are also trying desperately to figure out who they are supposed to be in their budding romantic endeavors. Students enjoy discussing (and eventually writing about) the play's many issues: the expectations of romantic love and marriage; the role of the mother and father in child-rearing; the nature of divorce; the idea of freedom for both sexes; the possible conflict between personal growth and the responsibilities of family; the gender roles played by men and women in emotional, sexual, and financial relationships; and the morality of lying for a good cause.

Before I teach any play or novel, I try to introduce it first (if necessary) in its historical context and then in terms of theme (preferably with a short story, poem, or essay). For *A Doll's House*, I begin with a look at "Girl," by Jamaica Kincaid, and a discussion of the assumptions made by people in power, regardless of the relationship (mother/daughter in this case). "Girl" prepares students for *A Doll's House* by getting them to think about the gender roles we learn as children and the kinds of authority imposed upon us by family or society. The girl in Kincaid's piece is silenced by her mother's power over her, and commanded not to grow up to be "the slut [she's] so bent on becoming." Nora is silenced by the conventions of her time, and by her husband's rigid morality. The imperative nature of Kincaid's piece also works nicely with the implied imperative of the play—that Nora must leave to grow up.

WRITING ASSIGNMENT

In order to write good essays, students must thoroughly analyze the play and use elements of persuasion in their writing—that's why I teach this play at the end of the year, when students have become familiar with some basic techniques of composition: analysis, argumentation, persuasion, and comparison/contrast. The play lends itself to any of these. The following are the prompts I assign:

- Compare and contrast the characters of Nora and Torvald: How does their "doll's house" serve them differently? How does each contribute to the world of illusion that they have created? Why does their masquerade work for as long as it does? Is the Helmer household—the "doll's house"—Nora's, as the possessive implies, or Torvald's? Who has the power in this family and why?

- Using examples from the play, answer the following question: "Does intending to 'do good' make a crime less severe?" Compare and contrast Nora's and Torvald's points of view on this issue. Was Nora justified in forging Torvald's signature, lying to her husband, and leaving her family after eight years of marriage? Is it possible to live by Torvald's strict moral code? How do their moral consciences collide?

To take students through the process of writing an essay, I usually have them complete the following steps:

- Write a free-form response to one of the prompts (students share these in groups so that they can hear other insights).

- Create a working thesis, which we discuss.

- Find examples from the play to support the ideas in the thesis and analyze accordingly.

- Make a rough outline.
- Write a first draft.
- Edit twice (in pairs): once for content and once for mechanics.
- Turn in final draft.

Reader-Response Analysis

Michael Matthews
TARRANT COUNTY JUNIOR COLLEGE
FORT WORTH, TEXAS

The experiences you bring to a text sensitize you to certain parts and desensitize you to other parts. Only you know what influences shape your reading of a text. Reading is an act of co-creation; when you read, you and the author create a text known only to you. Thus, by analyzing your particular reading of a text, you shed a unique light on it and learn to know yourself and the text better.

WRITING ASSIGNMENT

Write a reader-response analysis of Arthur Miller's *Death of a Salesman* (or any of the assigned plays). In your paper, identify the parts of the text to which you either respond positively or negatively. Then tell what personal influences cause those responses.

PROCESS

1. Mark passages in the text to which you have strong positive or negative responses (intellectual and/or emotional).

2. For each marked passage, write notes about why you respond that way (your immediate circumstances; your memories of previous texts, classes, people, and similar or different experiences; your attitudes and values about politics, religion, economics, families, marriage, parenting, ageism, sexism, and human nature).

3. Review the marked passages and your notes to identify recurring influences that affect your responses.

4. Select a major influence (or a series of related influences) that shape your responses.

5. Write an essay with an **introduction** that describes the text

and the major influence that affects your reading of the text; a **body** with three to five paragraphs that includes (a) supporting quotations from the text, (b) facts, examples, and narratives that influence your reading, and (c) connections between the text and the influence; and a **conclusion** that tells what you learned from this whole process.

FORMAT

Double-space your manuscript. Do not use a cover sheet; instead, put your name and the date at the top of each page and number pages at the bottom beginning with page two. Beneath the title on page one, write "Audience," and identify a specific reader or readers for the paper. The title should both describe the paper and interest readers in it.

In the essay, after quotations and references to specific passages, use parenthetical citations. Each citation should include the relevant page numbers of the work cited (142). If the author is not identified, also include the author's last name (Miller 1650). Use a hyphen to indicate a continuous sequence of pages (1652–53).

Using the following format, attach a "Works Cited" page that includes the primary source and any secondary sources that you use.

Miller, Arthur. *Death of a Salesman. Literature: An Introduction to Fiction, Poetry, and Drama.* Ed. X.J. Kennedy and Dana Gioia. 7th ed. New York: Longman, 1999. 1636–1706.

EVALUATION

Your paper should link influences in your life to parts of the text. Write about the text in present tense. With first-person "I" for present attitudes, beliefs, concerns, and situations, use present tense; but when reporting past experiences, use past tense.

Your grade will be determined by how well you:

1. Describe the text and quote its most relevant passages;

2. Include facts and report specific experiences that influence your response; and

3. Draw connections between the text and influences in your life.

Student Essay

The Suicidal Mind

Nancy Densmore
TARRANT COUNTY JUNIOR COLLEGE,
FORT WORTH, TEX

(Audience: People Curious about Suicidal Thinking)

In Arthur Miller's play *Death of a Salesman*, Willy Loman, a frustrated failure, makes a grave decision. He decides to commit suicide. Willy recognizes no alternative if he wants to improve the lives of those he loves. He earnestly believes that he has no value to his family beyond the twenty-thousand dollar insurance settlement payable upon his death. Americans enjoying good mental health do not consider suicide a rational or honorable solution to problems. Only someone who has dwelt in the bowels of major depression can understand the seeming logic, necessity, and even beauty of taking one's own life. I am that person. Along with Willy, I have lived in a twilight world where self-doubt and hopelessness are unceasing companions and where despair envelopes one even on a good day. The bond I share with Willy can be likened unto that of a terminally ill patient to whom death would be a sweet release.

Death of a Salesman opens up with Willy arriving home utterly exhausted after yet another unsuccessful sales trip. His wife, aware of the escalating number of suspicious auto accidents, fears that he has had another and asks if perhaps he isn't feeling well. Willy responds:

> I am tired to the death. I couldn't make it. I just couldn't make it, Linda. . . . The car kept going off the shoulder, y'know? . . . I'm—I can't seem to—keep my mind to it. (1637–38)

Willy feels depleted by all the wasted effort involved in a lifelong attempt to succeed. He is past sixty with nothing to show for his life except failed expectations concerning both his sons and career. Willy has not even remained faithful to his wife. He is overwhelmed by his decay; the turmoil in his mind blocks the concentration he needs for driving his car.

I see these auto mishaps as passive suicide attempts and can find parallels in my own life. Three years ago, my husband and I sought therapy to repair our relationship. We knew that our marriage was cracking but not that it had shattered into irretrievable pieces. Almost as a bonus, I learned that I was a chronic alcoholic. The next year consisted of marital and individual counseling, periods of sobriety, and ever-worsening relapses. Like Willy, my life appeared to be a series of failures to achieve what I most wanted. Willy Loman wanted his sons and his career to prosper; I wanted to restore my marriage and maintain long-term sobriety. A lifetime of chemical dependency coupled with twelve years of vegetating as a homemaker left me few, if any, marketable skills. I was stuck.

Suicide became an increasingly attractive and alluring prospect. Like Willy, I believed it was the logical path to follow. I understand Willy when he told Linda, "I have such thoughts, I have such strange thoughts" (1638). For Willy, it was driving off the road. I experienced compelling fantasies of driving into bridge supports whenever I was alone in my car. The closest I came to a car wreck was when I would drive down the freeway with my eyes closed. But I was never able to overcome the fear of crashing, surviving, and being left a helpless cripple. In my twisted mind, dying was desirable, but living as a paraplegic was intolerable. Abandoning this practice, I moved on to the next step: mixing alcohol and prescription drugs. Surely my death would be ruled an accidental overdose. After all, wasn't I participating in marital therapy, receiving individual counseling, taking antidepressants, going to church, attending AA, preparing to return to college, raising my children, running a household, reading self-help books—and telling everyone to have a nice day? No one would think I was suicidal. Just as Willy continued to go to work and run off the road, I worked at recovery while desperately seeking a way to die without leaving an obvious legacy of suicide to my sons.

Willy toys with another approach to suicide. Suspicious, Linda seeks help from her sons. She tells them that an insurance adjuster has evidence that Willy's car wrecks were intentional. She reports finding a rubber tube:

> There's a little attachment on the end of it. I knew right away. And sure enough, on the bottom of the water heater there's a new little nipple on the gas pipe. (1663)

With this act, Willy begins to take a more active role in his suicide. A car running off the road can be ruled an accident. A man's death from inhaling gas through a hose will be considered purposeful. Willy is anxious for a solution. He says, "The woods are burning, boys, you understand? There's a big blaze going on all around. I was fired today" (1688). In his mind, he can feel the hot tongue of the flames that encircle him. The flames are fueled by the wreckage of his failed life and doomed career. Supposedly he is a salesman whose gift of gab is his economic lifeline. He declares:

> I was fired. . . . the gist of it is that I haven't got a story left in my head, Biff. So don't give me a lecture about faces and aspects. I am not interested. (1688–89)

Willy's flirtation with the gas pipe shows how urgent the need to die has become. I, too, felt a similar necessity and urgency. I hadn't been able to wreck a car, and years of mixing alcohol and drugs had left me immune to lethal overdoses. It was time for me, like Willy, to go beyond the hopeful accident stage and seek a more overt method of suicide. Out came the razor blades. No longer would I pretend that my death would be judged an accident. Slashing my wrists would be a dead giveaway that I was not happy. I experimented by making small practice cuts to determine the best procedure. Should I slice horizontally, from side to side? How about tracing a vein lengthwise from wrist to elbow? What about timing? I didn't want my sons at home when I did it. Thoughts like these whipped through my fevered mind like a whirlwind. Like Willy, I was under much pressure. I was back in school after an absence of fourteen years. Having completed the Summer I session, I took English Composition II in Summer II. People told me I was crazy to take it in the summer. I had to hide my smile; what did they know about being crazy?

Unlike Willy, who definitely had the desire and courage to die, I was still unsure and scared. I had been sober for a while, but I reasoned that if I were to die I might as well enjoy my weekend. Thinking that the alcohol would give me the courage I needed to go through with it, I went sunbathing early the next day. I began drinking on the deck and continued as the sun crossed the sky. During the afternoon I went into a blackout. To an observer I must have appeared drunk, but aware and functioning. Unfortunately, once in a blackout, the drinker has no memory of events occurring during that period. One can't look at a drunk and determine that a blackout is happening. For someone in this condition, rational thought ceases to exist. At some point during that blackout, I went inside my house and slashed both my arms from wrist to elbow.

Willy abandoned the gas pipe idea, but not the suicide. The lure of the money was too strong. He told himself:

> What a proposition, ts, ts. Terrific, terrific. . . . Remember it's a guaranteed twenty-thousand-dollar proposition. . . . Oh, Ben, that's the whole beauty of it! (1699)

In Willy's mind his brother tells him, "It's called a cowardly thing [to do]." Willy replies, "Why, Does it take more guts to stand here the rest of my life ringing up a zero?" (1699). Willy is out of time, choices, and energy. Suicide becomes "the only way" (1699). Willy loses his will to live and does not recover it. I was luckier. Even in a blackout, after slashing my wrists, I still had something inside me that rejected death. Without alerting anyone, I drove myself to the hospital. Several hours later in the intensive care unit, I came out of my blackout. I was still alive.

My first reading of *Death of a Salesman* came after I had begun contemplating suicide. I very much identified with Willy's struggle. I envied what I thought was his courage in taking his own life. At that time I didn't view the play as a tragedy: I sincerely believed it had a happy ending. After all, Willy died, and the family collected the cash. I was very sick, and like countless others, I truly did not understand just how sick I was. Feeling a connection with Willy Loman reminds me of Luke Skywalker shuddering when he touches the Dark Side of the Force. I have seen my own dark side and know how powerful it is. People who have never lived through a severe depression can empathize but can never understand the horror of having their own mind become their worst enemy. Logic is lost, and bizarre fantasy can become reality. Two years after my suicide attempt, I no longer suffer from the depression I once had. I have a measure of sanity, serenity, and sobriety in my life. I now realize that *Death of a Salesman* does not have a happy ending but that perhaps my life will.

WORK CITED

Miller, Arthur. *Death of a Salesman. Literature: An Introduction to Fiction, Poetry, and Drama.* Ed. X.J. Kennedy and Dana Gioia. 7th ed. New York: Longman, 1999. 1636–1706.

Making Decisions:
Arthur Miller's
Death of a Salesman

Mary Alice Morgan
MERCER UNIVERSITY
MACON, GEORGIA

When I first began teaching this play twenty years ago, students were quick to discern Miller's critique of a capitalist ethic that defines a person's success in terms of wealth and status. They were also likely to see Willy's persistence in his job as heroic, though misguided. In this age of corporate downsizing, today's students are more likely to dismiss or condemn Willy for not dusting off his resumé, retraining, and changing careers to suit marketplace demands. Some feel he was a chump for not being more "entrepreneurial" like Ben. To encourage students to historicize the play and their own late-twentieth-century responses, I give the following two-part assignment.

CLASS DISCUSSION #1

Analyze Willy Loman's reasons for becoming a salesman and for persisting in his job despite his lack of success. What was his ultimate goal in life? Who or what is responsible for his downfall?

Given this open-ended question, some students will offer the critique of Willy I just described, and others will explain or "defend" Willy's actions. I let students discuss these issues generally for ten to fifteen minutes and then give them more specific study questions to consider for the next class period. I allow them to divide themselves into three small groups that focus on different aspects of Willy's character and career. They are to locate scenes and passages that pertain to their questions.

CLASS DISCUSSION #2—
TAKE A SECOND LOOK AT WILLY

Psychological Reasons

Why does Willy become a salesman in the first place? How does he feel about his job? Why doesn't he quit and do something else? What careers might he be better suited to? (This category allows students to think about why Willy went into selling rather than pursuing the building and craftsmanship that he loves. It also allows them to discuss Willy's psychological denial of his failure.)

Historical/Cultural Reasons

What kinds of jobs were available for a man of Willy's education and background during the time period of the play? Typically, how often did workers change jobs or move during the period? What is Willy's ambition in life or whom does he want to emulate? (Here students focus on the movement to a market and service economy as well as the theme of the American Dream. They also discuss the figures of Dave Singleman and Ben Loman as Willy's icons of success.)

Gender Reasons

To what degree is Willy driven to fulfill his notion of his proper role as a man, both in his job and in his marital and sexual life? Are his notions of manhood idiosyncratic or cultural? (Students in this group examine the importance of Willy's definitions of manhood in motivating his career choice and motivating his infidelity. Because Linda encourages Willy not to take a risk by going with Ben to Alaska but to stick with his job in New York, this question also allows students to examine the gender dynamics of the play.)

After students have had a chance to share their ideas in small groups, they bring their findings and analysis back to the large group for discussion. During this second discussion, students often discover that initially, they took Miller's play out of historical context and that they oversimplified the complex forces driving Willy toward his tragic end. They then use this second discussion as the springboard for the writing assignment that follows. This is the critical thinking assignment that encourages students to use what Martha Nussbaum calls "narrative imagination" (*Cultivating Humanity: A*

Classical Defense of Reform in Liberal Education, [Cambridge: Harvard UP, 1997]). That is, students are asked to combine careful examination of the text with rigorous self-examination.

WRITING ASSIGNMENT

Compare and contrast a major decision you have made or are in the process of making to Willy Loman's decision to remain a salesman. Two obvious choices might be your decision where to attend college or your decision about a major. Are such decisions easily made? Easily changed after the fact? Can one be fully aware of the factors influencing one's decision? In particular, examine the ways in which gender, your own historical or cultural circumstances, or your own personality influenced or might influence your decision.

At the end of your comparison/contrast, please address the following questions:

1. Having gone through our class discussions and your own self-examination, discuss whether you feel more compassionate toward Willy Loman and why.

2. Discuss whether you have come to an important insight about life decisions as a result of reading this play.

The essays generated by this assignment are quite varied. Some students will produce a "strong reading" in which they argue against Miller's portraying Willy as a tragic hero; they find Willy pitiable, but not heroic. Other students will come to a new understanding of hitherto unconscious factors guiding their own decision-making. Others come to a new appreciation of their parents' commitment to their jobs.

Casting *Othello*

Janet Eber
COUNTY COLLEGE OF MORRIS
RANDOLPH, NEW JERSEY

Shakespeare is surely the most formidable writer students face in our Freshman Composition II course. His language seems so remote from what they normally read that the majority become discouraged and disinterested. The difficulties are compounded with a play like *Othello* because the title character himself seems both distant and unsympathetic. One student, in our first class session on the play, threw up her hands and wailed "Why do we need to read about a jealous nut who murders his silly wife?" I replied that the work was one of the world's great tragedies, then instantly regretted so pat and pompous an answer that could only widen the chasm between the class's perception of the play and my own. "Who *is* he, anyway?" asked a voice in the back row. "You tell me," I challenged, then proceeded to ask the class how they saw Othello: tall or short, lithe or muscular, rugged or soft? Answers came slowly. We moved to Iago. What did he look like? Could they perhaps describe him in terms of a popular contemporary actor? Did Desdemona remind them of a particular actress? Did Emilia? Cassio? Before they knew it they had cast the play guided by the play itself, those very words that had been inaccessible at the beginning of the period. They quoted dialogue, description, defended their choices, disputed the merits of this or that actor. All they had to go on was the play, and they soon learned the rewards of close reading. I was little more than a moderator, joining in only when invited, because this was all their call; they were in control.

Some choices were traditional. They insisted that an African American play Othello, so James Earl Jones was their first suggestion. Even now he gets a number of votes, though in the past couple of years Denzel Washington has become the favorite. Actors ranging from Michael Keaton to Danny DeVito have been cast as Iago. By the character's own admission he lacks "beauty," and the students examine his soliloquies carefully before they make a final choice.

Someone once suggested Richard Gere, but in one voice the class voted him down; "too pretty," they said. He'd make a better Cassio.

Desdemona is harder to cast. Does she really need to be blonde, as she is often traditionally portrayed? Not according to some students who see Julia Roberts's strength and vulnerability as crucial to the role. Even Emilia inspires discussion, the most novel suggestion (pretty well substantiated, actually) being Cher.

The real point here is that students must make all recommendations based solely on the text and their own interpretations. I guide but do not impose my thoughts on them. The exercise is also fairly short, taking about a half hour. I've used it for years now and always with success. It breaks down that wall of resistance students often erect to protect themselves from great literature and also initiates a lively dialogue from which all benefit.

Virtue in *Othello*

Allen Ramsey
CENTRAL MISSOURI STATE UNIVERSITY
WARRENSBURG, MISSOURI

Othello is an excellent literature choice for generating freshman compositions because its plot is familiar and direct. Students understand the play's thematic thrust: Jealousy is self evident. The challenge is in expanding understanding to the less evident themes and plot devices. Lectures on Renaissance milieu can fill in some of the void, but these sessions quickly pall, and they do not do much to enhance perceptive essays. An approach that I have taken is a brief exploration of virtue and vice in the play, which leads to essay topics related to human virtues and vices. This assignment can be condensed and improvised, but I will describe the topics as I have used them at one time or another.

Perhaps because of relative ethics, we seem to be losing the sense of what the virtues are. Some brainstorming is possible, listing them on the chalkboard. I have also cited the twelve Aristotelian virtues as a matter of expediency. In either case, temperance (the mean between either extreme, "the golden mean") and magnanimity (the combination of the other eleven virtues) are valuable concepts to introduce early.

A virtue that students normally overlook in preliminary discussion is *self-control*, an idea that must be introduced by the instructor. This topic can open new insights about the play and give some direction to character analysis.

Self-control is a virtue attributable to civilization. It is a trait that allegedly sets people above the animals, giving them the control to eat enough but not too much; to compete, but to win and lose gracefully; to dress tastefully, not like a fop. Self-control is so important that civilized society has established numerous conventions surrounding the virtue.

Courting is an example. It requires a man to restrain his urges until a series of conventions are completed—introductions, public exposure, proposal, and so forth. (Cf. Juliet's reaction from the balcony: "I have no joy of this contract to-night, / It is too rash, too unadvis'd, too sudden" 2.2.117–18.) Control is proper to gentle people and requires the privileged classes to be a model for the underprivileged.

The irony (and interest) of this topic is in the specter Iago presents. Iago is a model of self-control, so that virtue is turned on its head. He reasons his way through a plan to destroy Othello, and he patiently waits for the right moment to strike. He comes from Venice, where wit easily gives way to deceit. Italy is the land of Machiavelli. The jarring point in this play, then, is that the person who possesses the virtue of self-control is the villain. Iago's villainy is unnerving partly because we can easily see ourselves in him. As we strive to be sophisticated, suave, or mature, we gain cunning in methods of exploiting others.

The opposite of self-control is impulsivity, a term that brings to mind the character of Othello. Othello is the magnanimous person. He is controlled and generous as he faces down Brabantio in court and explains that he did indeed court Desdemona, albeit secretly. Desdemona loves him for his worldliness, but a kind of worldliness that contrasts with that of Iago. The two characters portray similar traits, but their actions make the rules of society a formula for tragedy. In a handout the principals sort out as follows:

Self-Control vs. Impulsivity

Othello the Moor	*Iago the Italian*
Worldly—as a soldier	Worldly as a city person
Self controlled—as a military man	Self controlled as a schemer
Impulsive in matters of love	Cynical in matters of love
Virtuous in being naive ("primitive")	Evil in being sophisticated
Evil in being impulsive	Evil in being self-controlled

[I have worked through parts of this approach at various times in order to deal with primitivism, the term that I think best explains

Othello's condition. Primitivism is a virtue—because those who have not been corrupted by civilization retain the purity they are born with. Othello is virtuous in being primitive. The term resonates with meaning today, with our interest in our respective ethnic backgrounds. If we can appreciate a simpler, purer past, we may learn something about what our civilization is doing to us today. Yet, we should be aware that returning to our past can permit the prejudice of others to destroy us.]

This review of virtue offers several choices for writing assignments. If one were to teach *Hamlet,* too, Hamlet's urgent desire to be impulsive, but his maturity to be self-controlled, provides some material for a compare/contrast assignment (I have never done this). With *Othello*, the virtues can spin off of the play (fidelity/infidelity; honesty; jealousy; self-control; compassion; fair play; honor). Renaissance values can be contrasted with our own (pride, modesty, worldliness, chastity, submissiveness to one's husband). Or, these traits can be considered subjectively as topics for analysis or as sources of expressive writing.

Cruising with Woody Allen, or Writing Assignment #7,896,909

Louis Phillips
SCHOOL OF VISUAL ARTS
NEW YORK CITY

> Sports to me is like music. It's completely satisfying. There were times I would sit at a game with the old Knicks and think to myself in the fourth quarter, this is everything the theatre should be and isn't. There's an outcome that's unpredictable. The audience is not ahead of the dramatists. The drama is ahead of the audience.
>
> —Woody Allen
> *The New Yorker (June 6, 1994)*

Sure, we could go on forever writing and rewriting the same old themes—for example, comparing and contrasting old man Oedipus with foolish man Samson in the Book of Judges (they both have lives influenced by riddles, both have terrible tempers, both have sexual relations with the wrong woman, both end up blind in order to see the necessary tragic content of life, both die in exile), but suppose for now we take another tack (using tact) and concentrate a bit upon the structure of some of the plays included in this collection. Let's cruise with Woody Allen.

Given the choice, most persons on any given night would rather watch a sports event than a play (if you don't believe me, compare Public Television's *American Playhouse* ratings with the ratings for any major basketball, football, or baseball game). Why are sports more compelling than plays? Or are they? Do we root for Nora to walk out and slam the door the same way we root for our favorite team to win a game?

Do you agree or disagree with Woody Allen's notions about theater? For example, he believes basketball to be superior drama because the outcome is unpredictable. Think about the plays you have studied. How predictable were the outcomes? Could it not be true that one of the elements of drama is predictability—the inevitability of the outcome? How soon in reading *Oedipus Rex*, for example, do you know that Oedipus has murdered his father and has married his mother? Isn't the outcome of that play certain in the audience's mind long before the drama is played out? Greek audiences, of course, knew the stories before they ever entered the tragic festivals, but does such knowledge, not altogether forbidden, destroy the "fun" of theater-going or play reading? Isn't it obvious that Othello's jealousy is going to destroy his marriage?

Are surprise endings better drama than non-surprise endings? Oedipus goes off stage and blinds himself. Were you surprised? Was the dramatist ahead of you? Were you surprised that Hamlet died?

What does Woody Allen mean by the notion of the audience being ahead of the dramatist or the dramatist being ahead of the audience? Apply that notion to any play you have read. In *Hamlet*, how far ahead of us is Shakespeare? How did the playwright get so far ahead?

And, while we are lobbing questions for themes about, like so many life-consuming hand grenades, why not consider the repeatability of plays? Think how many times you could see or read *Hamlet*, *Death of a Salesman*, or *Oedipus the King*. How many times do we reread a mystery—a literary form whose endings most often depend upon a surprise? How many times will a sports fan sit through the replay of a contest whose ending is already known? Perhaps, true drama transcends the idea of an ending. Perhaps, true drama echoes, not on the bare stage or the hardwood floor, but in our heads—is that not true for sports as well?

EXTRA CREDIT

Imagine a society that preferred theater to sporting events. Would it be a "better" society than the one we are living in now? Why does Woody Allen persist in creating movies?

Literary and Extraliterary Devices in *The Glass Menagerie*

Gary A. Richardson
MERCER UNIVERSITY
MACON, GEORGIA

Like many freshman literature anthologies, *Literature: An Introduction to Fiction, Poetry, and Drama*'s generic progression allows instructors to hearken back to earlier discussions of fiction and poetry to explain elements of a specific play. In addition, late in a term such structure provides the opportunity to have students begin interrogating the very structure of knowledge they have been procuring. In the process, students begin to develop their own, more-conscious literary aesthetics by recognizing that the formal markers of genre may be less definite than they first appear, that exceptions to general rules often define the greatest art, and that art and imagination are often at odds with a rigid critical disposition. In addition, the mostly chronological organization of *Literature: An Introduction to Fiction, Poetry, and Drama*'s drama section makes it a simple matter to show how playwrights have often evidenced this recognition by writing in response to what they perceived as the narrow theatrical conventions of the day. *The Glass Menagerie* is a particularly apt play to use along these general lines, for Williams is brazen in his appropriation of devices from other literary and nonliterary art forms and is self-consciously attempting to break away from the dominant realistic ethos of American theater in the early 1940s.

I invariably teach *The Glass Menagerie* late in the term and use discussion of the play and the writing assignment below to synthesize some of the points that we have made over a semester and to propel students to begin thinking more critically about what they are being taught.

WRITING ASSIGNMENT

As his "Production Notes" in the "Writer's Perspective" make evident, Tennessee Williams felt free to borrow elements from other

293

art forms. He seems intent upon suffusing his "memory play" with nonrealistic qualities in order to come to what he perceived as a "closer approach to truth." Thus, the extraliterary devices—the music, screens, and lighting—are designed to give the audience a clearer sense of the truth as Williams sees it. But that truth comes not only from borrowed extraliterary elements in the play. After reading *The Glass Menagerie*, one is also often struck by how freely Williams has utilized devices often associated with other literary forms, particularly the narrative frame and the controlling metaphor of the "glass menagerie." Select either one of the extraliterary or one of the traditional literary devices and in an articulate, well-reasoned, well-supported, and interesting essay of 750 to 1000 words, discuss its impact upon the audience's understanding of the "truth" of *The Glass Menagerie*. In the course of your essay, you might wish to consider how the device specifically functions in the play; and how it relates to the theme.

Appendix:
A Model Course
Outline

Model Course Outline: A Literate Freshman Composition Course

Patricia Wagner
CALIFORNIA STATE UNIVERSITY, LONG BEACH
LONG BEACH, CALIFORNIA

SYLLABUS

COURSE DESCRIPTION

Freshman Composition is a course that satisfies one of the general education writing requirements. This class will introduce students to the types and functions of expository writing, focusing primarily on analytical reading and writing. Though we will read literature and address creatively the pieces we read, Freshman Composition is neither a literature nor a creative writing course. Its main activity is expository writing generated through observation, interview, survey, reading and discussion.

COURSE OBJECTIVES

Upon completion of this course, students should possess a working command of the writing skills necessary to face the challenges of college course work and the professional world. Students will also hone their ability to use language and be able to effectively communicate ideas using a variety of discourses. Most importantly, in developing their writing skills students should become more disciplined, organized thinkers and more effective communicators.

COURSE REQUIREMENTS

- Daily reading and writing assignments
- In-class writing exercises
- Final in-class exam
- 4 out-of-class essays
- Class participation and group discussions

REQUIRED TEXT

Kennedy, X.J., and Dana Gioia. *Literature: An Introduction to Fiction, Poetry, and Drama.* 7th ed.

SUGGESTED TEXTS

Gribaldi, Joseph, and Walter S. Achtert. *MLA Handbook for Writers of Research Papers.* 4th ed.

Hairston, Maxine, et al. *The Scott, Foresman Handbook for Writers.* 5th ed.

GRADING

Students will accumulate points based on the quality of completed writing assignments. To succeed, students must be prepared for each class meeting and have all work completed.

Attendance/Participation	10%
Reading Journal	10%
Essays	60%
Quizzes	5%
Final	15%

ATTENDANCE

Attendance is required. After three unexcused absences, the student's final grade will be reduced a minimum of one letter grade. Should any more than four absences occur, it will be up to my discretion to allow a student to remain in class. Keep in mind that coming to class unprepared will ultimately count as an absence.

CLASS PARTICIPATION

Students are expected to be prepared for each class meeting and discussion. This means that all reading and writing exercises must be completed before the class begins. In-class activities will also be assigned; workshops, in-class writings, peer response/critiques, and discussions of reading assignments will count toward this part of the grade. **Note:** Be prepared for a quiz on any assigned reading.

READING JOURNAL

To encourage creative ideas and critical thinking, you will be required to turn in responses to our assigned readings. This means that for every reading I assign, I will expect a journal entry of about a page or two that responds to or discusses that reading in some way. These entries must be typed and turned in the day we discuss the reading; late entries will not be accepted. I will not grade these journal entries, nor will I return them—be sure to keep a copy of the entries before turning them in.

ESSAYS

You will write four out-of-class essays. Because these essays are intended to build upon previous work, no work will be accepted after the agreed upon deadlines. All assignments must be typed and conform to the MLA format. Keep in mind the following "general" guidelines:

- Papers must be typed, preferably on a computer.
- Use white 81/2 by 11 paper (20# bond, no onionskin or erasable paper) and print in black ink on one side of the paper only.
- Have a 1-inch margin at the top, bottom, and sides.
- Unless told otherwise, all assignments are double-spaced.
- Use no binding, cover, or cover sheet.
- Documentation and style guidelines will follow MLA.

All of you are strongly encouraged to rewrite and revise your assignments. Practice improves writing skills, and the revision process teaches you to edit your own work critically and effectively. My office hours will be provided—everyone should feel free to stop by at anytime or set up an appointment.

WEEKLY PLAN

Week 1   Intro to Course
            Writing Process
            Diagnostic (In-class essay, ungraded)

Week 2   Intro to Fiction
            Theme: Progress/Change:
                "A Rose for Emily" by William Faulkner
                The Metamorphosis by Franz Kafka
                "The Tell-Tale Heart" by Edgar Allan Poe
            Abstract vs. Concrete Language

Week 3   In-Class Writing: "Where Are You Going,
                Where Have You Been?"
            Theme: Feminism/Roles:
                "The Story of an Hour" by Kate Chopin
                "The Yellow Wallpaper" by Charlotte
                    Perkins Gilman
                "Shiloh" by Bobbie Ann Mason
            Theme: Youth to Adult
                "A & P" by John Updike
                "Araby" by James Joyce
                "Where Are You Going, Where Have You Been?"
                    by Joyce Carol Oates
                "Greasy Lake" by T. Coraghessan Boyle

Week 4   In-Class Writing: "The Things They Carried"
            Theme: War/Friendship:
                "The Things They Carried" by Tim O'Brien
                "The Open Boat" by Stephen Crane
                "Cathedral" by Raymond Carver
            Peer response to 1st essay, bring three copies

Week 5   Thesis Statements
            1st essay due (attach peer responses, 1st drafts)
            Intro to Poetry
            Form:
                "Sestina" by Elizabeth Bishop

"My mistress' eyes are nothing like the sun"
    by WilliamShakespeare
"Leda and the Swan" by William Butler Yeats
"Do not go gentle into that good night"
    by Dylan Thomas
"Swan and Shadow" by John Hollander

Week 6   Robert Frost: Video *Voices and Visions*
        "Desert Places"
        "The Road Not Taken"
        "Acquainted with the Night"
        "Birches"
        "Mending Wall"
        "Stopping by Woods on a Snowy Evening"

Week 7   Paragraphing
        Imagery, Sound, Open Forms:
        "My Papa's Waltz" by Theodore Roethke
        "The Fish" by Elizabeth Bishop
        "Lake Isle of Innesfree" by William Butler Yeats
        "Jabberwocky" by Lewis Carroll
        "The Colonel" by Carolyn Forché
        "Buffalo Bill' s" by E. E. Cummings

Week 8   Introductions
        Group Conference draft of 2nd essay due, bring six copies

Week 9   Group conferences

Week 10   **2nd essay due** (attach peer responses, 1st drafts)
        Oral Presentation Techniques

Week 11   Biographical Presentations

Week 12   Methods of Compare and Contrast
        Transitions
        Peer response to 3rd essay, bring three copies

Week 13   Transitions
          3rd essay due (attach peer responses, 1st drafts)
          Intro to Drama
             Trifles

Week 14   *Oedipus the King*
          Film: *Oedipus the King*

Week 15   *The Glass Menagerie*
          Peer response to 4th essay, bring three copies

Finals   **4th essay due** (attach peer responses, 1st drafts)
          Final Exam

WRITING ASSIGNMENTS

IN-CLASS DIAGNOSTIC ESSAY (UNGRADED): "READING AND WRITING WITH AN ATTITUDE"

All of us have some sort of preconceived notion of reading and writing: We either hate it, love it, feel self-conscious, confident, inadequate—whatever. Sometimes we have such attitudes because of our background, the environment in which we live, or the teachers and family in our lives who have influenced us in their own notions and feelings toward reading and writing. Whatever this attitude may be, it has either helped or hindered you in your own work.

Assignment: In a thoughtful essay

- Describe this preconceived notion or attitude.
- Explain as best you can how you acquired it.
- Try to explain what effects this attitude has had on your scholastic career.

Before you begin writing, take a few minutes to plan what it is you want to say and the order in which you will say it. Be sure to fully develop your ideas into an essay of several paragraphs. You will have the rest of the class to write this essay—try to save a few minutes at the end to proofread your work. This will not be graded but will be used by me to assess your writing skills and to help plan lessons for the class. Don't worry! There's no right or wrong for this assignment—just do your best.

IN-CLASS TIMED WRITING: "WHERE ARE YOU GOING, WHERE HAVE YOU BEEN?"

Directions: You will have *the rest of the class period* to plan and write a unified essay on the topic assigned. Express your thoughts carefully, naturally, and effectively. Be sure to provide specific examples from the text, your own reading, personal experience, and/or observations.

DO NOT WRITE ON A TOPIC OTHER THAN
THE ONE ASSIGNED HERE.

Joyce Carol Oates's story "Where Are You Going, Where Have You Been?" is a story about an ordinary girl from an ordinary family living an ordinary life. However, her everyday life with her mother, father, and sister June changes when Arnold Friend and Ellie drive up in a bright gold open jalopy and invite her out for a ride. Describe the significance of Oates's title for the story and how it applies to the girl (Connie) both before and after Arnold Friend arrived. Does the title mean the same thing? Or does it have different meanings? (You might also discuss the significance of the numbers on Arnold Friend's car: "33, 19, 17.")

IN-CLASS TIMED WRITING:
"THE THINGS THEY CARRIED"

Directions: You will have *the rest of the class* period to plan and write a unified essay on the topic assigned. Express your thoughts carefully, naturally, and effectively. Be sure to provide specific examples from the text, your own reading, personal experience, and/or observations.

*DO NOT WRITE ON A TOPIC OTHER THAN
THE ONE ASSIGNED BELOW*

Short stories about the Vietnam war are not unusual. Many authors have written of their experiences in a variety of ways. However, Tim O'Brien's story "The Things They Carried" is anything but the typical Vietnam story of war and jungle and heroes. Relate the nature of this "untypical" story and the methods O'Brien uses. Discuss the significance of Lavender's death to the overall story—either to the structure or to the portrayal of the other characters. (You might also look at the repetitive quality of the story. For example, why do many of the sentences start with the same words? Or what, if anything, does the phrase "there's a moral here" mean?) Do you agree or disagree that this is an effective way of storytelling? Why or why not? You should support your response using examples from the text, your own reading, personal experience, and/or observation.

ESSAY #1: SHORT STORY SUMMARY

Introduction

The purpose of this essay is to learn how to summarize a piece of literature according to standard methods. You will be able to select a short story of your choice. For your summary, you might choose a theme and thoroughly explore how the author developed it. You might also explore a character or a specific line of action. The point is to condense the material without losing the overall meaning and without bringing in personal opinion or outside sources.

Writing Assignment

Choose a short story from our text and write a summary of the piece without verbalizing personal opinions or bringing in personal stories. This assignment is a first step in interpreting literature for more complicated essays (such as analysis), so I want you to isolate important information and present it in such a way that the writer's overall purpose and point remain abundantly clear. I also want you to practice paraphrasing the author's words into your own and pull out pieces of text and quoting it. (As you quote and paraphrase, practice using parenthetical documentation as presented in *A Writer's Reference*.)

Ways to Proceed

Carefully choose and read a story from our text and isolate the main points with the main support and/or the main events with the conflicts. Begin by listing and/or isolating the more significant aspects. From those aspects, look for overall trends. Then, see if you can't create a thesis that embodies the larger idea you think the author is trying to convey. Once you establish a thesis that delineates the author's point, elaborate on it; don't just present the thesis without developing it into a fully-fleshed introduction. (Be sure to introduce the writer and the story in your introduction.) The body of your paper will then be support to prove what you set up in the introduction. For the support, you will need to practice paraphrasing and quoting from the text so that the reader knows exactly what you mean and where you got it. Remember to be precise and don't take it for granted that the reader will understand everything that you present. In other words, go overboard to explain the connections you're making.

Basic Features of Summarization

- **Present a strong, controlling thesis which sets up the author's point.**

- **Condense the material:** A successful summarization boils down the material without losing important information. Yet it is more than simply restating the main points. Look for the main supporting points as well.

- **Use the same diction as the author:** The language you use should mirror the attitude and tone of the author. Any variation begins to take on an analytical aspect, which, though nice, is not what summarization does.

Considerations

- Your essay should not merely retell the reading with a series of quotes; you should paraphrase and selectively rearrange the chronology to best present the information.

- When you paraphrase and quote directly from the text, you'll need to use parenthetical documentation to cite the exact page.

- Do not use personal pronouns such as "I" or "we." Stay with the third person objective—which we will discuss more in depth later.

Guidelines

Your essay should be at least two to three typed and double-spaced pages and adhere to the MLA guidelines.

ESSAY #2: POEM ANALYSIS

Introduction

Academic writing means being able to read and write critically. There are several methods for doing this: analysis, explication, comparison, and contrast. For this essay, you will begin to practice the skills of critical reading and writing by analyzing a poem from our text. You will choose from a number of methods to discuss the poem, but remember to choose a poem that you react to in a positive or negative way, either emotionally or intellectually. The goal of this essay is to control your responses, pull together the techniques we've been practicing, and add another dimension to your essay by "responding" to the poem, "inferring" meanings from it, and/or "evaluating" both the author's intent and the text.

Assignment

Write an essay in which you state your opinion about a poem without actually saying "I think," "In my opinion," and/or bringing in personal stories. You will concentrate on analyzing the poem by breaking it down into separate parts to study the whole; you will look for important meanings and larger contexts. *Do not* do a stanza-by-stanza retelling of the poem; be more sophisticated! The goal is to push forward a point that you want to make about the poem using any of the following methods in any combination:

- The first and most obvious way to analyze a text is by **responding** to it. What are your initial reactions? What feelings does it evoke? What ideas does it raise? What questions does it pose? It will be tough to stay away from irrelevant digressions, and you still will have to prove what you say with relevant quotes and examples from the text, but you can see that this is a less academic analysis and more of a "gut" reaction.

- Another typical way to discuss a text is by finding the **inferences**. Look beyond the obvious meaning of the words and look for what isn't stated outright. What's between the lines? Finding the various subtleties is not easy, but it is usually a more interesting analysis.

- Because it also draws upon the response and inference methods, the most complicated and challenging method of analyzing a text is through **evaluation**. Evaluation uses initial responses, the author's inferences, and goes into what can be deduced about the author, the author's purpose, and the intended audience. It is a form of judgment or attitude about the text that is fully discussed using relevant quotes.

Ways to Proceed for the Analysis

Choose one of the assigned poems. Then, after reading it several times, begin by listing and/or isolating the more significant aspects. What do you see as being the important issues? Look for overall trends in theme, language, context, etc., and generate several ideas for the slant you wish to take. Isolate specific passages that support your ideas. Then, after brainstorming and/or freewriting, sort your ideas out and create a thesis that embodies what your point is about the poem. (Be sure to introduce the writer and the name of the poem in your introduction.) As usual, the body of your essay will support what you set up in the introduction. For the support, you will again practice paraphrasing and quoting techniques so that the reader knows exactly what you mean and where you got it. Remember to go overboard in explaining the connections you're making.

Basic Features of Analysis

- **A strong, controlling thesis that sets up the point *you* want to prove:** A successful analysis has more than a thesis; it has a strong point to prove on which it stays focused. All details, quotes, and paraphrasing advance that point.

- **A strong attitude/point of view:** The language you use should reflect your point of view. For example, if you disagree with a point the author makes, you would choose verbs and nouns that specifically tell the reader what your attitude is. You would not use "soft" language to express that disagreement.

- **No Assumptions:** Readers cannot read your mind. Remember to fully explain your ideas regarding the text—go overboard to make your connections clear.

Considerations

- Your essay should not merely retell the poem; you should have a point to prove about it.

- Focus on ONE aspect of the poem and discuss it in detail.

- When you paraphrase and quote directly from the text, you'll need to use parenthetical documentation to cite the exact page.

Guidelines

Your essay should be at least four to five typed and double-spaced pages. You might also look up in the library the name of the author as a "subject" and see what the critics have said or if there is some specific criticism about the poem itself. As we have discussed, you'll have to use the MLA format to document the story and any outside sources both within the text and in a "Works Cited" section.

ESSAY #3: COMPARE AND CONTRAST POEMS WITH SHORT STORIES

Purpose

The purpose of this essay is to teach you to compare and contrast two separate texts that may or may not have conflicting viewpoints. You will learn to see parallels between different treatments of the same subject, and be able to explore your own viewpoint regarding the pieces you have chosen. The object is for you to learn to choose subjects that will stimulate speculation *because* they are viewed in relationship to one another, and to express the various meanings that arise based upon the comparison.

Assignment

Choose one story and one poem from those we've already discussed and analyze their similarities and differences in a well-thought-out, organized essay that uses the MLA format for quoting, citing, and documenting sources. You may choose any story or poem from our assigned reading list. Whichever you choose, think about your two choices and point out both the obvious and the not so obvious connections between them. Pay particular attention to form, and stay on your topic.

Ways to proceed

First, brainstorm or cluster lists of words for both texts. For your lists, you might consider theme, character, voice, style, diction, point of view, social context, etc. Then, compare your lists for ideas that offer opportunities for comparing and contrasting. Immediately make notes or freewrite on the ideas that occur to you when comparing the lists. Continue to freewrite until you have several pages of ideas; keep writing until you have exhausted all the ideas that made you choose your two selections.

Block your ideas into organized chunks. Fill out any skimpy blocks with more brainstorming and freewriting. Once you have the ideas you want to pursue, write a rough draft of your essay making sure that you consult the blocks you created. Keep in mind that your blocks are not written in stone! You may change them if you think of other things you want to include. Just be sure that whatever you do include pertains to the rest of your material.

The conclusion should pull together the ideas you've been pursuing and re-emphasize your point. You must base your conclusion on what has been presented in the rest of the essay—no fair drawing a conclusion based on information that isn't there! After you have finished the first draft, go back and straighten up the form; flesh out undeveloped ideas; and *cut out* ideas you are unable to develop. Do not allow the essay to get away from you! Learning to compare and contrast effectively means that you must stay in control of your ideas.

Basic Features of Comparison/Contrast

- **An introduction that introduces both texts and the point of comparison:** Though you will set up each reading with an analytical statement or two, you will still need to forecast the overall point of discussion.

- **A strong point to prove about the comparison:** It is not enough to merely present the texts and show the comparisons and contrasts; you must have a point to prove about those comparisons and contrasts.

- **Strong transitions:** You have a couple of choices for your organizational strategy: point-by-point or text-by-text. Point-by-point means taking one aspect of each piece and discussing it thoroughly before moving on to the next. Text-by-text means fully discussing all the points for one text before switching to a full discussion of the other text. In either case, the transitions must be tight and make the overall flow of the essay smooth.

Considerations

- **Strong internal structure:** Because compare-and-contrast essays involve juggling sometimes complicated material, the reader may get lost if you don't keep a strong organizational strategy. Think about setting up your points of comparison and contrast in the same order for each reading.

- **Document your sources as you go:** You will need to document all quotes, paraphrasing, and ideas you get from the texts. Keep them straight right from the beginning! The worst thing is being unable to use the perfect quote because you don't know where you got it!

- **Control, control, control:** Don't let the essay get away from you. Keep in mind the main point you've set up, fully discuss the supporting points you're making, and don't move onto the next point of discussion unless you've given clear signals to the reader.

Guidelines

Your essay should be four to five pages long and follow MLA guidelines for parenthetical documentation and for a "Works Cited" section. Once again, you might also look up in the Library the name of the author as a "subject" and see what the critics have said or if there is some specific criticism about the story and poem.

ESSAY #4: ARGUMENT

Introduction

Effective academic discourses are usually arguments that take various forms: persuasion, pro/con, or classic argumentation. In all cases, the writer promotes a strong point and stays focused on that point throughout the essay. The differences come in with the treatment of opposing points of view. Persuasive writing does not present the opposition to any significant degree; pro/con writing presents both sides equally before drawing conclusions at the end; and formal argumentation presents the opposition only to refute it and make the author's point stronger.

Writing Assignment

For this essay, you will choose one short story, one poem, and one play from our assigned reading list and set up your essay in the form of a formal argument for which you have conducted library research. Remember to combine the techniques you have learned in previous assignments—comparing and contrasting, analyzing for significance, and condensing large amounts of material—while incorporating sources from the library and documenting those sources both within the text and in the "Works Cited" section of your paper. You may write on any aspect of the texts that you choose (do not choose a text handled in previous essay assignments) but will have to find four outside sources to support your point. Your focus will be to sell the reader on your point—something that appeals to both emotion and intellect.

Ways to proceed

Every essay has its own organizational needs. In the case of an argument, you will still allow your subject matter to dictate the flow and shape that your essay will take, but you will also write within the following guidelines:

1. Begin with a problem that needs a solution; your introduction should be a brief but penetrating analysis of the problem or topic under discussion.

2. Then, provide a solution/resolution in clear and concise statements that the reader can easily grasp.

3. Refute several opposing viewpoints—this will strengthen

your *authority*—by presenting the opposition and then showing why it is not true or does not pertain to your particular argument.

4. Conclude with a reaffirmation of your position.

Your essay does not have to follow the form that I have outlined exactly—though it must contain all these elements. You may repeat your solution for emphasis; save the solution for the end; the refutation can be before the affirmation, or the two may be mixed.

Basic Features of a Formal Argument

- **A fully-fleshed introduction:** The more thorough you are in setting up the problem in the introduction, the more clearly the reader will follow your argument. Don't leave anything out or unsaid. In fact, you might work your introduction into several paragraphs by setting up a context for the discussion with a general background of the texts or authors.

- **Awarding points to the opposition:** Seldom is one side completely wrong or right/better or worse. Remember to weigh the merits of both sides and then decide which has the most advantages. And don't be afraid of awarding merits to the opposing sides—you will sound so reasonable that it will only strengthen your position.

- **Forward-looking Conclusion:** Do not limit your conclusion to summarizing what you have already said. Often the conclusion of an argument will open up new possibilities, beyond the scope of your essay, and prompt suggestions for further research and/or discussion.

Considerations

- **An arguable point:** Much of the beauty in argumentation is the controversial stance the writer takes. Do not choose a problem already solved or an obvious point of discussion. Your thesis must be arguable.

- **Sound argumentation:** Do not skip over information or assume that the reader knows what you mean. We will go over logical fallacies and what makes an argument unsound. Keep these in mind as you write.

- **A survey of the research:** To adequately prove your point, you will need to survey the research done for your discussion. You must know what opposing arguments have been made and what other authors have said.

Guidelines

You will have to research at least four sources and attach photocopies of those sources to your essay. The essay itself should be four to six typed and double-spaced pages and strictly adhere to the MLA format.

ORAL PRESENTATION

STUDENT PANELS: BIOGRAPHICAL PRESENTATIONS

One method commonly used to write about literature is to examine the author. Critics might examine the text by how it fits historically into the author's surroundings or how it reflected the author's life at one particular time. For this assignment, you will work with other members of the class to gather and present biographical information about one of authors in our text (I will place you into groups). You will present your information as a group and give to me both a "Works Cited" page of the sources you used and a one- to two-page group letter describing your collaboration and its relative success.

Possibilities for the presentations are endless. How you present it is up to you—I have had students use visuals such as flip charts, overheads (transparencies), and videos. Whatever method you choose, remember to stay focused on specifics; refer to specific dates and times and provide specific quotes. Do not try to "read" into the author's mind or try to "guess" what he/she intended.

PRESENTATION OF READINGS

Preliminary Work
- Make contact with your group members and arrange meetings.

- Meet often, and assign tasks for each member.

- Go to the library and gather information.

Plan the Presentation
- Make a plan and stick to it.

- Determine focus/emphasis of the presentation.

- Organize the presentation into a series of points.

- Prepare readable notes ahead of time.

- Script visuals into your notes.

Presentation Techniques

- Introduce yourselves, the author, your point/emphasis.

- Give overview of the presentation (organization).

- Speak to the whole class, not just to me.

- Speak slowly and clearly.

- Repeat key words and phrases.

- Present visuals as needed; take down when through.

Take Questions

- Ask for questions, then pause and wait for a response. (Remember, everyone in the class has read the author's text and should have a comment and/or question.)

- Make responses either as a group or individually.

After the presentation

- Provide a one- to two-page group letter that discusses your methods for/success at collaboration.

- Provide a "Works Cited" page for the research conducted.

JOURNAL WRITING

See enough and write it down, I tell myself, and then some morning when the world seems drained of wonder, some day when I am only going through the motions of doing what I am supposed to do, which is write—on that bankrupt morning I will simply open my notebook and there it will all be, a forgotten account with accumulated interest, paid passage back to the world [of writing]. . . . It is a good idea, then, to keep in touch, and I suppose that keeping in touch is what notebooks are all about. And we are all on our own when it comes to keeping those lines open to ourselves: your notebook will never help me, nor mine you.

Joan Didion
Slouching Toward Bethlehem

While reading and underlining important passages from the texts, keep a pad of paper or a notebook next to you. You might rewrite those passages that strike you as significant and comment to yourself why. You might also record your impressions:

- What are your "gut" or initial reactions?
- What feelings does it evoke?
- What ideas does it raise?
- What questions does it pose?
- Where are you confused? Why?
- Are there things left out?

Make connections to other texts and events:

- What does the whole text evoke?
- What does a particular passage bring to mind?
- What theme or passage corresponds to other material you've studied?
- How can the text be applied to other material?

Stay focused on the text:

- Stay away from irrelevant digressions.
- Do not bring in personal stories.
- Isolate the discussion with relevant quotes and examples.

For all of our assigned readings, you will turn in to me a one full page response on the day we discuss the assigned text. These need to be typed and will not be accepted late. Be consistent! I will not return these responses, so be sure you have a copy for yourself.

PEER RESPONSE SHEET: ESSAY #1 (SUMMARY)

Completely fill out two (or three) peer response sheets for essay #1 during the peer response session. I will hold you responsible for these sheets and give you points accordingly. Be thorough, thoughtful, and honest! We are here to make the essays better, and this exercise helps both the reader and the author become better writers.

Author's Name_____   **Reviewer's Name**_____

Is the thesis identifiable? Underline it if you can.
Does the writer identify the names of the story and author?

Is the "point" of the story made clear? Does the writer clearly set it out and elaborate on it? Offer suggestions regarding how the "point" could be more developed and where the writer could elaborate on it more thoroughly.

Is the chosen support relevant? Could there be more quotes and paraphrasing? Discuss where the support could be more thorough.

Does the conclusion flow naturally out of the body of the essay? How could the conclusion be made stronger? Where could the conclusion be more developed?

In what place does the essay appeal to you? Find a passage you really like.

In what place does this essay confuse you? Find a passage that's not immediately clear.

GROUP CONFERENCES: ESSAY #2

Every member of the group will receive a copy of each essay—including myself. My copy will have prior drafts stapled to it.

- It is your responsibility to read each of the essays and provide a written commentary of approximately 200 words. These commentaries will be the basis of our discussions.
- We will take fifteen minutes per essay. I usually ask that the author remain silent throughout the discussion—though I will leave a few minutes at the end for any comments s/he might wish to make.
- When the conference session is over, the commentaries will be given to the author after I have briefly looked them over.

STRATEGIES FOR CRITIQUES

Write your initial response to the essay:

Sum up your first reactions to the whole essay: Was it an interesting topic? Was the essay successful? Did you like it?

Main point: Is it clear? Where is it?

Focus: Does the essay stay focused on the main point? Where does it go off topic?

Comment on the essay page by page:

Paragraphs: Do the paragraphs follow a logical progression? Are the paragraphs cohesive units? Which paragraphs get tangled up? Which paragraphs work particularly well?

Language: Are the words abstract? Are they concrete? Is the language consistent throughout?

Details and Examples: Does the author generalize instead of provide details and examples? Are there sufficient details and examples to illustrate the point? Where would you add more details and examples?

Improvements: What changes would you recommend to the author? Where would you cut material? Where would you add material? Is there something particularly interesting in the essay that you would have liked to see pursued?

What grade would you assign to this essay?

PEER RESPONSE SHEET: ESSAY #3
(COMPARE/CONTRAST)

Author: _____

Members of group:_____

In order to make the most of your time within a peer response group, determine before coming to class the types of questions you have about your essay and the kinds of problems you would like to address. Then, read the essay out loud to the group. Discuss some or all of the following issues as they apply to each essay:

> Is the point of comparison set up in the introduction?
> Does the author stay focused on that point?
> Where does the focus waver?
> How can the author get back on track?
> Does the author adequately develop and support the compare/contrast with quotes from the texts?
> Offer suggestions regarding how the compare/contrast could be developed more thoroughly.
> Indicate where the support is weak.
> What is the organizational strategy for the essay?
> Does the organization work? Is it interesting? Does it sound like a Ping-Pong ball?

During the discussion, and in your own language, write out your group's suggestions. After the peer response session is over, take a few minutes to plan out what steps you will take to revise your essay. I require that you staple your notes and this completed form to the final draft of the essay you turn in to me.

1. What specific questions or problems would you like your group to help you with?

2. List the major recommendations that members of your group have made.

3. Identify for yourself the next steps you need to follow to revise your draft.

PEER RESPONSE SHEET: ESSAY #4
(ARGUMENT)

Author: _____

Members of group: _____

In order to make the most of your time within a peer response group, determine before coming to class the types of questions you have about your essay and the kinds of problems you would like to address. Then, read the essay out loud to the group. Discuss some or all of the following issues as they apply to each essay:

> Is the problem/topic of the argument set up in the
>   introduction?
> Does the author stay focused on that problem/topic?
> Go through the essay paragraph-by-paragraph to see how
>   well focused the argument is.
> Where does the focus waver?
> Does the author refute and/or discuss opposing viewpoints?
>   If so, does the author set up the opposition fairly?
> What is the organizational strategy for the essay?
> Does the organization work? Is it interesting?
> Does the author adequately develop and support the
>   argument with quotes from relevant sources?
> Indicate where the support is weak.
> Is the "Works Cited" section of the paper complete? Has
>   the author brought photocopies of the source materials?

During the discussion, and in your own language, write out your group's suggestions. After the peer response session is over, take a few minutes to plan out what steps you will take to revise your essay. I require that you staple your notes and this completed form to the final draft of the essay you turn in to me.

1. What specific questions or problems would you like your group to help you with?

2. List the major recommendations that members of your group have made.

3. Identify for yourself the next steps you need to follow to revise your draft.

SAMPLE FINAL EXAM

I. Title-Author fill-in (1 point each): Write in the name of the story, poem, or play's author in the space provided.

_____ 1. A & P
_____ 2. The Colonel
_____ 3. Do not go gentle into that good night
_____ 4. The Glass Menagerie
_____ 5. Jabberwocky
_____ 6. Lake Isle of Innisfree
_____ 7. A Martian Sends a Postcard Home
_____ 8. The Metamorphosis
_____ 9. Musée des Beaux Arts
_____10. Oedipus the King
_____11. The Open Boat
_____12. A Rose for Emily
_____13. Sestina
_____14. Shiloh
_____15. The Sick Rose
_____16. The Story of an Hour
_____17. The Tell-Tale Heart
_____18. Trifles
_____19. The Unknown Citizen
_____20. The Yellow Wallpaper

II. Phrase-title Match-up (1 point each): Using the numbers 1–20 from Part I, identify the story, poem, or play that works best with the phrase below.

_____ 1. The window is filled with pieces of colored glass, tiny transparent bottles in delicate colors, like bits of shattered rainbow.

_____ 2. The whole store was like a pinball machine and I didn't know which tunnel they'd come out of.

_____ 3. None of them knew the color of the sky.

_____ 4. He worked in a factory and never got fired but satisfied his employers, Fudge Motors Inc.

_____ 5. Good men, the last wave by, crying how bright their frail deeds might have danced in a green bay.

_____ 6. Rain is when the earth is television. It has the properties of making colors darker.

_____ 7. We remembered all the young men her father had driven away.

_____ 8. If you still think me mad, you will think so no longer when I describe the wise precautions I took for the concealment of the body.

_____ 9. Some of the ears on the floor caught this scrap of his voice. Some of the ears on the floor were pressed to the ground.

_____ 10. About suffering they were never wrong, The old Masters: how well they understood its human position.

_____ 11. And I shall have some peace there, for peace comes dropping slow.

_____ 12. While usually at this time his father made a habit of reading the afternoon newspaper in a loud voice to his mother and occasionally to his sister as well, not a sound was now to be heard.

_____ 13. He took his vorpal sword in hand: Long time the manxome foe he sought.

_____ 14. The invisible worm . . . Has found out thy bed of crimson joy.

_____ 15. But the double lash of your parents' curse will whip you out of this land some day, with only night upon your precious eyes.

_____ 16. The grandmother sings to the marvelous stove and the child draws another inscrutable house.

_____ 17. I want to make her this beautiful home. . . . I don't think she even wants it. Maybe she was happier with me gone.

_____ 18. I get positively angry with the impertinence of it and the everlastingness. Up and down and sideways they crawl, and those absurd unblinking eyes are everywhere.

_____ 19. She saw beyond that bitter moment a long procession of years to come that would belong to her absolutely.

_____ 20. I know what stillness is. When we homesteaded in Dakota, and my first baby died—after he was two years old, and me with no other then. . . . I know what stillness is.

III. Vocabulary-Definition match (1 point each): Match the correct definition to the vocabulary word and write the letter in the space provided.

_____ 1. Dénouement
_____ 2. Implied speaker
_____ 3. The main character of a literary work
_____ 4. A group of characters who comment on the action of the play
_____ 5. Context in place and time
_____ 6. Static or dynamic
_____ 7. Causal sequence of incidents
_____ 8. A highly repetitive closed form with 19 lines
_____ 9. Poetic paragraph
_____ 10. Rhythmic measure

A. Alliteration
B. Anapest
C. Assonance
D. Character
E. Chorus
F. Climax
G. Dactyl
H. Exposition
I. Falling Action
J. Foot
K. Iamb
L. Meter
M. Narrator
N. Plot
O. Protagonist
P. Resolution
Q. Sestina
R. Setting
S. Simile
T. Sonnet
U. Stanza
V. Tragic Hero
W. Trochee
X. Villanelle

IV. Short Answers (10 points each): In paragraph form, being as specific as possible and writing in complete sentences, answer the following questions. Avoid oversummarizing and answer all aspects of the question.

1. In *Trifles*, what is the significance of the bird cage and the dead bird? Why do Mrs. Hale and Mrs. Peters respond so strongly to them?

2. In *The Glass Menagerie*, Mr. Wingfield's picture is illuminated at significant moments. What purpose does Mr. Wingfield's picture serve in the play? What events does it foreshadow? Though he is not present, is he still a character?

3. In *Oedipus the King*, it is the blind seer Teiresias who reveals to Oedipus the reason for the plague. What does he reveal? Why is it important that Teiresias is blind? What symbolic nature does his blindness serve?

4. In "The Open Boat," why does the sea gull seem "somehow gruesome and ominous" to the men in the boat? Compare and contrast the sea gull with the shark that appears later.

5. In *The Metamorphosis*, Gregor has conflicting feelings about the furniture being taken out of his room. Discuss those feelings. Why does he try to save the picture? What might the author's intention be in stressing that it is on this occasion that Grete calls Gregor by his name for the first time since his metamorphosis?

SAMPLE FINAL EXAM (KEY)

I. Title-Author fill-in

John Updike	1.	A & P
Carolyn Forché	2.	The Colonel
Dylan Thomas	3.	Do not go gentle into that good night
Tennessee Williams	4.	The Glass Menagerie
Lewis Carroll	5.	Jabberwocky
W. B. Yeats	6.	Lake Isle of Innisfree
Craig Raine	7.	A Martian Sends a Postcard Home
Franz Kafka	8.	The Metamorphosis
W. H. Auden	9.	Musée des Beaux Arts
Sophocles	10.	Oedipus the King
Stephen Crane	11.	The Open Boat
William Faulkner	12.	A Rose for Emily
Elizabeth Bishop	13.	Sestina
Bobbie Ann Mason	14.	Shiloh
William Blake	15.	The Sick Rose
Kate Chopin	16.	The Story of an Hour
Edgar Allan Poe	17.	The Tell-Tale Heart
Susan Glaspell	18.	Trifles
W. H. Auden	19.	The Unknown Citizen
Charlotte Perkins Gilman	20.	The Yellow Wallpaper

II. Phrase-title Match-up

__4__ 1. The window is filled with pieces of colored glass, tiny transparent bottles in delicate colors, like bits of shattered rainbow.

__1__ 2. The whole store was like a pinball machine and I didn't know which tunnel they'd come out of.

__11__ 3. None of them knew the color of the sky.

__19__ 4. He worked in a factory and never got fired but satisfied his employers, Fudge Motors Inc.

__3__ 5. Good men, the last wave by, crying how bright their frail deeds might have danced in a green bay.

   7   6. Rain is when the earth is television. It has the properties of making colors darker.

   12   7. We remembered all the young men her father had driven away.

   17   8. If you still think me mad, you will think so no longer when I describe the wise precautions I took for the concealment of the body.

   2   9. Some of the ears on the floor caught this scrap of his voice. Some of the ears on the floor were pressed to the ground.

   9   10. About suffering they were never wrong, The old Masters: how well they understood its human position.

   6   11. And I shall have some peace there, for peace comes dropping slow.

   8   12. While usually at this time his father made a habit of reading the afternoon newspaper in a loud voice to his mother and occasionally to his sister as well, not a sound was now to be heard.

   5   13. He took his vorpal sword in hand: Long time the manxome foe he sought.

   15   14. The invisible worm . . . Has found out thy bed of crimson joy.

   10   15. But the double lash of your parents' curse will whip you out of this land some day, with only night upon your precious eyes.

   13   16. The grandmother sings to the marvelous stove and the child draws another inscrutable house.

   14   17. I want to make her this beautiful home. . . . I don't think she even wants it. Maybe she was happier with me gone.

   20   18. I get positively angry with the impertinence of it and the everlastingness. Up and down and sideways they crawl, and those absurd unblinking eyes are everywhere.

   16   19. She saw beyond that bitter moment a long procession of years to come that would belong to her absolutely.

   18   20. I know what stillness is. When we homesteaded in Dakota, and my first baby died—after he was two

years old, and me with no other then. . . . I know what stillness is.

III. Vocabulary-Definition match

__P__	1.	Dénouement
__M__	2.	Implied speaker
__O__	3.	The main character of a literary work
__E__	4.	A group of characters who comment on the action of the play
__R__	5.	Context in place and time
__D__	6.	Static or dynamic
__N__	7.	Causal sequence of incidents
__X__	8.	A highly repetitive closed form with 19 lines
__U__	9.	Poetic paragraph
__J__	10	Rhythmic measure

A. Alliteration
B. Anapest
C. Assonance
D. Character
E. Chorus
F. Climax
G. Dactyl
H. Exposition
I. Falling Action
J. Foot
K. Iamb
L. Meter
M. Narrator
N. Plot
O. Protagonist
P. Resolution
Q. Sestina
R. Setting
S. Simile
T. Sonnet
U. Stanza
V. Tragic Hero
W. Trochee

IV. Short Answers
answers vary

Index of Authors
and Titles

Page numbers are of the opening pages of the relevant Assignments.